LONDON RECORD SOCIETY
PUBLICATIONS

VOLUME XXIII
FOR THE YEAR 1986

THE COMMISSIONS FOR BUILDING FIFTY NEW CHURCHES

THE MINUTE BOOKS, 1711–27, A CALENDAR

EDITED BY
M. H. PORT
Professor of Modern History
Queen Mary College
(University of London)

LONDON RECORD SOCIETY
1986

SBN 90095223 7

The publication of this volume has been assisted by a grant from the late Miss Isobel Thornley's Bequest to the University of London

Phototypeset by
Wyvern Typesetting Ltd, Bristol
Printed in Great Britain by
The Bath Press

CONTENTS

ABBREVIATIONS

Arch. Rev.	*Architectural Review*
Atterbury	*The Epistolary Correspondence . . . of the Rt Rev. Francis Atterbury, D.D. . . .*, ed. J. Nichols (1783)
CJ	*Commons' Journals*
DNB	*Dictionary of National Biography*
George, *London Life*	D. M. George, *London Life in the Eighteenth Century* (1925)
HMC	Royal Commission on Historical Manuscripts
LPL	Lambeth Palace Library
SPG	Society for the Propagation of the Gospel
Wren Soc. xvi	A. T. Bolton and H. D. Henry, eds, *The Wren Society*, vol. xvi (Oxford 1939).
church, etc.	church, church yard, and minister's house

INTRODUCTION

The Creation of the Commission

The spiritual flame burned brightly in the Church of England at the opening of the eighteenth century, and nowhere more brightly than in London. It was naturally there that the two great proselytizing societies, those for Promoting Christian Knowledge and the Propagation of the Gospel in Foreign Parts, gathered their forces, not confined to any one church party, but embracing men of a wide range of opinion.[1] Controversy within the Church was keen, but that in itself served to raise the general consciousness of religious issues; and the battle was fought too against external enemies: Dissenters, Papists, Atheism and licentiousness. Associations of the faithful sought to inculcate a keener sense of Christian vocation in men's private lives. Charity schools were organised to teach Christianity to the poor; and to provide mental sustenance for the laity Dr Thomas Bray* organised a scheme to establish parochial libraries.[2]

Yet despite this exhilarating climate, the enormous growth of London since the Great Fire left the metropolitan area seriously lacking in provision for organised worship: the performance of divine service and the preaching of the Word. Thanks to the legal difficulties stemming from its being the State Church, the parochial arrangement of the Church of England was resistant to modification, and the necessary legislation could often be blocked by interested parties. For Dissenters, it was now an easy matter to open a meeting-house, and there was a prevalent, if unjustified, fear among churchmen that the Dissenters were spreading rapidly in the suburbs: a parliamentary committee estimated that 100,000 people, a quarter of the population of London's suburbs, were Dissenters[3]—and

* See entry in *Dictionary of National Biography*.

1. W. O. B. Allen and E. McClure, *Two Hundred Years, 1698–1898, the History of the Society for Promoting Christian Knowledge* (1898).

2. M. G. Jones, *The Charity School Movement* (1938).

3. The evidence we have suggests that such guesses were much exaggerated. The most recent calculation, based on contemporary returns, does not amount to half that figure. M. R. Watts, *The Dissenters* (1978), estimates the five main Protestant Dissenting sects in London and Middlesex at 33,220 persons, with a further 12,080 in Surrey, including Southwark—respectively 5.71 and 7.17 per cent of the estimated population of those districts (p. 509, table xii). Watts bases his calculations on the 'Evans list' (Dr Williams's Library, MS 38.4), compiled from a national survey of Dissenting congregations set on foot in 1715 by the 'Committee of the Three Denominations' (Presbyterians, Independents and Baptists both Particular and General), supplemented by recent studies of the Quakers.

There seem to have been some 74 Dissenting congregations in the metropolis in 1715–18, of which 27 were 'Within the Walls'. Probably many worshippers at this time attended church or meeting-houses indiscriminately, and Watts suggests this was also that papists were proselytizing among the unshepherded masses.[4] The building of proprietary chapels for Anglican worship met only the needs of well-to-do pew renters. In an anonymous pamphlet of 1709 suggesting various ways of improving the moral condition of the nation without resort to legislation, Swift commented on the endless number of defects requiring legislative remedy, particularly noting as a scandal to Christianity that where towns had grown prodigiously 'so little care should be taken for the building of churches, that five parts in six of the people are absolutely hindered from hearing divine service. Particularly here in London, where a single minister, with one or two sorry curates, hath the care sometimes of above twenty thousand souls incumbent on him.'[5] Legislative attempts to suppress Dissent by outlawing occasional conformity and destroying the Nonconformist educational system sharpened the obligation to provide churches in the new centres of population.

The Church of England itself, however, was riven by quarrels. Meetings of Convocation at the start of the new century had been characterized by dissension between the Lower House, dominated by Tory parsons, and the largely Whig bench of bishops who formed the Upper House.[6] So sharp had their differences become that Convocation was not allowed to debate again for several years. The Tory victory in the general election of 1710 gave it new life. Royal letters issued on 29 January 1710/11 put at the head of the agenda 'The drawing up of a representation of the present state of religion among us, with regard to the late excessive growth of infidelity, heresy, and profaneness'. A joint committee of the two houses produced a draft, said to be mainly the work of Francis Atterbury,* the High Church prolocutor of the Lower House.[7]

particularly true of the Presbyterians, by far the largest of the sects in London and Middlesex with 38 congregations. The inhabitants of Deptford complained that 'the want of convenient reception in our parish church' had 'kept many . . . in Ignorance and Irreligion, and driven Others to the separate Congregations' (LPL, MS 2727, pp. 64–5). Similarly, many of the inhabitants of Limehouse were allegedly, for want of a church, 'seduced to resort to Meeting Houses' (LPL, MS 2712, p. 80). But particularly alarming to High Churchmen were the Dissenting Academies (see L. Timberland, *Proceedings of the House of Lords,* ii, 158 for a warning from Archbishop Sharp of York in 1705), and it was against these that the Schism Bills were directed.

4. Several bishops complained of the diligence of papists in converting and seducing Anglicans and stirring up strife within the national church (e.g. Wm. Talbot, Bishop of Oxford, *Charge to the Clergy of his Diocese . . . 1712* (1712); Edm. Gibson, *Charge of . . . Lord Bishop of Lincoln . . . 1717* (1717)). Fears of the Jacobites also stimulated political attacks on papists (cp. Bishop Fleetwood, *A Charge delivered to the Clergy of the Diocese of Ely . . . 1716* (Cambridge, 1716)). But a return of papists ordered by the Privy Council in 1706 in response to an Address from the House of Lords showed derisorily little evidence from London, only four parishes discovering more than two dozen individuals, headed by St Clement Danes with 146 and St Giles in the Fields with 136 housekeepers and 25 lodgers (Guildhall MS 9800). Nevertheless, ungrounded fears may have been a potent stimulus to action.

5. [J. Swift], *A Project for the Advancement of Religion and the Reformation of Manners* (1709).

6. G. Every, *The High Church Party 1688–1718* (1956), chap. 5.

7. T. Lathbury, *History of the Convocation of the Church of England* (2nd edn, 1853), 409–10; G. V. Bennett, 'The Convocation of 1710: An Anglican Attempt at Counter-Reformation', *Studies in Church History,* vii, ed. G. J. Cuming and D. Baker (Cam-

Their representation, though drawing hope from the setting up of church societies and the development of the charity school movement, deplored the licentiousness and infidelity of the age; it called for a renewed censorship of press and stage, and, as soon as more church accommodation should have been provided, the enforcement of the law against those who 'abstain from all sorts of religious tendencies'. This call for the re-establishment of the Church of England was one aspect of a wide-ranging programme for church reform, which was aborted by disagreement between the two houses of Convocation. Any remaining hopes for major reforms were bogged down in Lord Treasurer Harley's* 'political calculating dilatoriness'.[8] Only the proposals for building new churches were to be implemented.

That anything at all was achieved was doubtless because the House of Commons was involved. Atterbury was a 'particular friend' of William Bromley,* Speaker in the 1710 Parliament.[9] On 14 February 1710/11 a petition was read to the Commons from the parish of Greenwich, praying that their church, ruined in a storm the previous November, might be rebuilt out of the surplus of the coal dues allocated for the rebuilding of St Paul's cathedral. It was doubtless Bromley who exploited the opportunity thus created by instructing the committee considering the petition not only to report on the finances of the rebuilding of St Paul's, but also the wider question of 'what Churches are wanting within the cities of London and Westminster, and the Suburbs thereof'.[10]

Waves of petitions from metropolitan parishes then kept up the pressure: St Mary le Strand (demolished in 1549 for building Somerset House), Deptford (the steeple in danger of falling), St Botolph without Aldersgate (damaged in the Great Fire), on 27 February; Kingston on Thames (damaged in a storm, 1703), St George the Martyr Southwark (in a dangerous state), St Botolph Bishopsgate ('supported by props'), Gravesend (the steeple ruinous), on 2 April; and, as the ripples spread, West Tilbury (nave collapsed), St Leonard Shoreditch (ruinous), Malden (in danger of collapse), St Alphage Cripplegate (shored up).[11]

Meanwhile Atterbury and his High Church friends had been following up the Speaker's initiative. Convocation agreed on 28 February that the prolocutor, attended by Drs Stanhope,* Stanley,* Smalbridge* and Delaune, should formally convey to the Speaker a statement of the 'great satisfaction' with which they had noted the instruction given by the Commons that a committee should 'consider what Churches are wanting within the cities of London and Westminster, and the suburbs thereof'. 'It was in our thoughts', the message declared, 'to have done what in us lay towards setting forward so pious a design; but we are glad to find ourselves happily prevented by the zeal of the Honourable House'.[12] The

bridge, 1971), 322 ff.

8. Bennett, *op.cit.*, and *The Tory Crisis in Church and State 1688–1730* (Oxford, 1975), 131–2.

9. J. Nichols, ed., *The Epistolary Correspondence . . . of the Rt. Rev. Francis Atterbury D.D.* . . (1783), i, 26; ii, 311.

10. *Commons Journals* [*CJ*], XVI, 495.

11. Ibid.

12. *Atterbury*, ii, 312.

next day, the deputation waited on the Speaker and offered Convocation's assistance in the work. The Commons then resolved that they would 'have particular regard to such applications as shall at any time be made to them from the clergy in convocation assembled'. Bromley announced on 10 March that Atterbury had on the previous evening presented him with a scheme showing the parishes most in need of additional churches, which also was referred to the committee. Petitioned by Convocation to support the scheme, the Queen commended it to the Commons on 29 March.[13]

The proposals for new churches were, of course, a means of overcoming the inherent difficulties that hindered the Established Church in any attempts to build new churches and divide parishes. The financial interest of patrons, incumbents and parishioners alike in preserving the status quo created an enormously strong *vis inertiae* which could only be overcome by means of parliamentary action, and not always even then. The interests of the individual often proved stronger than the common good. But the growth of London was so formidable a phenomenon that the need to enable the building of new churches was coming to be widely accepted. Defoe, in the early 1720s, could refer to London 'in the modern acceptation' as 'all that vast mass of buildings, reaching from Black-Wall in the east, to Tot-Hill Fields in the west . . . and all the new buildings by, and beyond, Hannover Square, by which the city of London . . . is extended to Hide Park Corner . . . and almost to Maribone in the Acton Road, and how much farther it may spread, who knows? . . . nothing in the world does, or ever did, equal it, except old Rome in Trajan's time'. 'The great and more eminent increase of buildings . . . and the vast extent of ground taken in' had been made, Defoe remarked, 'not only within our memory, but even within a few years'.[14]

This general impression is supported in detail by parochial returns made to the Fifty New Churches Commission. In the ring of parishes immediately outside the City walls, in 1711 the larger parishes were already too populous for the old structure: St Giles Cripplegate was reported to have 4,600 houses, St Andrew Holborn and its liberties 3,785 houses.[15] Beyond the City boundaries, St Clement Danes had 1,690 houses, Shoreditch 2,278, and in Stepney, Spitalfields claimed nearly 20,000 inhabitants by 1715, and Wapping 18,000. On the edge of the urban area, districts such as Limehouse with 910 houses in 1711 and St James Clerkenwell with 1,619 in 1720, were either without churches or quite inadequately supplied.[16]

In its report, on 6 April, the Commons' committee remarked on the care with which Convocation's scheme had been drawn up, and declared that fifty new churches were necessary in London and the vicinity, a recommendation adopted by the House.[17] Twenty six metropolitan

13. *CJ* XVI, 567.
14. D. Defoe, *A Tour through England and Wales* (1724–6), Everyman edn. i, 314, 324.
15. Lambeth Palace Library [LPL], MS 2714, f.252; 2712, f.4.
16. LPL MS 2712, f. 78; 2713, f.98.
17. *CJ* XVI, 580–3. A somewhat cynical view of the Commons' proceedings was taken by Bishop Gilbert Burnet, *History of his own Time* (2nd edn, Oxford, 1833), vi, 48.

parishes and the seven hamlets of Stepney were computed in Convocation's scheme to contain rather more than eighty thousand families. Allowing six per family for the most part,[18] the total population of these districts was estimated—probably overestimated—at some 513,000. The total provision for public worship was stated to be 46 Anglican churches, chapels and tabernacles, 61 Dissenting and 14 Quaker meeting-houses, and 13 French congregations.[19] Dr George, having compared the Convocation's population figures with those of the 1801 census, regards many of the former as 'clearly exaggerated';[20] but it may well be that the inner suburb populations were not markedly larger in 1801, the main growth occurring in the outer ring. On the basis of these statistics, of 32 parishes and hamlets, by 1801 ten had grown more than 20 per cent; seven were significantly smaller; and fifteen much the same. Allowing 4,750 souls to each of the existing Anglican places of worship, the committee calculated that an additional 72 churches would be required. However, an allowance for the number of Dissenters and French Protestants reduced the estimated need to the conveniently round figure of 50 new churches: approximately as many as were rebuilt in the City after the Fire.[21]

A bill was thereupon passed for imposing an additional duty on coals brought into the Port of London to finance building the new churches. This proposal would have seemed entirely reasonable to a Parliament dominated by High Churchmen. A generation or so earlier no one had questioned that after the Great Fire an adequate number of churches should be rebuilt at the public expense. Duties on coals brought into the Port of London had between 1667 and 1688 raised £265,000 for the churches.[22] By 1709 the consumption of coal in London was such that a tax of 3*s*. per chaldron or ton would yield more than £50,000.[23] This revenue, however, was up to 1716 committed to the completion of St Paul's and Greenwich Hospital, and the repair of Westminster Abbey. The duty was therefore renewed for a further eight years, out of which £10,000 p.a. were allotted to Westminster Abbey and Greenwich (Statute 9 Anne, c.22). The remaining sum, considerably larger than that for the rebuilding of the City churches, would have seemed ample for providing the fifty new churches stipulated, even allowing for having to buy sites for them. An invitation, however, to go for a more costly architectural character than that of the Wren churches, was provided by the requirement that the churches were to be built 'of stone and other proper materials . . . with towers or steeples to each of them'. The Act also provided for the appointment of commissioners to determine where the new churches should be sited, and to report to Queen and Parliament by 24 December 1711, 'to the end such further Directions may be given thereupon as may be pursuant to Her Majesties pious Intentions'.

18. St Martin in the Fields and St James Westminster parishes were computed at ten persons per family, and St Margaret Westminster at seven.
19. *CJ* XVI, 542.
20. M. D. George, *London Life in the Eighteenth Century* (1925), 415.
21. *CJ* XVI, 542.
22. T. F. Reddaway, *The Rebuilding of London after the Great Fire* (1940), 186–7.
23. See M. D. George, *London Life*, 330, n.6, for consumption of coals in years 1709 to 1716.

This Commission, of which the Minute Books are calendared in this volume, first met accordingly at Lambeth on 28 September 1711. Unable to complete its labours in the allotted time, it duly reported to that effect, whereupon a further Act, 10 Anne, cap. 11, continued the Commission until its work should be completed. The Commissioners received powers to contract for sites for churches, churchyards and parsonage houses; to erect churches, and to make chapels into parish churches; to borrow on the credit of the future coal dues, paying interest up to six per cent; to treat with patrons of existing parishes; to appoint select vestries for the new churches; and make a perpetual division of parish rates. Intra-mural burials in the new churches were forbidden. One church was required to be in Greenwich (the immediate occasion of the 1711 act) and that of St Mary Woolnoth in the city was to be rebuilt, the Commissioners being reimbursed from the proceeds of a one shilling duty on coals levied under an Act of 1685.

Membership of the Commissions

Thus the Commissioners for Building Fifty New Churches came into existence, and such, broadly, were their powers. They were active from 1711 to 1734, meeting at first in the Banqueting Hall, Whitehall, and then acquiring chambers in Lincoln's Inn. During the session of Parliament, however, they found it more convenient to meet in the house of their Treasurer, Henry Smith, in Old Palace Yard (**79**), and, their new Treasurer acquiring the lease in 1716 (**147**), it was there from October 1716 to August 1734 that they regularly met—usually weekly, but from 1728 generally monthly. They continued to meet occasionally until February 1749. In 1758, their remaining functions having been terminated by Act of Parliament, their papers were transferred to Lambeth Palace Library, to be lost from sight for nearly two hundred years.[24] Strictly, there were four Commissions: those of 1711, 1712, 1715 and 1727. Effectively, however, we may group these in two. The 1712 Commission was an augmentation of that of 1711; that of 1727 a topping-up of the 1715 body consequent upon the death of George I.

The Queen Anne Commissioners formed a relatively homogeneous body, characterised by Toryism, High Anglicanism, devotion to good works, and London associations. They were no random congregation, but a hand-picked body of supporters of Harley's ministry, with the exception of a few whose dignities made their inclusion obligatory: Archbishop Tenison,* the Whig Lord Mayor Sir Gilbert Heathcote,* John Vanbrugh,* Comptroller of the Queen's Works (whose ideas about the new churches were any way such as to be warmly welcomed by his High Church colleagues). Tenison attended only one meeting, and the lead in the first Commission was taken by Robinson,* Bishop of Bristol, who was soon to return to his earlier functions as a diplomatist, becoming plenipotentiary in the peace negotiations at Utrecht. His role was taken

24. The papers of the Commissioners, with the exception of the minute books, are catalogued in E. G. W. Bill, compiler, *The Queen Anne Churches,* with an introduction by Howard Colvin (1979).

in the second Commission (from mid 1712) by Dawes,* Bishop of Chester (promoted to York in March 1714), a favourite of the Queen's, celebrated as a preacher, and Bisse* of St David's (translated to Hereford in February 1713), Harley's 'urbane and socially-minded cousin'.[25] The lesser clergy largely consisted of Atterbury's own circle—Smalridge* and Gastrell* from Christ Church, Stanley,* Stanhope* and Moss,* silver tongues of London pulpits, Freind* of Westminster School—but the irascible dean himself played strangely little part in the proceedings of the Commission that he had done so much to bring into being.

The Commissioners may be classed in five groups: lawyers, City magnates, philanthropists, men of business, and architects. Although outranked by law officers past and present (Powys,* Northey,* Raymond*), pre-eminent among the lawyers was Edward Jennings, Q.C. He was energetically assisted by his fellow Inner Templars, Annesley and Box (both Benchers in 1713) and Manlove. The two masters in Chancery, Hiccocks and Meller, were of the Middle Temple. The City men were those marked out by the electoral triumphs of 1710: the four MPs for the City of London (Withers, Newland, Cass* and Richard Hoare*) and two for Westminster (Crosse and Medlicott); the sheriffs (Stewart and Cass again). The lord mayor, Heathcote,* a survivor of the Whig ascendancy, rarely attended. The City Tories were closely connected with the philanthropists. Cass, a High Churchman, was treasurer of Bethlem and Bridewell Hospitals, Stewart president of St Bartholomew's, well known as Tory strongholds.[26] Henry Hoare and Jennings were trustees of the London Charity schools, and both were closely associated with the pious Robert Nelson* in the Society for the Promoting of Christian Knowledge and the Society for the Propagation of the Gospel. Nelson was intimate also with Smalridge, Gastrell and Stanhope.[27] Whitlock Bulstrode* too was associated with the religious societies, though as a commissioner of excise and later a commissioner for St Paul's Cathedral and chairman of Middlesex Quarter Sessions he may perhaps be more appropriately classified as a man of business, along with John Isham, a former Tory under-secretary of state, Reginald Marriott, auditor for St Paul's and the City churches, and Wren's assistant Thomas Bateman.[28] The architects were inevitably the gentlemen of the Board of Works: Sir Christopher Wren* and his like-named son and John Vanbrugh;* to whom was added the Tory courtier Thomas Archer.*

Not all these men played a conspicuous role in the Commission's work.[29] The detailed planning was entrusted initially to a committee, chaired usually by Smalridge, Atterbury's successor as dean first of

25. G. V. Bennett, *Tory Crisis*, 141.
26. A. B. Beaven, *The Aldermen of the City of London,* ii (1912), 195; N. J. M. Kerling, 'The Relations between St Bartholomew's Hospital and the City of London, 1546–1948', *Guildhall Miscellany,* iv (1971), 16, 18.
27. C. F. Secretan, *Memoirs of the Life and Times of the Pious Robert Nelson* (1860), 118, 125, 129–30, 132, 136–7, 211.
28. *Wren Soc.* xvi (1939), 116; 68; 86, 99, 100, 142.
29. A list of Commissioners present heads the record of each meeting. These have not been reproduced, for economy's sake, but information about attendance is included in the Index, which lists all Commissioners who are recorded as attending a meeting.

Carlisle and then of Christ Church. His most active clerical colleagues were Sherlock,* Master of the Temple, son of a late Dean of St Paul's, and a London pluralist, Robert Moss (Dean of Ely in 1713). But more numerous were the active laymen: Thomas Crosse, MP for Westminster, where his family were established as brewers, a power in St Margaret's vestry; the great banker Sir Richard Hoare, Lord Mayor in 1712, and his son Henry, zealous in the great church societies, and his colleague Robert Nelson; several lawyers—Jennings, Box and Annesley (a leading member of the October Club); Isham and Bulstrode; and the four architects. In addition to their attendance at committee or Board meetings, the lay members were much employed in inspecting sites, (e.g. **484**, **488**, **502**, **507**, **532**).

When an enlarged Commission was appointed in 1712, taking up its labours in June, a committee was again appointed, but there was less consistency in attendance over the longer period of its labours. Smalridge attended less regularly, Moss but little, Sir Richard Hoare hardly at all, perhaps because of his mayoral duties, the aged Sir Christopher Wren only the first two meetings. Nelson, Jennings and Cross were the constant figures, closely followed by Annesley and Sherlock; but from October 1712 they were joined by three new clerical stalwarts, Bisse, Dawes,* and Dawes's friend John King,* rector of Chelsea. Attendance at the main Board was very similar, with two other new members scoring a considerable though irregular attendance: the Revd Lord Willoughby de Broke and Dr John Bettesworth, Dean of the Arches, a leading ecclesiastical lawyer. Others whose attendance was not negligible included Stanhope, Dean of Canterbury, Rector of Lewisham and Vicar of Deptford, the stentorian Stanley, Archdeacon of London and Dean of St Asaph, and the Hon. James Bertie, MP for Middlesex. An outer circle of members who came seldom to meetings nevertheless formed part of a valuable network of influence. Lord Rochester was a useful channel of communication with the Queen, whose cousin he was. The royal physician Dr John Arbuthnot* was well liked among the aristocracy. Alderman Robert Child was a power in the City, John Ward Q.C., MP, a Tory legal luminary frequently consulted, Viscount Weymouth and the Earl of Thanet conspicuous supporters of the SPG.[30]

This High Tory commission was doomed by the death of Queen Anne. It continued to meet for a year thereafter; but then a gap of four months elapsed before a new Commission of a much more Whiggish character began to function. Dawes, now Archbishop of York, could hardly be overlooked, but Bisse was dropped with Gastrell, by now Bishop of Chester. Robinson, whose diplomatic services had been rewarded with translation to London on Compton's death, and Smalridge, his successor at Bristol, had deserted Harley in good time and retained their seats, as did Sherlock, who 'reeking hot' from the Tory ranks had through Lord Nottingham's influence lately secured the deanery of Chichester.[31] Stanhope, always a moderate, and Stanley were, along with Moss, other clerical survivors. They were now joined by Archbishop Tenison's successor

30. Secretan, *Nelson*, 144. Cp. G.E.C., *Complete Peerage*.
31. N. Sykes, *William Wake* (1957), ii, 100, quoting Bishop Gibson.

Wake,* the influential Whig bishops Trimnell* of Norwich and Willis* of Gloucester, and the 'unblushing Whig' propagandist John Wynne* (an Oxford divine lately promoted, again through Nottingham's influence, to the see of St Asaph),[32] supported by several metropolitan clergy: Canon Lynford* and Doctors Bradford* and Cannon,[33] Whig prebendaries of Westminster, and three City incumbents, Gooch,* Waddington* and White Kennett* (also Dean of Peterborough, Atterbury's chief opponent in the Convocation controversy of 1701, and friend of Trimnell). These made up the clerical workhorses of the new Commission.

Notable Tory laymen also vanished from the new Commission. Robert Nelson had died in 1715. Now Jennings, Crosse, and Henry Hoare were swept away, and the City Tories replaced by Whigs. Meller and Hiccocks, masters in Chancery, were retained, as was Bettesworth with his significant role as an ecclesiastical lawyer, but the most active lay commissioners were new men: Sir John Philipps, Bt,[34] active in the church societies and the charity school movement, but of Whig tendencies—uncle by marriage of Robert Walpole; John Ellis,* a former under-secretary of state who had been deprived of the mastership of the Mint by Harley; a City man, Sir Harcourt Masters; and Edward Peck, probably a scion of a distinguished family of lawyers.

The political differences in the Queen Anne and King George Commissions were further evidenced in their officials. The Treasurer was nominated by the crown; the other officers elected by the Commissioners themselves. The first Treasurer was Henry Smith, Esq. of Old Palace Yard, Westminster, whose security was the Jacobite Robert Cotton (later 5th Bt of Connington), taken prisoner at Preston in 1715 (**107**). Thomas Rous was appointed Secretary, probably the same who acted as secretary of Convocation in 1710. Two Surveyors were elected, Dickinson and Hawksmoor,* both pupils of Wren, the one surveyor to the Dean and Chapter of Westminster, the other a clerk of works in the Queen's Works. John Skeat was appointed Agent, to conduct business about sites: although he was a solicitor, it was soon found necessary to appoint Simon Beckley as Solicitor to inquire into estates and interests, and draw abstracts of title deeds (**9**). Dickinson resigned in 1713 on appointment as clerk of works for Whitehall, St James and Westminster in the Royal Works. John James, Hawksmoor's assistant at Greenwich Hospital and carpentry contractor for four of the new churches, sought the post, but after much deliberation the Commissioners elected James Gibbs* (**54–8, 62**), who had the advantages of study in Italy and Harley's patronage.[35] It

32. Ibid. 99.

33. G. V. Bennett, *White Kennet 1660–1728* (1957), 83, 123.

34. T. Shankland, 'Sir John Philipps; the Society for Promoting Christian Knowledge; and the Charity-School Movement in Wales, 1699–1737', *Transactions of Hon. Society of Cymmrodorion 1904–5*, 74 ff.

35. See T. Friedman, *James Gibbs* (1984), 9–10, citing *HMC Portland* V and X. Gibbs' belief that Vanbrugh was plotting against him receives little support from the Minute Books, Vanbrugh being absent from the meetings on 7 October (when the date for electing a new Surveyor was fixed) and 21 October (when the election was postponed) as well as 18 November when balloting resulted in Gibbs' election. The date of Gibbs' letter to Harley, *HMC Portland* V, 331–2, given as 13 September 1713, must be queried,

need hardly be said that he was not re-elected in 1716, James securing the post in his stead. Hawksmoor was luckier, and held on to his Surveyorship. But Treasurer, Secretary and Solicitor went, being replaced by John Leacroft, Jenkin Thomas Philipps, and Vigerus Edwards respectively (**130**). Leacroft died in 1721 and was succeeded by Hawksmoor's son-in-law, Nathaniel Blackerby (**294**, **296**).

The Queen Anne Commission at work

How did the Commissioners set about their business? Bishop Robinson set out the Commission's business (**1a**), officers were appointed and the secretary ordered to send to twenty suburban parishes a letter drafted by the Dean of Canterbury and Dr Moss asking for information about their populations (**1b**). Where best to put even as many as fifty new churches was clearly a major problem, and the Dean of St Paul's suggested a means of deciding based on his observations of City parishes: 'For I find that in the biggest of them, of which some are very large and numerous (at least now since two or three parishes was laid to one church) there have never been buried 200 in one year. And yet the clergy find those parishes rather too large to looke after as they ought, though with the help of a Reader and other Assistant sometimes.'[36] He suggested that where of late years 350 or 400 had been buried annually, a new church should be built; allowing in the largest parishes one new church for every 250 or 300 burials. With one or two variations, it was to the parishes listed by Godolphin that the inquiry was sent.

A week later the Commissioners met again. They nominated Dickinson and Hawksmoor as their Surveyors, and appointed a committee to draft instructions for them and to consider proposals from parishes (**2**). Doubtless the choice of Surveyors was governed by the recommendations of Sir Christopher Wren and Vanbrugh, who both attended these early meetings. The committee instructed their new officers to supply them with a large up-dated map of London and its suburbs, and to consider possible sites, and how certain parishes might be divided (**480**). By 2 November the committee was able to propose a general allocation of 48 new churches to parishes, accepted by the Board at their next meeting with some modifications, for 38 churches (**6**, **483**). On 21 November, the Board accepted six more recommendations for churches in Westminster (**8**), at the same time laying down that sites were to be determined before any new district parishes were formed, and that churches were normally to lie east-west. They instructed the Secretary to buy as many maps as possible of parishes in which new churches were proposed (**8**). With the appointment of Beckley to investigate complexities of title (**9**), the work of fixing on sites could go on apace. The price the Commissioners were prepared to pay varied according to the location: in East London £400 was regarded as a reasonable price for two or three acres (**10**, **507**); in

as the Commissioners did not meet between 19 August and 7 October. It may perhaps be 13 August, the date of the Board's meeting at which Dickinson submitted his resignation, and the decision about the date for a new election was put on the agenda for the next meeting.

36. LPL, MS 2727, ff. 3–4, 3 Oct. 1711.

Bloomsbury £1,000 was necessary (**144**); but £2,200 for the Three Cups Inn in Holborn was thought unreasonable (**491**).[37] At the first committee's last meeting, 4 December 1711, Hawksmoor's design for a church to be built in Lincoln's Inn Fields (but no bells or burials) was directed to be laid before the Board.

The selection of sites was, however, full of perils, only hinted at in the minute books: 'Upon a debate arising about the two sites for churches, churchyards and ministers' houses proposed by the inhabitants of . . . Limehouse the Commissioners came to the following resolutions, viz. That Rigby's Garden ground . . . ought to be preferred before West's Field (the proprietor undertaking to fill up the ditch between the ground and the Rope Walk to make convenient approaches thereto), provided the same can be had upon reasonable terms.' (**9**). The details of controversy lacking in the minutes can be supplied, however, from other papers of the Commission:[38] petitions and counter petitions from the inhabitants of Limehouse in November and December 1711 show that West's Field, offered at £400 for three acres, was recommended by the parish officers and 242 inhabitants, but was said by the opposition to lie at the edge of the hamlet, and five feet lower than Rigby's Garden (and this in a riverine hamlet); approached by a dangerous bridge 'where coaches have several times fell in'. The West-ites retorted that only a few persons lived beyond the bridge; that there was no coach-way at all to Rigby's Garden, which was near a powder-mill; and that 'a great number . . . who are Dissenters from the Established Church of England have declared they would constantly frequent' a new church built on West's field. The Commissioners were persuaded to change their minds, but the Rigby-ites fought on (**11**, **16**, **501**). Eighty-four plans of sites serve to elucidate such problems (MS 2750).

Of a similar character were the difficulties concerning proposals for the divisions of parishes, which often provoked sharp local dissensions. Unusually, the patronage of St James Clerkenwell belonged to the parish; the minister's stipend of £11 was augmented by fees and contributions. The parish petitioned in 1718 for the parish church to be rebuilt as one of the fifty; but the Commissioners' proposal to buy the proprietary St John's or Aylesbury Chapel—the choir of the ancient church of St John of Jerusalem—and divide the parish met with local resistance (**332**, **337**). It was alleged that one-third of the ratepayers were Dissenters, and that St James's church was large enough to hold another thousand, besides the conveniency of very large aisles for the inferior sort to stand in; whereas ever since the conversion of St John's to be a chapel for the Aylesbury family, it had been used to store wine and tobacco, and also as a meeting-

37. The Secretary's 'Account of Sites Purchased', 8 July 1715, is printed in *CJ* XVIII, 216–17. Sites already purchased for churches were in Deptford, £710; St Margaret Westminster, £700; St George's Chapel (Ormond Street), £1,100; Limehouse, £400; Spitalfields, £1,260; Upper Wapping (St George in the East), £400; St Paul Shadwell, £1,000. Prices are also there given of sites of which the purchase had not yet been completed or that were still under treaty.

38. LPL, MS 2712, ff. 60–70. For the difficulties of choosing and purchasing a suitable site in nearby Spitalfields, see *Survey of London* XXVII, *Spitalfields and Mile End New Town* (1957), 151–3.

house. Furthermore, an experienced surveyor had reported that it would soon need rebuilding. The minister, churchwardens and inhabitants of St James petitioned the Commission against the division, as did inhabitants of the district allocated to St John, who objected to the new church as a burden. The rector and churchwardens of St John, for their part, petitioned for the legal endowment of the new parish, some parishioners offering a capital sum of £1,500 to prevent endowment by a church rate raising opposition 'which there is too much reason to expect'. Again, it is the papers of the Commission that enable us to flesh out the bare record of the Minute Books.[39] The scheme for dividing the old parish gives the number of houses and the value of rents, distinguishing those of more than £20, those between £8 and £20, and those under £8, as well as how many actually paid poor rate; and shows how all these were to be apportioned between the two parishes.[40]

Design

Having determined where to build, in general terms, the Commissioners had to determine how to build. The principal officers of the Royal Works, Sir Christopher Wren and John Vanbrugh, both appointed to the Commission, were ready with their advice.[41] Wren recommended that the new churches should be built in main thoroughfares, where coaches might have easy access, and in the midst of the 'better Inhabitants' who would pay most of the expenses. An east-west orientation should not be strictly insisted upon, and 'plainness and Duration' should principally be studied for the exterior: porticoes for the fronts most in view and handsome spires 'rising in good Proportion above the neighbouring Houses' would afford sufficient ornament to the town, without incurring the great expense of lofty steeples. For materials he advised well-made brick with stone quoins and oak roofs covered with lead. Considering the number of inhabitants to be provided for, it was clear that the churches must be large; but they must not be larger, Wren pointed out, 'than that all present can both hear and see'. Even with galleries, it was not practicable to build for more than 2,000 persons. He therefore recommended a nave of 60 ft by 90 ft, and pointed to St James Piccadilly as an economic model. Pews, he acknowledged, were necessary for the financial support of the minister, but space should be provided for the poor, 'for to them equally is the Gospel preached'. Intramural burials should, he thought, be forbidden.

His colleague Vanbrugh, however—perhaps influenced by Hawksmoor—had much grander notions: the new churches should not only enable the inhabitants to worship publicly, but also 'remain Monuments to posterity' of the Queen's piety and grandeur, 'ornaments to the Town,

39. LPL, MS 2713, ff. 77–105. See also *CJ* XX, 785, 801, 813; XXI, 669, 706, 720.

40. LPL, MS 2713, f. 98.

41. C. Wren, compiler, *Parentalia* (1750), 318–21. Vanbrugh's proposals survive in two MS copies in the Bodleian Library. That in MS Eng. Hist. C 2, printed in *Arch. Rev.* 107 (1950), 209, is by a contemporary copyist. The other, in Bishop Robinson's papers, MS Rawl, B 376, ff. 351–2 (printed in K. Downes, *Vanbrugh* (1977), 257–8), is in Vanbrugh's hand but may, Professor Downes suggests, be the work of Hawksmoor (ibid. 84).

and a credit to the Nation'. Striking an historical note, he pointed out that all religions had placed their churches in the first rank of buildings, no expense being thought too much. 'Their magnificence had been esteemed a pious expression of the People's great and profound veneration towards their Deitys; and the contemplation of that magnificence has at the same time augmented that veneration'. He recommended a 'plain but just and noble style', adding a number of specific requirements: the new churches should stand free of other buildings, for both dignity and security against fire, and be so sited that they made features in the town; they should be adorned with porticoes (both useful and magnificent) and towers; built in the most durable manner; and possess a 'solemn and awfull appearance', not over-lighted by many windows. Vanbrugh, like Wren, condemned intra-mural burials and advocated cemeteries on the outskirts of the town.

The building committee appointed by the second Queen Anne Commission handled many of these detailed questions of both site and design. Not until June 1712 was the second Commission able to take up its work, the necessary legislation and formalities imposing a half-year's hiatus. One of the new committee's first tasks was to consider alternative plans for Greenwich church, those of the Commissioners' own Surveyor, Hawksmoor, being preferred to a design by John James, though Hawksmoor was told to amend his plan pursuant to the committee's verbal orders (**494**).

On 11 July the committee agreed that 'one general model be made and agreed upon for all the fifty new churches' (**495**), and laid down general rules; the churches to stand isolated where possible; to be built of stone (as required by the act), lined with brick; with handsome porticoes at the west, as well as a large room for parish business, and at the east two small rooms for vestments and consecrated vessels; the pews to be of equal height so that every one might be seen either kneeling or sitting—no doubt so that the beadle might rouse those sleeping during the sermon, or deal with graver offences against decorum—and so contrived that all might kneel towards the communion table. Chancels were to be raised three steps above the nave. And—in accordance with Wren's preferred practice—contracts were to be made with every artificer separately for his trade.[42] Though neither Wren nor Vanbrugh was then present, they had attended the previous meeting, and the character of these rules suggests very clearly that their observations were given due weight.

These recommendations were adopted by the Board, with some modifications; e.g. that the new churches should have different towers or steeples. Towards the end of the month they received some designs from an ambitious architect, Colen Campbell,* and agreed that a time be fixed for persons to lay designs before them (**498–9**). Hawksmoor's design for

42. The architectural aspects of the Commissioners' operations were studied in a notable article by Mr H. M. Colvin, 'Fifty New Churches', *Arch. Rev.* (Mar. 1950), 189–96; as well as in Professor K. Downes's monographs, *Hawksmoor* (1969) and *Vanbrugh* (1977) and Dr T. Friedman's *James Gibbs* (1984); and are therefore not further pursued here. See also F. H. W. Sheppard, ed., *Survey of London* XXVII, *Spitalfields and Mile End New Town* (1957), chap. xii.

Greenwich, having been improved by Archer, was approved, and estimates called for (**18**). It was then decided, although no general design had yet been decided upon, to go ahead with Greenwich (**21**). In August the Board considered the matter further, and chose one of two designs then submitted by Hawksmoor (**22**), the committee ordering him to finish the 'modell' in detail, so that exact plans could be drawn for annexing to the building agreements with the tradesmen (**502**). This was not the end of discussion, however, for in February 1713, after construction had begun , there was further debate before a design was agreed upon, though a decision whether to continue the north and south arcades was left until Hawksmoor and the masons and bricklayers provided estimates of the cost with and without arcades. They were finally authorized in March 1713 (**526**, **528**). Thus the Commissioners were intervening in the design process well into the construction of the building, tenders having been considered and adopted as early as 13 August 1712 (**23**).

Building

The committee's principal concerns were questions of sites and artificers. Decisions about closing dates for the submission of designs were taken by the Board. When only Dickinson and Archer handed in designs by the due date, three weeks more were allowed (**30**). Hawksmoor then gave in four designs (**31**). There was however no general inflow from architects, which was perhaps why the Commissioners silently abandoned their decision to have one general model, though Gibbs in May 1713 presented several designs (**41**). In April 1713 the committee agreed to choose designs for churches at Westminster (Millbank) and Deptford at its next meeting (**534**); but no further meeting is recorded until more than a year later. It was the Board that chose Archer's four-towered proposal for Millbank (**39**). A week later, his designs for both sites were considered, and he was asked for estimates (**40**). At the same time the Board ordered notice to be given in the *London Gazette* that on 4 June they would receive proposals or tenders for these two churches from masons, carpenters and bricklayers; an advertisement that would, they hoped, encourage country workmen to compete. The masons' and carpenters' tenders on this occasion were tabulated by the Surveyors, whose report was referred to the four architect-commissioners (**46**, **47**). Subsequently the Surveyors drew blank schedules or specifications for the submission of tenders (**59**, **83**, **86**), but the Board still found it necessary to refer them to the Surveyors, to report which were the lowest (**98**, **128**, **329**). It is unlikely that the tenderers had the benefit of seeing the plans, but as the system of measure and prices was the basis of the artificers' contracts (**19**), there would not have been the same need to see the plans as in the competitive lump-sum contracting of the nineteenth century. But Archer's new proposal of 2 July 1713 for the roof and foundations of Millbank church was copied for the tendering carpenters, so that they might 'set down their prices for the articles mentioned in the new design' (**48**). For his part, the appointed carpenter found 'several of the said articles exceedingly difficult to judge of, and the said roof in many respects very different from what hath been done in any other church'.[43]

From the selection of a site to the completion of a church, the Surveyors had an active role to play. In July 1714 the Board ordered that no site be approved before the Surveyors should furnish a section of the ground down to the lowest part of the foundation (**93**). In December 1713 they were ordered to make monthly written reports on all the works in progress (**65**). At Millbank and Deptford they were instructed to take Archer's directions in all matters relating to building the churches (**50**), and had to measure the work done and report on its quality (**56**). The question of foundations on the riverside site at Millbank was carefully considered, and Hawksmoor had to prepare estimates under headings of the various trades (**57**). A little later, he was called upon to estimate the cost of alternative designs for the west end of Deptford church: one steeple, two steeples, or two and a portico (**60**). Was this work above or below the gentleman architect? Hawksmoor's detailed estimates survive among the Commission's papers.[44]

The Commissioners' need for professional advice may be illustrated by the Surveyors' report on plasterers' proposals by Hands & Ellis and Wetherill & Wilkins.[45] In most particulars, the former firm was the cheaper, but the Surveyors thought that both might be induced to reduce their prices. But 'whether each proposer understands the several articles directly in the same way, and intends to perform equally well, is a doubt with us'. They therefore suggested that the two firms should be employed in distinct places 'by way of specimen . . . which will infallibly shew their skill and ingenuity in performance; and this emulation between the proposers will make them do their utmost to give the Commissioners satisfaction'.

That this sort of doubt, whether the lowest price would 'perform equally well', was justified, is shown by the sad tale of the mason for St George Hanover Square. Tenders by Cass (contractor for the balustrade crowning St Paul's Cathedral) and Dunn (employed by the Commissioners at Spitalfields and St Mary Woolnoth) were underbid by Joshua Fletcher, sometime William Kempster's foreman at St Paul's and subsequently employed at Blenheim.[46] Having agreed for the work at 'the lowest prices that any Church hath been yet built', he had, with the encouragement of some leading inhabitants, used part of Hanover Square for storing and working his stone. Although this speeded the work, it involved, Fletcher claimed, a double charge of loading and carriage, so that in April 1722 he petitioned for compensation (**303**). In the summer of the next year, the leading inhabitants were complaining that Fletcher was 'very negligent and unfaithful in the discharge of his duty, employing very few hands . . . and often applying those hands to other uses'. He alleged that contrary winds had held up shipments of stone (**330**). Further complaints came a year later (**377**). The upshot was that the Board ordered two other masons, Strong and Cass, to finish the

43. LPL, MS 2715, f. 196.
44. LPL, MS 2717, f. 85, 10 Dec. 1713.
45. LPL, MS 2724, f. 51.
46. *Wren Soc.* xvi, 165–8.

church (**391**). Fletcher whined that he had 'laboured under unseen difficulties and extraordinary charge'; that he had been in 'a declining condition for a long time'; and thought it 'very hard that my business should be disposed of to other people before I am dead'. 'My Lords it is very Hard to Bury me before I am dead'.[47]

Once the work was firmly in their hands, it was not uncommon for building tradesmen to seek to alter their contracts. Thus Edward Tufnell and Edward Strong, masons, petitioned for double wharfage, cranage and lighterage for their work at Limehouse, the river being so shallow that not above one vessel in five could unload, and the crane had twice broken down, so that stone had to be delivered at Wapping.[48]

The Commissioners' counsel pointed out that when they accepted a tender, the agreement was entered in the Minute Book in some such form as that the proposal be accepted and the solicitor prepare a contract accordingly. 'The Workman', Mr Ward remarked, 'is not careful in what words . . . the Commissioners' secretary takes the minute for if he is permitted to do the work he is sure to be paid according to the proposal or perhaps better by a Jury [if the matter be taken to law]. And the solicitor's care is to make him explain his proposal fully and clearly and to take from him such agreement as may be a hold on the workman'.[49]

One of the chief difficulties the Commissioners experienced in the execution of their work was to procure bricks of good enough quality. Several contractors were threatened with dismissal for providing poor bricks (**114–16**, **173**); the problem was referred several times to the Surveyors (**66**, **155**, **195**); and on occasion the Commissioners decided to supply bricks themselves to the craftsmen (**78**, **207**). Two practices were particularly objected to: the use of 'samel' bricks, i.e. those that being furthest from the fire in the clamp (or pile of bricks) had not received sufficient heat to burn them thoroughly, so that they were soft and uneven in texture; and the use of 'ashes' or 'Spanish', the character of which is revealed in a report obtained from the Company of Tylers and Bricklayers, which ascribed the practice to bricks having been made after the Great Fire from fields 'much dunged with Ashes'. 'It was observed the Brick made with Earth in those Fields would be sufficiently burned with one half of the Coles commonly used; since which Times the Coles being by the high duties on them of more value where the quantity of Spanish is increased; especially since the custom of strawing the houses with sand hath prevailed, the Dust Basket in every house being the common receptacle of sand as well as ashes, so that the Spanish have not the force as formerly; since the corrupt mixture of it; which excessive quantity so corruptly mixed we take to be a great occasion of the badness of the Bricks.'[50] At Greenwich, the Surveyors complained of the use of 'common place bricks [i.e. 'common worthless bricks', used for the foundation of the clamp, J. Gwilt, *An Encyclopedia of Architecture,* revised by Wyatt Papworth, 1899, para. 1817], mixt with seacole ashes after the

47. LPL, MS 2714, ff. 20–2, 25, 50, 65, 67, 69, 73.
48. LPL, MS 2715, f. 109v.
49. LPL, MS 2728, f. 164.
50. LPL, MS 2723, ff. 21v–22.

infamous way of the City of London'. Most were burnt to a cinder, and the others were not burnt enough. They recommended the use only of bricks 'of pure virgin clay well and hard burnt, without any mixture of ashes or other distructive composition'.[51]

It was not only the artificers who tried to take advantage of loosely-drawn contracts. Cleave, a smith, accused Hawksmoor of 'always [taking] such care as never to let slip through his hands any one article . . . that was not in contract without abatement', though other smiths had 'little or no abatement at all in what they charged'.[52]

One important aspect of the work of church-building on which neither the Minute Books nor the other papers of the Commission throw much light is the making of estimates. Hawksmoor was required to produce a 'particular' or detailed estimate for the Greenwich church design he submitted in June 1712 (**493**), and both he and James particular estimates for building their designs in brickwork or in ashlar, with various alternative features such as a stone cornice or a wooden one (for this was outside the range of the Building Act), and a roof of deal or of oak (**18**). But these estimates do not survive, and the actual cost of the churches greatly exceeded the Commissioners' expectations.[53]

As the Queen Anne Commission drew near to expiry, the Board called for a general report on the progress of their churches. The Surveyors reported to the House of Commons on 8 July 1715 that there were seven under way. Greenwich indeed was 'entirely finished, except some small matters'. At Deptford the roof was being put on; Millbank would shortly be ready for the roof; of the church in the Strand the lower storey was erected; and Spitalfields and Upper Wapping (St George in the East) were respectively 14 ft and 8 ft above ground level; Limehouse was raised above the ground and advancing with expedition.[54] Some £40,000 had already been paid to the workmen, and a further £23,000 was due. For sites, £7,000 had been paid, and others had been contracted for at a cost of £5,800. Officers' salaries and incidentals brought total expenditure up to about £80,000.[55] As yet, of course, nothing had been received from the coal dues, which were only appropriated to the fifty new churches from 14 May 1716 to the extent of 2*s*., and wholly (3*s*. per chalder or ton) from Michaelmas 1716. The Commissioners must have been disconcerted by this statement of their affairs: if each of the new churches was to cost something like £15,000 or £20,000, then fifty would cost at least twice as

51. LPL, MS 2717, f. 83.
52. LPL, MS 2723, f. 91.
53. An 'Abstract of charge of the churches built', dated 31 Dec. 1726, gives the following totals (to nearest £): Bloomsbury £23,792, Cornhill (St Michael, tower) £6,440, Deptford £22,088, St George the Martyr (Ormond Street) £2,033, St George Hanover Square £19,079, Greenwich £18,260, Limehouse £31,251, Spitalfields £34,140, Wapping (St George in the East) £25,885, Westminster (St John) £35,243, Woolnoth (St Mary) £16,234 (LPL MS 2711, f. 55). Further sums were spent subsequently on most of these, e.g. the total for St John Westminster to the end of 1733 was £38,311 (LPL, MSS 2697–2702). St Luke Old Street, supposed (like St George Hanover Square) to cost no more than £10,000, actually cost £15,579 (LPL, MSS 2701, 2702).
54. LPL, MS 2711, p. 6.
55. Ibid. pp. 4–5, expenditure to 8 July 1715, reported to King and Parliament, 24 Mar. 1716.

much as the total funding likely to be available. The Board after receiving their Surveyors' report ordered that no church was to be started without a plan, model and estimate; when approved, no alteration was to be made in the design without the Board's direction, and an agreement made for the charge of such alteration (**119**). The Surveyors were directed to make progress reports each month (**123**), as had already been ordered in December 1713 (**65**), and were again to be called for in 1718 (**198**). And a committee was appointed to consider rules for bringing in plans and estimates (**119**). It was of course too late to be effective: a few months later the Queen Anne Commission expired, though not before it had secured an Act providing for the maintenance of the ministers of the new churches and the appointment of a further commission (1 Geo. I, Stat. 2, c. 23).

The Commission of 1716

The King George Commission that met for the first time on 5 January 1715/16 must have been aware that there was now little hope of completing the fifty new churches. The search for sites was largely abandoned. Before Hawksmoor's design for a church on Lady Russell's ground in Bloomsbury was approved, an estimate was required (**145**, **148–9**). At £9,791 it would have seemed the sort of price they could afford. It finally cost them £23,800. Cost control was an art yet to be acquired.

New methods of keeping the accounts were considered. Thriftiness became more essential as parliamentary alarms began to sound. A report to Parliament was one of their first considerations, and a watchful eye had to be kept on parliamentary proceedings.[56] In 1717 the Lord Mayor produced a bill for rebuilding ten City churches left ruinous after the Fire as part of the fifty: the Commissioners despatched delegations which successfully wooed the Speaker's support and persuaded the Lord Mayor to drop his project (**174–5**). But the next year, although the Speaker promised to do what he could, the Board was not able to stop a bill for rebuilding St Giles in the Fields parish church at their expense; and the rebuilding of the tower of St Michael Cornhill was similarly provided for.[57] In January 1717/18 they determined to consider the great expense incurred in building the new churches (**195**), perhaps in consequence of a Treasury decision to appoint a new Treasurer and 16 sub-commissioners (rescinded in February).[58] Meanwhile, they insisted that all the master workmen were to seal their contracts, and resolved that no parsonage house was to cost more than £1,000 (**204**), and the Surveyors were once again ordered to make monthly written progress reports (**198**). Thus they stood in better order when the House of Commons early in 1719 opened an inquiry into their expenditure, and proposals to rebuild St Martin in

56. *CJ* XVIII, 216–18. The Commissioners' report, laid before the House of Lords on 23 Mar. 1716, is printed in summary, with a full transcript of the accounts, in *The Manuscripts of the House of Lords,* XII, 264–7.

57. *CJ* XVIII, 698, 704, 715, 731–2; statutes 4 Geo. I, c.5 and c.14. See *MSS of the House of Lords,* XII, 523.

58. W. A. Shaw, ed., *Calendar of Treasury Books,* XXXII, pt. II (1957), 18, 162, 164.

the Fields and a dozen other churches as part of the fifty were successfully combatted.[59]

The result of the Commons' investigation was a complex measure by which the Commission's funds were more strictly limited and the government turned the coal tax to its own purposes, thereby avoiding the need to impose new taxes.[60] To meet their debts and carry on their pious work the Commissioners were authorized to borrow up to £360,000, the estimated yield of the three shilling coal duty from Lady Day 1719 to Michaelmas 1725, when it was due to expire. The duty was now extended to 1751. However, instead of receiving the annual receipts from the duty, the Commissioners were allocated only a fund of £21,000 p.a., which included the payments they had to make under the acts of Anne to Greenwich Hospital (£40,000) and Westminster Abbey (£36,000). Of the remainder of the revenue, over £30,000 p.a. went to meet the expenses of the state lottery, which was the ministry's painless device for raising sufficient monies to meet current expenditure. Since, under the Act of 1715, the yield of the coal tax for its final year, from Michaelmas 1724, was to provide the fund for endowing the incumbents of the new churches, the total sum available for church-building was limited to about £230,000. The Commissioners were deprived of the incremental yield on the tax, which by 1724–5 was producing more than £65,000.[61]

The immediate result of this measure was to bring work on the churches almost to a halt. Against bills of £1,450 for Millbank church from 1 January 1718 to 25 March 1719, expenditure in the next twelve months fell to £32, and for 1720–1 was only £130. Similarly on St Mary le Strand, expenditure fell from £4,198 (1718–19) to £406 in 1719–20 and £107 in 1720–1.[62] The King George Commissioners had begun only two churches from the time of their appointment to 1719: St Mary Woolnoth, for which there was special financial provision out of the St Paul's monies,[63] and Bloomsbury, where the site had been lately purchased.[64] Yet by 1721 they were nearly £67,000 in debt to the workmen, and they took the drastic step of reducing their officers' salaries (**279**, **280**). During 1718 their accounts had fallen further into arrears, as the Treasury refused to issue further funds until it had completed raising a loan (**209**, **210**). An order for the Secretary to draw an abstract of the workmen's bills and enter it on the books was doubtless another attempt by the Board to control expenditure (**213**). By 1719 £148,000 had already been issued, but further large sums had been incurred by works not yet brought

59. *CJ* XIX, 27, 67–70. Samuel Tufnell, an Essex M.P. born into the City aristocracy, led an attack on the Commissioners' 'unthrifty management', especially criticising the expense of Millbank church, *Historical Register,* XIII (1719), 73, cited Colvin, *Arch. Rev.* (Mar. 1950), 190n. For petitions to include St Martin in the Fields and other old churches in the Fifty see *CJ* XIX, 21–2, 28–9, 31–2, 40–1, 45 and 49. St Martin was rebuilt under a special act by means of a parish rate, ibid. 234, 336, 353.

60. Statute 5 Geo. I, c. 9.

61. LPL, MS 2711, pp. 49, 51. The Commissioners were not relieved of the onerous obligation to build in stone, as they had requested (**222**).

62. LPL, MS 2697, pp. 204, 208, 213, 481, 488, 495.

63. Statutes 10 Anne, c. 11; 1 Geo. I, Stat. 2, c. 23.

64. LPL, MS 2711, pp. 20–1.

to account.[65] As the works were measured periodically, and payments generally made on the basis of works so measured and brought to account, there were always considerable sums outstanding due to the workmen. For example, the Millbank books of works for 1713–15 were not approved until May 1717.[66]

In consequence of this sorry state of affairs, plans to build in St Olave's parish, Southwark, and in St Giles Cripplegate were frozen in February 1719 until the churches already under construction could be paid for (**223**). Archer's supervision of St Paul Deptford was dispensed with, and the Board's own Surveyors told to direct the roofing and ceiling of the north portico, and do it as soon and cheaply as possible (**226**). At St Mary le Strand, Gibbs was not superseded, but ordered to supply the Board with design and estimate for any carving or painting, so that contracts might be made before the work was begun (**227**).

Meanwhile, the workmen were pressing for payment (**229**). Bills made up to Christmas 1717 were settled about twelve months later (**218**). In March 1719, the Surveyors were ordered to measure work executed and make up accounts to Christmas 1718 (**226**); and a month later, to bring them up to Lady Day 1719 (**229**), when the new financial regime commenced. In June, the Surveyors submitted their accounts, articles for which there were no contracts being referred to the Board's consideration (**232–3**); and application was made to the Treasury for the issue of tallies for £45,000. Legal problems about the issue of tallies to workmen however deferred settlement, the Treasury again delayed, and the Board took the view that to issue so large a sum in interest-bearing tallies would impose an excessive burden on their resources (**234**). Accordingly only £23,000 was issued in March 1720 (**251**). In April some £8,600 was paid to clear the accounts for 1717 (**253**) and in May arrangements were made for paying five shillings in the pound on the 1718 accounts (**255**). It was not until September that the second £23,000 was obtained. Thus the new churches were in part financed by delayed payment, and it is a tribute to the creditworthiness of the contractors (or to their success in charging high prices) that few collapsed under such exacting conditions. Presumably they could sell their orders or tallies as interest-bearing securities, though perhaps at a discount.

Although local initiatives persuaded the Commissioners to approve the building of a church near Hanover Square, a wealthy district, late in 1720 (**266**), on a site given by General Steuart, a design by Gibbs commissioned by the inhabitants was rejected in favour of one by the Board's own Surveyor, James, which was not to cost more than £10,000 (**268–9**). The workmen were to be paid in tallies (**272**), but a further examination of the Commission's finances showed debts of some £66,700, as mentioned above, and the parish authorities were told that they would have to procure the tallies (**274**). Perhaps because of the lack of money for their

65. According to the preamble of the act 5 Geo. I, c. 9, the Commissioners had received £161,175. 16*s*. 7*d*., presumably by the end of 1718, and incurred further large sums, but the ledgers show issues from the Exchequer of only some £148,600 up to October 1718. Another £23,000 was issued on 24 Mar. 1720 under the new act (LPL, MS 2710, f. 1).
66. LPL, MS 2697, pp. 155, 165, 175.

operations, the Commissioners did not meet between May and October 1721.

Parishes and Endowments

In addition to building new churches, the Commissioners had to carry through the whole process of devising new parishes for them. This involved not only the carving out a district from the old parish, but also obtaining churchyards or cemeteries for burying the dead of the new districts, and establishing a scale of fees for burials, sometimes a contentious business, because the rights of the rector and parish officers had to be considered, as well as the interests of consumers. Burials in the upper ground of St George the Martyr cemetery were fixed at £1. 14*s* .6*d*. for those aged over ten, of which sum the rector and churchwardens received 6*s*.8*d*. each, the curate 3*s*.4*d*., the clerk 2*s*.6*d*., bell and knell 6*s*. (including 1*s*. for the sexton), and the gravedigger 2*s*.6*d*. In the middle ground the fees totalled 18*s*.6*d*., in the lower, 9*s*. Strangers were charged double; burials after 10 in the summer or 8 o'clock in the winter surcharged one third. The poor receiving alms were buried free (**415**).

Furthermore, it was necessary to provide for the government of the new parishes. The Commissioners were empowered to set up select vestries, and they took considerable care over this work, employing Commissioners with local knowledge to draw up lists of persons suitable to be parish officers and vestrymen; each Commissioner present took a copy and brought to the next meeting a rolled-up paper with his own selection of names to the requisite number of vestrymen: in St George Hanover Square district parish with its large aristocratic population, as many as one hundred (all the great men had to be accommodated) including four plain 'Mr's (**408**, **414**). St George the Martyr Queen Square was more mixed, with 4 knights, 15 esquires and 5 tradesmen among its 30 members (**347**); while St Mary le Strand was composed overwhelmingly of tradesmen, including the celebrated book seller Jacob Tonson (**365**).

In all this work it was necessary to bear in mind the rights or claims derived from the old parishes: the fees of which incumbents, curates and clerks might be deprived by marriages and burials in the new parishes, the property rights of the patron in the presentation to the living; the burden of poor rate on the inhabitants at large.[67] And perhaps the most difficult question of all—at least, so one would judge from the time the Commissioners devoted to it—was that of providing an endowment or maintenance for the ministers of the new parishes. Robert Moss had attempted in November 1713 to get the Board to adopt a plan, but the subject was constantly deferred to the next meeting—whether after incomplete discussion or undiscussed is not clear. A committee was appointed to examine the plan on 13 January 1713/14, but a week later it

67. LPL, MS 2714 contains a petition dated 18 Jan. 1724/5 from the parish clerks of three Westminster parishes praying that their rights be secured in any division of the parishes, (ff. 71–2); MS 2725, legal opinions on the rights of bishops and patrons in the new parishes (f. 3).

was dissolved, and not until 29 April was it determined to address the Queen on the subject, the address itself being agreed the following week. The question was then taken up again with the new King (**118**) and it may be claimed as one of the final achievements of the Queen Anne commission that an act early in George I's reign extended the three shilling coal duty for a further twelve months (to Michaelmas 1725) specifically to provide a fund to endow the ministers of the new churches, as well as providing for the appointment of a new Commission to carry out the work.

Endowment was one of the first problems considered by the new Commission (**138**) but as no church was finished, the issue was postponed. In March 1718 a committee recommended a plan by Dean Stanhope (**224**), and a representation to king and parliament was drawn up (**226**). A draft bill was referred to Farrer, chairman of the Committees of Supply and Ways & Means, and the Commission's masters in chancery in January 1720 (**242**), but by April it was clear there would be no bill that session (**252**). Attempts were renewed in subsequent years (**271**, **287**, **312**), and early in 1723 a bill secured Robert Walpole's promise of support (**322**). Objections however blocked further progress (**327**). Year after year, the Minute Books tell the same story: the bill considered, remodelled with the advice of leading MPs (**359**, **385**, **392**), parliamentary agents appointed (**360**). But even Bishop Gibson's discoursing with Sir Robert Walpole (**359**) failed to bring it into the House, let alone achieve its passage. One ground of objection was the amount of perquisites or surplice fees that the ministers might obtain (**362**), another the burden on the inhabitants, whether of the old or the new parish (**373**). In 1725 success at last looked within the Commission's grasp, but its hopes were dashed by strong local opposition to the principle of endowment chiefly by means of a rate levied on the parish: large, rich parishes (e.g. St George Hanover Square) were to be endowed entirely by rate; large parishes with many poor might receive £80 p.a. from the parliamentary fund, smaller or even poorer ones as much as £100 or £120; so establishing stipends ranging from £200 to £270 for rectors and £50–80 for curates (**396**). But in Hanover Square parish a $\frac{3}{4}$*d*. rate would raise as much as one of 16*d*. in Stratford Bow.[68] Petition after petition from threatened persons or interests protracted proceedings until Lord Chancellor Macclesfield's impeachment absorbed the Commons' energies.[69]

68. LPL, MS 2724, f. 135. On 12 Apr. 1725, the Commissioners reported to the House of Commons that the new parishes would be of at least 6,000 souls in each. Considering the great number of births and burials, requiring the minister's personal attendance, and 'often times at unseasonable hours to baptise children in danger of death and to bury the deceased late in the night', the number of sick to be visited, applications by persons of all sorts, the daily duty of public prayers and 'the time necessary to prepare seasonable and well digested discourses for the pulpit', as well as time for their unavoidable private avocations, it was necessary to have at least two ministers. Parishes in and about London requiring 'men of the best education, learning and experience, whose service besides their constant attendance upon their ordinary duties, may be wanting for the public defence of Religion'; and considering the very great expense of maintaining a family in London, and the decline in the value of coin since 1660, they thought that at least £200 p.a. was necessary, with a maximum of £350—not more than would support a family in 'a modest decent manner'. LPL, MS 2727, ff. 65 et seq.

69. *CJ* XX, 451–2, 460, 467–8, 471, 473, 476. The Commissioners' report to the House

Faced with the impossibility of carrying a general endowment act[70]—even for parishes willing to submit to a pound rate (**408–9**)[71]—the Commission had to proceed by a separate measure for each parish, and the distribution of the parliamentary fund that eventuated was quite different from that described above. Sums of between £2,500 (for St Mary le Strand) and £3,500 (Limehouse) were invested in South Sea Annuities until lands could be purchased to provide the endowment. These annuities produced between £94 (St John Smith Square) and £145 (St John Horsley Down), according to the price of the stock at the time of investment, and, of course, the capital allocated.[72]

The last years

By the spring of 1726 the Commission's finances were on a sound footing and the building work was well forward. After a period from 1719 to 1722 when shortage of funds had brought building almost to a halt, as debts had been cleared off, work picked up again, and the officers' reduced salaries were restored (**443**). Several new churches were begun, and by the end of 1726, some £249,000 had been spent on twelve churches and St Michael Cornhill tower;[73] but only three had been completed and consecrated. It was obvious that, as the Board reported in opposing a bid from the Dean and Chapter of Westminster for a larger share of the coal tax, 'the expense of building with stone and purchasing sites is so great, and so far exceeds calculations formerly made, that it will be utterly impracticable to build half the churches first purposed' (**436**). Yet several parishes still contained thirty or forty thousand souls, many at considerable distances from the parish church. To meet necessity so far as their very limited funds would now permit, the Commissioners considered their Surveyors' models for a new church, and ordered them jointly to prepare a design for a tower to be as cheap as possible (**464–5**). In June 1727 they approved plans for long-held sites in Old Street (Cripplegate) and Horsleydown (Southwark): churches that were to be built in a

of Commons, 12 Apr. 1725, attacked 'printed papers' that had been 'handed about' claiming that no provision was necessary for the clergy of the new churches because of the great amount of dues and perquisites; the real income from such sources was much lower. LPL, MS 2727, ff. 65–70; for surplice fees, see MS 2713, f. 234.

70. The fate of this proposal was not reported in the Minute Books, but one item appears to have been omitted from the minutes for 23 Apr. 1725. On the next day, Dean Stanhope wrote: '. . . We are all surprised at being told, the business of the Church Bill stands still from any Delay on our part; after so many particulars sent to the Lord Bishop of London five months ago'. LPL, MS 2727, f. 30.

71. Attempts to pass a single measure for the whole parish of Stepney failed in 1727 and 1728, partly because the rectors of the old parish resisted anything that might diminish their income, and partly because of hostility to select vestries, as well as the dislike of a church rate (*CJ* XX, 772, 814, 847; XXI, 94, 134, 156–7); but separate acts were later passed for Spitalfields and Wapping (royal assent 14 May 1729), Stratford Bow (24 Mar. 1730), and Deptford, Bloomsbury and Limehouse (15 May 1730). Millbank had secured its act in 1728 (royal assent 28 May), having failed in 1727 (*CJ* XX, 798, 514, 831; XXI 182); but St John Clerkennwell never succeeded because of the opposition of the mother parish (p. xx above).

72. LPL, MS 2711, pp. 65, 98; MS 2725, ff. 26, 130, 132.

73. LPL, MS 2711, p. 55.

cheaper fashion than their predecessors (**467**). An act in 1728 tied up some loose financial ends, and in July 1729 it was calculated that some £37,000 was available in the building fund.[74] By 1732, there was only £10,000 left for building,[75] and the officers' salaries were cut by half. In May 1731 an act had allocated £5,000 from the Commission's funds to trustees for rebuilding Gravesend parish church, and in March 1732 a further £3,000 was similarly allocated for rebuilding Woolwich church. A year later St George the Martyr, Southwark, obtained a similar rebuilding act.[76] Their funds thus drained, the Commissioners began to shut shop: the Surveyors were discharged at Midsummer 1733, the Secretary in 1734.[77] The house in Old Palace Yard was given up, the models of churches moved across to the Abbey, the furniture sold. Only the Agent and the Treasurer remained, involved in the purchase of lands for endowing the livings and administering the incumbents' endowments. No meetings were held after February 1749. By 1757 all the original Commissioners of 1727 were dead, and the Treasurer wished to resign. An act in 1758 enabled the sale of the remaining sites and transfer of the endowments to the beneficiaries.[78] At a last meeting on 14 December 1758, the archbishop, lord chancellor, lord mayor and sheriffs appointed trustees, and ordered the papers of the Commission to be deposited in Lambeth Palace.[79]

Editorial Note

I am grateful to the Librarian, Lambeth Palace Library, for permission to publish this calendar of the Minutes of the Commissioners for Building Fifty New Churches.

The original Minutes (which are no longer extant) of the four commissions were contemporaneously copied into four vellum-bound volumes. MS 2690 contains the minutes of both Queen Anne Commissions and of the first Georgian Commission up to 20 March 1718 (numbered in ink, pp. 1–393). It also contains at the end (pp. 396–446) and written from the back, minutes of a standing committee, 10 October–21 December 1711. (These have also their own numeration, facing pages being given the same number in ink.) MS 2691, of 465 pages, continues the Commissioners' minutes from 3 April 1718 to the last meeting of the first Georgian Commission on 10 November 1727. It also contains the minutes of the second Georgian Commission from 5 December 1727 to 17 May 1728. MS 2692 contains the remaining minutes of this fourth Commission until its abolition in December 1758. The minutes of committees of the

74. Statute 1 Geo. II, Stat. 2, c. 8; LPL, MS 2711, pp. 59–60.
75. LPL, MS 2711, p. 80.
76. Statutes 4 Geo. II, c. 20 (see *CJ* XXI, 667, 698–9, 755), 5 Geo. II, c. 14 (*CJ* XXI, 791–2, 855), and 6 Geo. II, c. 8 (see *CJ* XXII, 43–4, 99). £8,000 had already been allocated for rebuilding St Giles in the Fields (4 Geo. I, c. 14 and 3 Geo. II, c. 3); and in 1733 the Dean and Chapter of Westminster obtained from the Commission's funds another £4,000 for the repair of the abbey church and £1,200 for finishing the dormitory (6 Geo. II, c. 25)—though another £4,000 in 1734 came from the national revenue (*CJ* XXII, 260, 273; 7 Geo. II, c. 12).
77. LPL, MS 2692.
78. Private Act, 31 Geo. II, 2.
79. LPL, MS 2692.

second Anne and first George commissions are in MS 2693. There are also indexes to the minute books (MSS 2694–6). It is the minutes of the first three Commissions and their committees that are calendared in the present volume (i.e. MSS 2690; 2691, pp. 1–434; 2693). The fourth Commission was almost entirely concerned with the endowment of the new churches begun by their predecessors, and its minutes are therefore not included here.

In preparing this calendar I have attempted to stay as close to the original as the need for succinctness permitted. There is considerable variation in the original MSS in the spelling of proper names, and these I have standardised, giving variants in the index. The adopted spelling generally follows that of Dr Bill's *The Queen Anne Churches,* a calendar of and index to the general mass of the Commission's papers excluding the minute books, a work that has greatly lightened my labours. Capitalization follows modern practice except that offices under the Commission are distinguished by initial capitals. A list is given of the holders of these offices.

Each meeting of the Commission has been given a serial number in bold, and each meeting of the committees is similarly numbered in a continuing sequence. These numbers are used in the Introduction and as the only location references in the Indexes (Persons, Places, and Subjects). The number of the page of the MS minute book on which each meeting entry begins is also given. The place at which the meeting was held is stated only when there is a change of venue. The names of those attending have not been reproduced, but the Index of Persons gives abstracted details for those Commissioners who attended any meetings, with dates of first and last attendance, distinguishing the three Commissions and two successive committees, as well as showing any periods of prolonged absence (i.e. of approximately a year or more), and the number of meetings attended. The lengthy lists of men nominated to the new vestries have not been included in the Index of Persons.

My work on the Commissioners' papers was facilitated by a grant from the University of London Central Research Fund.

I should like to thank the staff of Lambeth Palace Library for their co-operation over a long period; Dr Bill for permission to reproduce the list of Commissioners from *The Queen Anne Churches* (Mansell, 1979); Mrs Jean Chapman and my daughters Helen and Elisabeth for help with the Indexes; my colleague Dr John Miller for reading the Introduction; Mr David Johnson for looking through the House of Lords papers; Mr Ralph Hyde, Mr J. Fisher, Mr D. J. Thomas, Mr D. A. Armstrong, and the Department of Geography, Queen Mary College, for help with the map of parishes; and the former general editors of the London Record Society, William Kellaway and Michael Collinge, for their forbearance over the too many years it has taken to prepare this calendar.

LIST OF COMMISSIONERS AND OFFICERS OF THE COMMISSION FOR BUILDING FIFTY NEW CHURCHES

The Commissioners
Reproduced by permission from E. G. W. Bill, *The Queen Anne Churches* (1979).

1. Commissioners appointed by letters patent dated 21 September 1711
Thomas Tenison (Archbishop of Canterbury), John Sharp (Archbishop of York), John Robinson (Bishop of Bristol), Henry Compton (Bishop of London), Jonathan Trelawney (Bishop of Winchester), Nathaniel Crewe (Bishop of Durham), Thomas Sprat (Bishop of Rochester), Francis Atterbury, D.D. (Prolocutor of the House of Convocation and Dean of Christ Church, Oxford), George Stanhope, D.D. (Dean of Canterbury), Henry Godolphin (Dean of St. Paul's), William Stanley, D.D. (Archdeacon of London), George Smalridge, D.D., Francis Gastrell, D.D., Robert Moss, D.D., Robert Freind, D.D., Thomas Sherlock (Master of the Temple).
The Earl of Thanet, the Earl of Anglesea, the Earl of Rochester, the Earl of Dartmouth (Secretary of State), Viscount Weymouth, Lord Guernsey, William Bromley (Speaker of the House of Commons), Robert Benson (Chancellor of the Exchequer), the Lord Mayor of London, Sir Thomas Powys (Sergeant at Law), Sir Edward Northey (Attorney-General), Sir Robert Raymond (Solicitor-General), James Bertie, Hugh Smithson, Thomas Medlicott, Thomas Crosse, Sir William Withers (Alderman of London), Sir Richard Hoare (Alderman of London), Sir George Newland (Alderman of London), John Cass (Alderman of London), the Sheriffs of London, Sir Christopher Wren (Surveyor of the Queen's Works), Edward Harley (Auditor of the Imprests), John Hoskyns, Edward Jennings, John Isham, Robert Nelson, Henry Hoare, Francis Annesley, Nathaniel Manlove, Dr John Radcliffe, Thomas Archer, Christopher Wren (Chief Clerk of the Queen's Works), John Vanbrugh (Comptroller of the Queen's Works), Henry Box, Whitlock Bulstrode.

2. Commissioners appointed by letters patent dated 7 September 1712
Thomas Tenison (Archbishop of Canterbury), John Sharp (Archbishop of York), John Robinson (Bishop of Bristol), Henry Compton (Bishop of London), and the Bishop of London for the time being, Jonathan Trelawney (Bishop of Winchester), Nathaniel Crewe (Bishop of Durham), Thomas Sprat (Bishop of Rochester), William Dawes (Bishop of Chester), Philip Bisse (Bishop of St. David's), Francis Atterbury, D.D. (Prolocutor of the House of Convocation and

Dean of Christ Church, Oxford), George Stanhope, D.D. (Dean of Canterbury), Henry Godolphin, D.D. (Dean of St. Paul's), William Stanley, D.D. (Archdeacon of London), George Smalridge, D.D., Francis Gastrell, D.D., Robert Moss, D.D., Robert Freind, D.D., John King, D.D., Thomas Sherlock (Master of the Temple).

The Duke of Buckingham (President of the Council), the Earl of Thanet, the Earl of Anglesea, the Earl of Rochester, the Earl of Dartmouth (Secretary of State), Viscount Bolingbroke (Secretary of State), Viscount Weymouth, Lord Guernsey, Lord Harcourt (Lord Chancellor), Lord Willoughby de Broke, William Bromley (Speaker of the House of Commons), Robert Benson (Chancellor of the Exchequer), the Lord Mayor of London, Sir Thomas Powys (Sergeant at Law), Sir Edward Northey (Attorney-General), Sir Robert Raymond (Solicitor-General), Sir Nathaniel Lloyd (Advocate General), John Bettesworth, LL.D. (Principal Official of the Court of Arches and Vicar-General), James Bertie, Hugh Smithson, Thomas Medlicott, Thomas Crosse, Sir William Withers (Alderman of London), Sir Gilbert Heathcote (Alderman of London), Sir Richard Hoare (Alderman of London), Sir George Newland (Alderman of London), Sir John Cass (Alderman of London), the Sheriffs of London, Sir Christopher Wren (Surveyor of the Queen's Works), Edward Harley (Auditor of the Imprests), John Hoskyns, Edward Jennings, Robert Nelson, Henry Hoare, Francis Annesley, Nathaniel Manlove, Dr John Radcliffe, Dr John Arbuthnott, Thomas Archer, Christopher Wren (Chief Clerk of the Queen's Works), John Vanbrugh (Comptroller of the Queen's Works), Henry Box, Whitlock Bulstrode, Sir James Bateman, Sir Ambrose Crawley, Thomas Foley, John Aislabie, George Clarke, Sir Isaac Newton, Edmund Halley (Professor of Astronomy at Oxford), Richard Hill, John Ward (of the Middle Temple), Erasmus Lewis, Robert Child, Thomas Bateman, Reginald Marriott.

3. Commissioners appointed by letters patent dated 2 December 1715
Thomas Tenison (Archbishop of Canterbury), William Dawes (Archbishop of York), John Robinson (Bishop of London), and the Bishop of London for the time being, Jonathan Trelawney (Bishop of Winchester), John Hough (Bishop of Coventry and Lichfield), William Talbot (Bishop of Salisbury), John Evans (Bishop of Bangor), William Wake (Bishop of Lincoln), Charles Trimnell (Bishop of Norwich), William Fleetwood (Bishop of Ely), George Smalridge (Bishop of Bristol), Richard Willis (Bishop of Gloucester), John Wynne (Bishop of St. Asaph), George Stanhope, D.D. (Prolocutor of the House of Convocation and Dean of Canterbury), Henry Godolphin, D.D. (Dean of St. Paul's), White Kennett, D.D. (Dean of Peterborough), Robert Moss, D.D. (Dean of Ely), Francis Hare, D.D. (Dean of Worcester), Thomas Sherlock, D.D. (Dean of Chichester), William Stanley, D.D. (Archdeacon of London), Thomas Lynford, D.D., Lilly Butler, D.D., Samuel Bradford, D.D., Robert Cannon, D.D., John Waugh, D.D., Edward Waddington, D.D., Thomas Gooch, D.D.

Sir Thomas Parker (Chief Justice of the King's Bench), Sir Peter King (Chief Justice of the Common Pleas), Sir Samuel Dodd (Chief Baron of the Exchequer), Sir Robert Eyre (Judge of the King's Bench), the Lord Mayor of London, Sir Joseph Jekyll (Sergeant at Law), Sir Edward Northey (Attorney-General), the Solicitor-General, Sir Gilbert Heathcote (Alderman of London), the Sheriffs of London, Sir John Philipps, Bart., Sir George Markham, Bart., Sir Randolph Knipe, Sir Isaac Newton, Sir Harcourt Masters, John Bettesworth, LL.D. (Principal Official of the Court of Arches and Judge of the Prerogative Court of Canterbury), George Paul, LL.D. (Vicar-General), Sir Nathaniel Lloyd, L.L.D. (Advocate-General), John Hiccocks (Master in Chancery), John Meller (Master in Chancery), William Melmoth (Barrister), John Pulteney, George Naylor, William Falkner, William Clayton, John Ellys, John Hoskins, John Aislabie, William Farrer, Thomas Pitt senior, Thomas Micklethwait, Edward Peck.

4. Commissioners appointed by letters patent dated 24 November 1727
William Wake (Archbishop of Canterbury), and the Archbishop of Canterbury for the time being, Lancelot Blackburn (Archbishop of York), Edmund Gibson (Bishop of London), and the Bishop of London for the time being, William Talbot (Bishop of Durham), Richard Willis (Bishop of Winchester), John Wynne (Bishop of Bath and Wells), Benjamin Hoadly (Bishop of Salisbury), Thomas Greene (Bishop of Ely), Samuel Bradford (Bishop of Rochester), White Kennet (Bishop of Peterborough), William Baker (Bishop of Bangor), John Waugh (Bishop of Carlisle), John Leng (Bishop of Norwich), Richard Smallbrooke (Bishop of St. David's), Edward Waddington (Bishop of Chichester), Samuel Peploe (Bishop of Chester), George Stanhope, D.D. (Dean of Canterbury), Francis Hare, D.D. (Dean of St. Paul's), Robert Moss, D.D. (Dean of Ely), Thomas Sherlock, D.D. (Dean of Chichester), Nicholas Claget, D.D. (Dean of Rochester), William Stanley, D.D. (Archdeacon of London), Thomas Gooch, D.D. (Archdeacon of Essex).

Sir Robert Raymond (Chief Justice of the King's Bench), Sir Joseph Jekyll (Master of the Rolls), Sir Robert Eyre (Chief Justice of the Common Pleas), Sir Thomas Pengelly (Chief Baron of the Exchequer), Robert Price (Judge of the Court of Common Pleas), the Lord Mayor of London, Sir John Cheshyre (Sergeant at Law), Sir Philip Yorke (Attorney-General), Charles Talbot (Solicitor-General), and the Attorney- and Solicitor-General for the time being, the Sheriffs of London, Sir Robert Walpole (Chancellor of the Exchequer), and the Chancellor of the Exchequer for the time being, Sir Spencer Compton, Sir Charles Turner, Bart., Sir John Philipps, Bart., Sir Daniel Dolins, Sir Richard Hopkins, Sir William Ogbourne, John Bettesworth, LL.D. (Principal Official of the Court of Arches and Judge of the Prerogative Court of Canterbury), George Paul, LL.D. (Advocate-General), William Pulteney, P.C., John Verney, William Clayton, Francis Annesley, John Meller, William Melmoth,

List of commissioners and officers

John Ellis, Martin Blayden, John Scroop, William Farrer, John Conduit, Robert Jacomb, Edward Peck.

The Officers

1. The Queen Anne Commissions, 1711–15

Secretary	Thomas Rous
Agent and solicitor	John Skeat
Messenger	Thomas Crocker
Doorkeeper	Thomas Brookes
Solicitor	Simon Beckley (appointed 28 Nov. 1711)
Treasurer	Henry Smith (appointed July 1712)
Surveyors	Nicholas Hawksmoor
	William Dickinson (resigned 13 August 1713)
	James Gibbs (appointed 18 Nov. 1713)

2. The King George Commissions, 1716–58

Secretary	Jenkin Thomas Phillips (discontinued 1734)
Agent	John Skeat (died September 1724)
	John Prichard (appointed 14 Sept. 1724; died February 1727)
	John Sherman (appointed 27 Feb. 1727; died May 1744)
	Edward Sleech (appointed May 1744)
Messenger	William Waters (died May 1729)
	Richard Bowman (appointed May 1729)
Solicitor	Vigerus Edwards (discontinued 1734)
Treasurer	John Leacroft (died November 1721)
	Nathaniel Blackerby (appointed 10 Jan. 1722, died June 1742)
	Henry Fane (appointed June 1742; resigned 1758)
Surveyors	Nicholas Hawksmoor and John James (discontinued, Midsummer 1733)

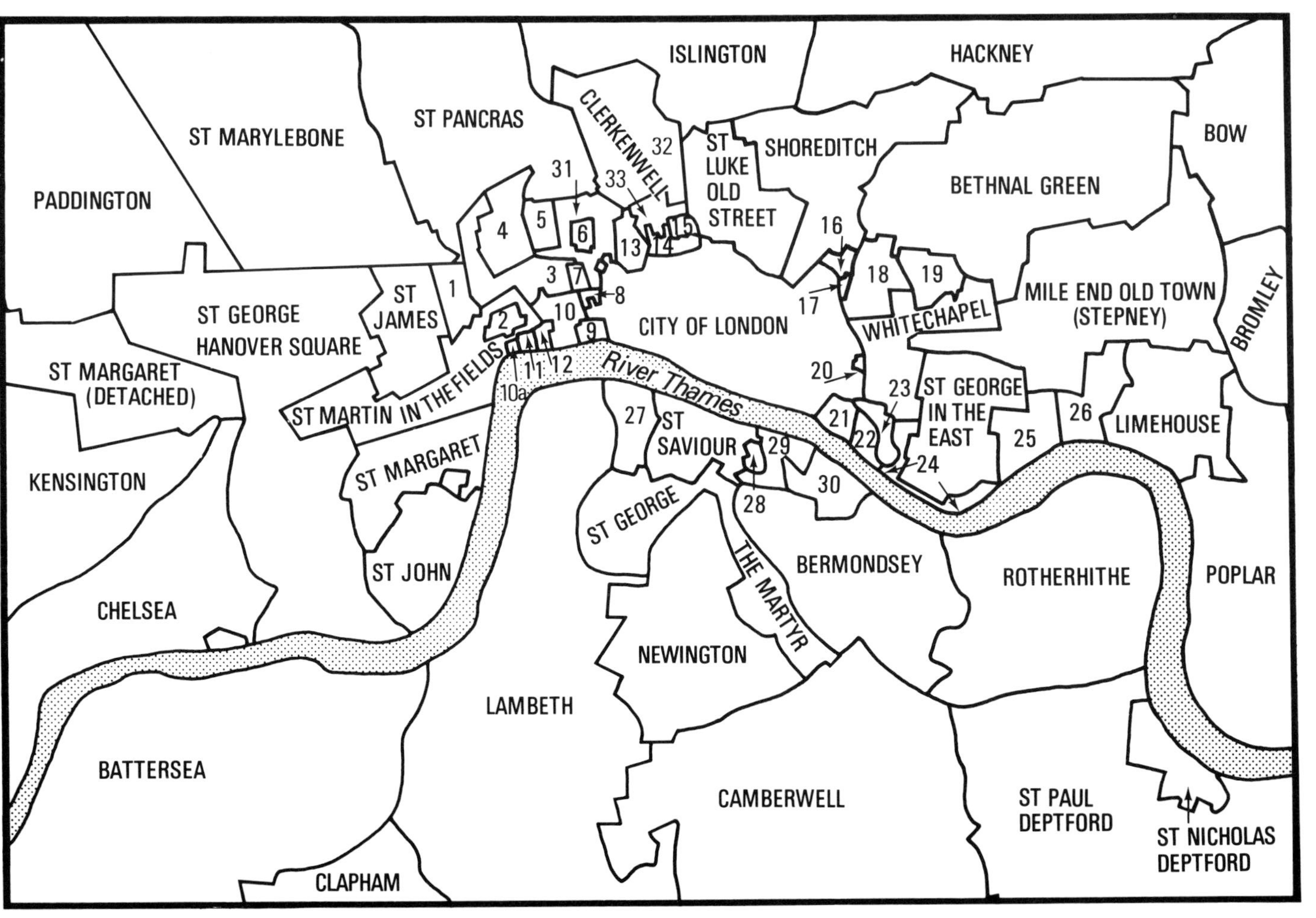

ISLINGTON
HACKNEY
ST PANCRAS
ST MARYLEBONE
PADDINGTON
CLERKENWELL
ST LUKE OLD STREET
SHOREDITCH
BOW
BETHNAL GREEN
MILE END OLD TOWN (STEPNEY)
BROMLEY
WHITECHAPEL
CITY OF LONDON
ST JAMES
ST GEORGE HANOVER SQUARE
ST MARGARET (DETACHED)
ST MARTIN IN THE FIELDS
River Thames
ST GEORGE IN THE EAST
LIMEHOUSE
ST SAVIOUR
ST MARGARET
KENSINGTON
ST GEORGE
BERMONDSEY
ROTHERHITHE
POPLAR
ST JOHN
THE MARTYR
CHELSEA
NEWINGTON
LAMBETH
BATTERSEA
CAMBERWELL
ST PAUL DEPTFORD
ST NICHOLAS DEPTFORD
CLAPHAM

Parishes in London and Westminster, outside the City of London

The map on the facing page has been redrawn from those accompanying W. Loftie's *History of London* (1884), for which the base map was Rocque's 'Environs of London' (1763).

Key to numbers

1. St Anne Soho
2. St Paul Covent Garden
3. St Giles in the Fields
4. St George Bloomsbury
5. St George the Martyr Queen's Square (Ormond Street)
6. Gray's Inn (extra-parochial)
7. Lincoln's Inn (extra-parochial)
8. Liberty of the Rolls
9. Temple (extra-parochial)
10. St Clement Danes

10a. St Clement Danes (detached)

11. Precinct of the Savoy
12. St Mary le Strand
13. Liberty of Saffron Hill
14. St Sepulchre
15. Charterhouse (extra-parochial)
16. Liberty of Norton Folgate
17. Old Artillery Ground (extra-parochial)
18. Christ Church Spitalfields
19. Mile End New Town
20. Holy Trinity Minories
21. Tower Liberty
22. St Katharine by the Tower (royal peculiar)
23. St Botolph without Aldgate
24. St John Wapping
25. St Paul Shadwell
26. Ratcliff
27. Christ Church Southwark
28. St Thomas Southwark
29. St Olave Southwark
30. St John Horsleydown
31. St Andrew Holborn
32. St James Clerkenwell
33. St John Clerkenwell

CHURCHES BUILT BY THE COMMISSIONERS FOR BUILDING FIFTY NEW CHURCHES

Church	Architect	Date
Christ Church Spitalfields	N. Hawksmoor	1714–29
St Alphege Greenwich	N. Hawksmoor	1712–18
St Anne Limehouse	N. Hawksmoor	1714–30
St George Bloomsbury	N. Hawksmoor	1716–31
St George in the East (Upper Wapping)	N. Hawksmoor	1714–29
St George Hanover Square	J. James	1720–5
St John Horsleydown (Southwark)	N. Hawksmoor and J. James	1727–33
St John Smith Square, Millbank (Westminster)	T. Archer	1713–28
St Luke Old Street (Cripplegate)	N. Hawksmoor and J. James	1727–33
St Mary le Strand	J. Gibbs	1714–23
St Mary Woolnoth (rebuilt)	N. Hawksmoor	1716–24
St Paul Deptford	T. Archer	1713–30

Churches subsidised from the Commissioners' funds

Church	Architect	Date
St George Gravesend	Charles Sloane	1731–3
St George the Martyr, Southwark	John Price	1734–6
St Giles in the Fields	Henry Flitcroft	1731–4
St Mary Magdalen, Woolwich	? Matthew Spray	1727–40
St Michael Cornhill (tower completed)	N. Hawksmoor	1718–24

Church bought by the Commissioners and altered

Church	Architect	Date
St George the Martyr, Ormond Street (Queen Square)	N. Hawksmoor	1717–20

Church bought by the Commissioners

Church	Architect	Date
St John Clerkenwell		1723

THE COMMISSIONS FOR BUILDING FIFTY NEW CHURCHES

MINUTES OF THE COMMISSIONERS, 1711–18

Lambeth MS 2690

1a. [p. iii] 'The Rt Honble Ld Bishop of Bristol, Lord Privy Seal, his abstract of what business lies before the Rt Honble and Honble Commissioners appointed by Her Majesty for building Churches etc. Vizt

To enquire into what parishes the said churches, cemeteries and minister's houses are needed.

What chapels now in being may be converted into parish churches.

What limits to be fixed for the said new parishes.

In what part of those limits the churches are to be placed.

What houses, ground, etc. necessary to be purchased for that end.

What estates and interests are in the houses, grounds, etc., that are to be purchased for those ends.

To return an answer in writing by the 24th of December 1711 to Her Majesty; and a duplicate of the same to each House of Parliament.'

1b. [p. 1] 3 Oct. 1711, at Banqueting House, Whitehall
1. Jennings reported what passed at Lambeth House, upon opening the commission, on Friday, 28 September: commission was opened and read; Commissioners present chose Mr Thos Rous their Secretary, adjourning till Wednesday, 3 October 1711 to the Banqueting House, Whitehall.
2–3. Mr John Skeat to be Agent and Solicitor; Thos Crocker, Messenger; Thos Brookes, Doorkeeper; if hereafter occasion for another Messenger, Edward Stanley to be used.
4. Secretary to write to Minister, churchwardens and vestrymen of the following parishes, according to the draft proposed by Dean of Canterbury and Dr Moss: St Andrew Holborn, St Ann Westminster, St Botolph Aldgate, St Botolph Aldersgate, St Clement Danes, St Giles Cripplegate, St James Clerkenwell, St Sepulchre, St Giles in the Fields, St Martin in the Fields, St Mary Magdalen Bermondsey, St Paul Shadwell, St James Westminster, St Leonard Shoreditch, St Margaret Westminster, St Olave Southwark, St Saviour Southwark, St Mary Whitechapel, Deptford, and St Dunstan Stepney. To the following chapels: New chapel in St Margaret Westminster, St George's chapel in St Andrew Holborn, Hatton Garden

chapel, and King Street chapel near St James Westminster, and St Mary le Strand.

5. 'The Commissioners appointed by Her Majesty, pursuant to a late Act of Parliament (entitled etc.) being desirous to proceed in so pious and useful a work with all possible expedition, have thought fit hereby to request that you would inform them concerning the number and condition of your inhabitants, that so they may the better be enabled to judge, what new church or churches will be necessary to be erected in your parish.

You are also desired to inform them of proper places for the sites of the said church or churches, and for church yards, and also for houses for the habitation of the respective ministers; and lastly, whether there be in your parish any chapel or chapels fit to be made parish churches.

All which you are desired to signify under your hands, with all convenient speed, that the Commissioners may proceed accordingly.'

6. 'To the Minister and Trustees of St George's Chapel, etc.

The Commissioners . . . do desire you with all convenient speed to lay before them the constitution, state and condition of St George's Chapel; and whether the same may be fit to be made a parochial church; and what terms you shall propose proper for that purpose; as also what place may be found commodious for a church yard, and for the habitation of the minister.'

2. [p. 2] 10 Oct. 1711

1,2. Read representation from minister and churchwardens of Stepney. Churchwarden and parish clerk of St James Westminster delivered reasons why, at present, they could not make any return.

3. William Dickinson and Mr Nicholas Hawksmoor appointed Surveyors.

4–6. Sir C. Wren, Stanhope, Annesley, Smalridge, Bertie, Archer, Vanbrugh, Sir R. Hoare, Jennings, Mr Wren, Mosse, Isham, Sir R. Raymond, Sherlock, Mr Hy Hoare and Bulstrode, and all other Commissioners that attend (any three being a quorum), appointed as a committee to prepare instructions for the Surveyors, consider proposals already received, and receive any further proposals from parishes, and report. All Commissioners present to have votes. Committee to meet in this place immediately after the Commissioners adjourn.

7. Messenger to give notice when and where the Committee to meet.

8. A conveniency to be made in this room for the Secretary to lock up books and papers for the Commissioners' use.

3. [p. 4] 17 Oct. 1711

Read minutes of Commissioners, 10 Oct. (**2**), and of Committee, 16 Oct. (**479**).

1. Read representation of St George's chapel, Ormond Street, St Andrew Holborn.

2. Resolved that St George's chapel is fit to be made a parochial church, being capable of holding about 2,000 people for Divine Service.

3,4. Bishop of London to apply to Lady Russell for a piece of ground near the chapel for a church yard, when made parochial.
5. Read resolutions of the Committee relating to erecting five new churches in Stepney parish.
6. Resolved that the chapel at Poplar is fit to be made a parochial church.
7,8. Sir R. Hoare and the two present sheriffs of London and Middlesex to apply to the East India Company, to know their interest in the chapel, and desire their concurrence that it be made a parochial church.
9. The rest of the Committee's resolutions relating to Stepney to be re-committed; the Committee to consider the recent act of Parliament relating to the division of the parish after the death of the present incumbent.
10. Read the memorial of the minister and churchwardens of Deptford, relating to erecting a new parish church, and the Committee's resolutions thereon.
11. Resolved that one of the fifty new churches ought to be erected in Deptford.

4. [p. 6] 24 Oct. 1711
1,2. Bishop of London reported that Lady Russell agreed to sell the piece of ground mentioned in the representation of the trustees of St George's chapel for a church yard; she would desire Mr Hoskins, one of this Commission, to treat with any that the Commissioners should appoint. Also that she has some old houses in the parish of St Giles, of which the leases are nearly expired, which she had deferred renewing, thinking to pull them down and erect a place for public worship. Being since informed that there were new churches to be built in that parish, she would suspend renewing the leases till she knew whether the Commissioners thought it a proper site for a new church.
3. Sir R. Hoare reported he had seen the Directors of the East India Company about Poplar chapel; they would reply in writing.
4. Agreed with the Committee that a letter should be written to the Principal and Fellows of Brasenose College Oxford, signifying the division intended to be made of the parish of Stepney, and to desire their concurrence.
5. Approved draft of such letter prepared by Dean of Canterbury.
6. Secretary to write and subscribe the said letter, and send it forthwith by the General Post.
7. Letter to be sent to Sir Nat. Curzon and John Kent, Esq., about the terms for church yard for St George's chapel, Ormond Street.
8. John Hoskins to be added to the Committee.

5. [p. 8] 31 Oct. 1711
1. Lord Privy Seal reported that the Lord Treasurer had promised to order £200 to be issued towards defraying incident charges about executing this Commission.
2,3. Read letter from secretary of East India Co. presented by Sir R. Hoare, about Poplar chapel. Consideration adjourned until reply received about Stepney from Brasenose College.

4. Dr Landon, minister of Poplar, attended; Sir R. Hoare to desire East India Co. directors for early reply about making the chapel parochial.
5. Committee empowered to treat with any persons, as required, for carrying on more speedily and effectually the purpose of this Commission, reporting the result.
6. Agreed with the Committee that one of the fifty new churches ought to be erected in Bishopsgate parish, including the precincts of Norton Folgate, the Old Artillery Ground and St Mary le Spittle.
7. Dean of Canterbury to draft letter to parishes that have not made returns to the letter of 4 October, desiring them to make their returns to the Committee by 9 November; otherwise the Commissioners will proceed without them.
8. Secretary to provide one of the best and largest maps of the Cities of London and Westminster and suburbs thereof, to be hung in this room for the Commissioners' use.

6. [p. 10] 7 Nov. 1711
1. No church to be built at the end of Albemarle Street.
2–4. Dean and Chapter of Westminster thanked for offer of a free site.
5,6. Dean of Rochester and inhabitants of St Mary le Strand given leave to state in petition to the Queen that in Commissioners' opinion one of the new churches should be for their benefit.
7. Received letter from the Principal of Brasenose College.
8. Letter to Brasenose College states that churches are to be apportioned to population; hope that Parliament will provide for ministers' maintenance.
9. Resolved that new churches ought to be built in the following parishes, according to the numbers there allotted to each parish:

St Andrew Holborn	3	St Leonard Shoreditch	2
St Botolph Aldgate	2	St Mary Magdalen Bermondsey	
St Bride's including White Friars	1	St James Clerkenwell	1
St Botolph Bishopsgate	1	St Mary Whitechapel	2
St George Southwark	1	St Paul Shadwell	1
St Giles Cripplegate	1	St Ann Westminster	1
St Saviour Southwark	1	St Clement Danes	1
St Olave Southwark	2	St Margaret Westminster	2
St Sepulchre	2	Lambeth	1
St Dunstan Stepney	5	St Mary le Strand	1
St Giles in the Fields	4	Deptford	1
		Rotherhithe	1

Sir C. Wren, Thos Archer, John Vanbrugh and Chr. Wren, Esquires, to view the sites agreed upon by the Surveyors, and report.

7. [p. 12] 14 Nov. 1711
Agreed with Committee that:

1. One of the new churches ought to be erected within St John Wapping parish.
2. Bow chapel in Stepney parish ought to be made a parochial church.
3. The hamlet of Bethnal Green in Stepney parish be made a parish, and a new church be erected there.
4. The hamlet of Limehouse in Stepney parish be made a parish, and a new church be erected there.
5. The hamlet of Upper Wapping be made a parish, and a new church be erected there.
6. The hamlet of Lower Wapping in Stepney parish be made a parish, and a new church be erected there.
7. The hamlet of Spitalfields in Stepney parish be divided into two districts or parishes, and two new churches be erected there.
8. Where cemeteries can conveniently be had, at some distance from the churches, they ought to be so appointed.
9. A new church ought to be erected in St Botolph Aldgate parish.

10,11. Resolved that Great Lincoln's Inn Square is a proper site for one of the new churches in St Giles in the Fields parish, provided there be no church yard, nor burials in the church, nor a ring of bells. Notice of the resolution to be given to the inhabitants, and to the Society of Lincoln's Inn.

12. Upon reconsidering the state of St Sepulchre parish, resolved that only one new church ought to be erected there, viz in that part without the Liberty.

13,14. Representation of the trustees of King Street Chapel, St James Westminster, to be laid before Archbishop of Canterbury by Freind, Bulstrode and Hoskins, to know his opinion and the nature of the trust.

15. The first part of Lady Russell's answer, relating to a church yard for Ormond Street chapel, to be communicated to the trustees of the chapel.
16. The site of the Maypole in the Strand, proposed for a parish church for St Mary le Strand parish, to be recommitted.
17. Nelson to be added to the Committee.

8. [p. 15] 21 Nov. 1711

Agreed to the following resolutions of the Committee, reported by Smalridge:

1. That the parish of St James Westminster should be divided into four distinct parishes.
2. That the parish of St Martin's in the Fields should be divided into four distinct parishes.
3. Resolved, that the site proposed in Upper Wapping, next Ratcliff Highway, Cannon Street, etc., is a convenient site for a church, church yard and minister's house.
4. The site proposed by Archer, at the low end of the Minories on Little Tower Hill, is a proper site for one of the two new churches in the parish of St Botolph Aldgate; Archer to ascertain of John Jefferys, Esq., of Sheen, Surrey, what he demands.
5. Read Committee's resolution relating to the site proposed for a church, etc. in Harefields, Bethnal Green; resolved that if there were no

greater objections than what has already been made, there ought to be a church there erected for Bethnal Green hamlet.
6. The sites for churches, church yards and ministers' houses to be fixed upon before any districts of parishes be made; reserving liberty to alter such sites as required.
10.* Resolved that Westfield in Limehouse hamlet is a proper site for a church and minister's house, unless a more convenient site can be proposed nearer the centre of the hamlet.
7. Surveyors to enquire chiefly after ground to build ministers' houses on; unless they propose houses to be pulled down in order to erect new ones.
8. No site to be pitched upon for erecting a new church, where it will not admit that the church be placed east and west, without special reasons, to be particularly approved of by the Commissioners.
9. As many maps as can be got of the several parishes wherein new churches are to be built to be bought by the Secretary.

* Postscript, numbered 10, but marked to be inserted after 6.

9. [p. 18] 28 Nov. 1711
Agreed with the Committee that:
1. The district formerly proposed for a parish by the trustees of St George's chapel, Ormond Street, is a proper district.
2. The demand made by Sir N. Curzon and John Kent, Esq. for the inheritance of the ground whereon St George's chapel stands is unreasonable.
3,4. Unless they propose more reasonable terms, the Commissioners will erect a new church in Red Lion Square, or elsewhere within the district. Mr Box to acquaint the said proprietors accordingly.
5,6. A debate arising about the two sites for churches, etc., proposed by the inhabitants of Limehouse, resolved that Rigby's Garden ground ought to be preferred before West's Field (the proprietor making convenient approaches), if it can be had on reasonable terms.
7. Further agreed with the Committee that:
(1.) The Three Cups Inn, Holborn, is a proper site for a new church within the parish of St Andrew Holborn.
8–10.(2.) A solicitor ought to be appointed to enquire into the interests of such sites as the Commissioners wish to purchase, and to make abstracts of deeds, in order to lay them before some of the Commissioners. Simon Beckley to be appointed Solicitor for the purposes mentioned. Messrs Jennings, Box and Annesley to inspect such titles as the Solicitor prepares for them.
11. Also agreed with the Committee that the sites proposed for churches and ministers' houses, to be taken out of St Olave Southwark, are proper; the former is in Stoney Lane and Unicorn Yard; the latter in Horsleydown Lane.
12. Two acres of ground to be allowed for each church yard when so much can be obtained on reasonable terms.
The district proposed by the Committee for the lower parish within St Botolph Aldgate is proper.

13. To the districts proposed by Rev. Dr Bray for the middle parish in St Botolph Aldgate there ought to be added all the houses on both sides the way from the north side of Trinity Minories to Whitechapel Street and all the south side of Whitechapel from Aldgate to the Bars.
14,15. The new church in Lambeth parish ought to be erected within the Liberty of Stockwell, on the ground offered gratis by Sir John Thornicroft. Robt Nelson, Esq., to return the Commissioners' thanks to Sir John for his generous offer.
16. The gentlemen who appeared for the Liberty of Stockwell to procure the consent of all who have right of commonage there, that an act of Parliament may be obtained for erecting a church thereon.
17. The site proposed at the Maypole in the Strand is a proper site for a new church for the parish of St Mary le Strand; the district commonly called the Savoy Ward (part of St Clement Danes parish) ought to be added to the parish of St Mary le Strand.
18. Read Hawksmoor's report that the approaches for coaches from Harefields to Bethnal Green may be made convenient; resolved that the new church for Bethnal Green ought to be erected in Crossfields by Hare Street.

10. [p. 21] 1 Dec. 1711
Agreed with the Committee that:
1. Mr Watts' demand of £400 for two acres of ground for the site of a church, etc., in Upper Wapping is reasonable.
2. All that part of St Saviour Southwark parish known as the Borough Liberty, and part of Clink Liberty beginning at Deadman's place on the south, and all the east side of Stoney Street toward the Thames ought to be continued to the mother church.
3. The Tenterfields on the north side of Castle Street is a proper site for a church, etc. to be taken out of the parish of St Saviour.
4. Its district ought to be bounded by Bandy Leg Walk, Maiden Lane on the north and north-west, and on the north by the Bear Garden down Rope Alley, to be terminated by the Thames on the north.
5. The site proposed in Pye Garden on the south side of Maiden Lane is a proper site for a second church, etc. within the said parish; its district ought to consist of the remaining part of the parish, lying south-west of Maiden Lane.
6. Mr Slaughter's demand of £300 for the site of a church, etc. in Hare alias Cross fields, Bethnal Green, as set out by Hawksmoor, is reasonable.
7. When they make their report to the Queen and Parliament, they will represent how convenient it will be to add some part of St Giles Cripplegate parish, lying contiguous to St Alphage, to that parish, which is very small.
8. Mr Smith's ground on Millbank, St Margaret Westminster parish, is a proper site for a church and minister's house for one of the new churches.
9. The site and district proposed by Hawksmoor for a church, etc., to be taken out of Bermondsey parish is proper.
10. The parish of St Sepulchre should be divided into two by a line drawn

from [blank's] house in Long Lane through the centre of the lane and thence across Smithfield on the north side of the sheep pens and down the middle of Check Lane to Fleet Ditch.
11. The two sites and districts proposed by Dickinson for the new parishes to be taken out of St Olave Southwark are proper.
12. Earl of Rochester to speak with Earl of Salisbury, to persuade him to set a moderate price on his ground, proposed for the site of a church, etc. in Bermondsey.
13. Hoskins to remind Archbishop of Canterbury of the written answer he promised, relating to King Street chapel, St James Westminster.
14. Dean of Carlisle and Annesley to draft report from the Commissioners to Queen and Parliament.

11. [p. 24] 5 Dec. 1711
1. Mr Willmers offered a site for a church, etc., called the Mermaid Brewhouse in White Cross Street, in St Giles Cripplegate, at £550.
2,3. Read petition of Wm Richardson, clerk, relating to a chapel in St Jones's [*sic*], in St James Clerkenwell parish. Dickinson to report thereon, and discourse Dr Carr, the proprietor, about his demand.
4,5. Read a second demand from Sir N. Curzon and John Kent, Esq., for the inheritance of the site of St George's chapel [Ormond Street]; the sum of £1,000 demanded is reasonable.
6,7. Read petitions of several inhabitants of Limehouse that a church be built on Westfield; and of others that Rigby's Garden be chosen. Heard the petitioners. Resolved that, for the reasons offered in and upon the petition for Westfield, the order relating to erecting a church in Rigby's Garden be revoked, and that the church ought to be erected in Westfield.
8. Accepted Mr Kemp's demand for ground proposed for a house for minister of Bow and Old Ford.

12. [p. 26] 12 Dec. 1711
1–3. Received representation from St Saviour Southwark; and letter from Archbishop of Canterbury on King Street chapel.
4. Agreed with committee in two resolutions:
5. The case of the parishioners of Rotherhithe to be particularly represented to Queen and Parliament.
6. The chapel in Hatton Garden is not fit to be made a parochial church.
7,8. Bulstrode, accompanied by Hawksmoor, to enquire what ground or houses can be purchased about the chapel to make it a proper site for a church, with the several demands for the property.
9,10. Disagreed to the Committee's resolution relating to the district for the new parish of St Clement Danes. The churchwardens of the liberties within the parish to attend the Committee on Friday next, to inform them about the division of the parish.
11. Read, the consent of freeholders of Common Green, Stockwell, Lambeth.

13. [p. 28] 17 Dec. 1711
1. Reported that pulling down some houses adjacent to Hatton Garden

chapel might make it a proper site for parochial church and minister's house.

2. Bulstrode to enquire their demands of the proprietors, and ask Bishop of Ely his views and terms for his interest.

3. Read Archbishop of Canterbury's letter relating to King Street chapel. His Grace having been a great benefactor and unwilling that the chapel should be made parochial, resolved that it should not be made parochial.

4,5. Surveyors to enquire for three sites for churches, etc., within St James Westminster parish. Freind, Hoskins and Bulstrode, or either of them, to inform Archbishop.

6. Agreed with the Committee that:
The districts proposed by Hawksmoor in two plans before them, of St Giles in the Fields and St Paul Shadwell parishes, are proper for the division of the parishes.

7. Mr Rous's demand of £350 for site for church and minister's house for the parish to be taken out of Shadwell is reasonable.

8. Dean of Carlisle brought draft report to the Queen, which was unanimously agreed to.

The officers to bring their accounts of disbursements to the Committee on Friday, 21 December at 3 p.m.; Committee to distribute the £200 advanced towards incidental charges among the officers.

Copy of the report above mentioned [minute 8]:

> 'To the Queen's most excellent Majesty.
>
> Whereas by your Majesty's commission . . . bearing date the 21st day of September 1711 . . . the Commissioners therein named are directed, authorized and commanded to enquire and inform themselves, in what parishes in and about the Cities of London and Westminster, fifty new churches except one for Greenwich were most necessary to be built, and of proper places for the sites of the respective new churches, and, also, a cemetery or church yard for each of the said churches, for the burial of Christian people, to be purchased; and also what chapels in the respective parishes aforesaid are fit to be made parish churches, and to ascertain the several houses, lands, tenements and hereditaments, and bonds and limits which may be fit to be made distinct parishes: and to enquire and inform themselves by the best means they could of the value of such lands, tenements and houses, and of the respective estates and interests therein as they, or any five or more of them, should think necessary to be purchased for the said sites and cemeteries, and for the houses for the habitations for the respective ministers, and that they, or any five or more of them, do on or before the 24th day of December 1711 report or certify to your Majesty, in writing under their hands and seals, such matters and things as should appear to them upon their inquiries aforesaid with their opinions thereupon, to the end such further directions might be given thereupon, as might be pursuant to your Majesty's intentions . . .
>
> Your Commissioners have had frequent meetings and consul-

tations; and have caused schemes and plans of the several parishes, and of sites for churches to be drawn and laid before them; the delineation of which by proper and skilful persons hath taken up much time and they have made diligent enquiries and informed themselves by the best means they could of the several matters aforesaid; but they do with all humility represent to your Majesty that they have not with their utmost industry and application been able within the time laid down for the purposes aforesaid to lay before your Majesty a representation of all those facts which it is necessary for your Majesty to be fully informed, in order to the putting in execution your pious intentions for completing a work which tends so much to the honour of God, to the spiritual welfare of your subjects, to the interest of the Established Church, and to the glory of your Majesty's reign: But from what progress they have already made, they are humbly of opinion that if farther time were given them, for the purposes aforesaid, they should then be able fully and satisfactorily to answer your Majesty's expectations: And they do think it a duty incumbent upon them, humbly to represent to your Majesty that one great obstruction they found in carrying on this pious good work was the want of power to contract with the several proprietors of lands, proper for sites for churches and cemeteries, and for houses for the habitations of the respective ministers, which defect of power the Commissioners do conceive hath created a backwardness in several of the proprietors, either to lay before the Commissioners their titles, whereby it might appear what estates and interests the respective proprietors had in [the sites] . . . or even so much as to treat with the Commissioners about the sale or purchase thereof. All which matters are . . . humbly submitted to your Majesty . . .' 18 December 1711.

14. [p. 32] 6 June 1712
1. Read act of Parliament for enlarging time and giving further powers to the Commissioners.
2. Jennings and Annesley to make an abstract of powers in the act.
3. The Committee formerly appointed to consider what is proper to be done for executing the act, and report to next meeting.
4. Commissioners to meet here on Wed. next at 10 a.m.

15. [p. 33] 18 June 1712
1–3. Sites proposed for new church, etc., at Limehouse to be reviewed by the Dean of Canterbury, Sir John Cass, Nelson, Hoskins, Vanbrugh and Chris. Wren, of whom Vanbrugh and Wren to be two. Godfrey to have notice thereof. Only three petitioners for each site to attend committee.
4. Resolved that whatever was done by the Commissioners before expiration of their Commission, 24 Dec. 1711, shall stand confirmed.
5. Hawksmoor to submit plan of the ground of old church and church yard at Greenwich, with an upright plan or draught of a new church, and detailed estimate, with value of old materials fit to be used or disposed of.

6,7. Hawksmoor, being called in, produced plan and estimate. Consideration referred to the Committee.
8,9. Committee to consider of proper models for the new churches. All models offered by any of the Comissioners to be considered by Committee.
10. Beckley to settle title and purchase of site of St George's chapel [Ormond Street], on terms formerly agreed; and to do the like for all other proposals formerly agreed to, or hereafter to be agreed to by the Commissioners.
11. Secretary to give Beckley copies of such proposals.
12. All such reports made by Beckley to be in writing.
13. Bertie, Jennings, Annesley, and Nelson to consider of some proper way to treat with patrons of parishes where new churches are intended to be built, about patronage thereof.
14. Committee's resolution relating to assigning certain times and places for meetings to be considered on Wednesday next; notice to be given by Messenger.

16. [p. 36] 25 June 1712
Read minutes of last meeting.
1. Earl of Rochester to request Queen to assign Commissioners some place in Somerset House for their public meeting, for putting into execution the powers granted by Parliament.
2–4. Considered Hawksmoor's report on the two sites proposed for a church for Limehouse hamlet. Curate of Stepney and one from each party were heard. Resolved that the church be built on Westfield.
5. Hawksmoor to leave plan of Greenwich church with Secretary.

17. [p. 38] 2 July 1712
1. Read minutes of last meeting.
2,3. Lord Treasurer to be desired to direct Exchequer to receive by loan £10,000 upon credit of the coal duties. Signed draft to Lord Treasurer.
Committee to consider Dean of Canterbury's proposal about site for new church at Deptford.
Committee to consider designs and estimates proposed and to be proposed for new church at East Greenwich.

19. [p. 40] 9 July 1712
1. Considered two several plans proposed by Hawksmoor and James for Greenwich new church; they were severally heard.
2. James's plan not to be received; Hawksmoor's, as improved by Archer, is preferable.
3. Hawksmoor to submit particular estimate of his design so corrected; and with the following materials:
Brickwork, well banded with good brick and mortar.
2nd, ashler with coins, and banded with stone.
3rd, estimate of a stone cornish.
4th, a timber cornish.
5th, a roof of oak.

6th, a deal roof.
7th, a basement two feet above ground.
8th, covering with best Derbyshire lead, eight lbs to the sq. ft.

12 [*sic*]. James to have liberty to propose any other plan, with estimates of each sort of building.

13. Committee to consider Deptford site at next meeting.

14. Committee to meet at Secretary's house on Friday, 11 July at 4 p.m.

19. [p. 42] 16 July 1712

1. Read Wise's resolution about site for church, etc. in Deptford; referred to the committee.

2. Read and approved letter proposed by Secretary pursuant to order of the committee of 11 July.

3. Letter to be sent forthwith to N. Curzon, Esq.

4. Agreed to resolutions of the Committee made on 11 July [see **495**], with amendments; that:

  5. One general design or form be agreed upon for all the fifty new intended churches, where sites will admit thereof; the steeples or towers excepted.

  6. Situations of all the churches be insular, where sites will admit thereof.

  7. Ministers' houses be as near the churches as conveniently may be.

  8. There be at East end of each church two small rooms, one for vestments, another for vessels or other consecrated things.

  9. There be at West end of each church a convenient large room for parish business.

  10. Fonts in each church be so large as to permit Baptism by dipping when desired.

  11. All pews be single and of equal height, so low that every person in them may be seen either kneeling or sitting, and all facing the communion table.

  12. Movable forms or seats be so contrived in the middle aisles as to run under the seats of the pews, and draw out into aisles.

  13. Chancel be raised three steps above nave or body of church.

  14. There be handsome porticoes to each church.

  15. No person be admitted as a general undertaker to build any new intended churches, but every artificer be separately agreed with to perform all the work belonging to his particular trade or business.

16. Hawksmoor to see Sir J. Thornicroft about site he offered at Stockwell.

17. Committee to meet at Church house at the east end of St Clements Danes on Friday 18 July at 4 p.m.

18. Committee to draw an application to be delivered to Queen by Bishops of London and Winchester and Earl of Rochester, or any two, for assigning Commissioners the place they now make use of, or some other, for their public meetings.

20. [p. 45] 23 July 1712

1. Read letter of 19 July from N. Curzon, Esq.

2. Curzon to be informed Commissioners accept his offer of £1,000 for site of St George's chapel, Ormond Street; ready to complete as soon as title laid before their counsel.
3. Advowson not in their power to grant; if they have a power to grant him a seat, they shall be ready to gratify him.
4. Beckley to ask Kent to concur in Curzon's proposal.
5. Dean of Carlisle, Nelson, Jennings and Vanbrugh to enquire after a proper meeting place for Commissioners and their Committees.
6. Hy Smith, Esq. presented a patent under Broad Seal constituting him Treasurer; read by Secretary; to be entered into Book of Muniments.
7. Agreed to Wise's demand, delivered by Dean of Canterbury, 16 July, in all things except his having a pew in the new church [at Deptford], settled to himself and family, and Sam. Prestman's being sexton, neither being in the Commissioners' power to grant.
8. Secretary to acquaint Wise with Commissioners' resolution.
9. Rev. Dr Browne's demand of £200 for his interest in Pardon church yard, proposed for site of new church in St James Clerkenwell parish, is reasonable, provided tenant has a customary right to renew his lease for 21 years, before its expiration, for £3. 10*s*.
10. No site to be approved as proper for a new church, etc., until it be viewed by some of the Commissioners.
11. Proposed site at Goulstone Square, Whitechapel.
12. Plans to be prepared of all sites purchased by the Commissioners for new churches, etc., to annex them to conveyances.
13. Hawksmoor to submit plan of a church to be built conformable to Commissioners' resolutions of 16 July.
14. Committee to meet at Secretary's house on Friday, 25 July at 4 p.m.

21. [p. 48] 30 July 1712
1. Sir Jas Etheridge offers his interest in two houses next the Snuff house in Goulstone Square, Whitechapel, at usual rates.
2–4. Concerning St Alphage's parish, and annexing part of St James [*sc.* Giles] Cripplegate thereto.
5. Any persons delivering estimates for building churches to set down the thickness of the stone they design to use in each part, and sort of stone they intend to use; calculations to be on supposition that ashlar nine inches thick one part with another.
6. A time to be fixed by the Commissioners for persons to submit designs and models for new churches.
7. Resolved to proceed upon building Greenwich church, although a general design be not yet agreed upon for the fifty new churches.
8. A model for East Greenwich church to be fixed upon by this day fortnight.
9. A general design or form for the rest of the new churches to be fixed upon before Christmas next.
10. Referred to Committee the Lord Treasurer's reference about the sufficiency of Hy Smith's security as Treasurer.
12. Committee to meet at Secretary's house, Friday, 1 August, at 5 p.m.

22. [p. 50] 6 Aug. 1712
1,2. Smith's security of £5,000, Rob. Cotton being bound with him for the whole, considered sufficient.
3. Ministers of St Alphage and Cripplegate to attend.
4. Considered designs submitted for East Greenwich church.
5–10. Fixed upon the smallest of Hawksmoor's designs. The pillars to support the gallery only; only one portico, at east end; to be 37 ft high within, 90 ft long, and 65 ft wide; to be built with stone, ashlar nine inches thick. To be proceeded upon with all convenient speed.
11. Committee to meet at Secretary's house on Tuesday next at 4 p.m. and receive proposals from masons and bricklayers for said church.

23. [p. 52] 13 Aug. 1712
1,2. Petitions received for and against annexing part of St Giles Cripplegate to St Alphage parish. Consideration deferred.
3–6. Question of a church yard in St Pancras parish for St George's chapel, Ormond Street.
7. Mr Wren and Vanbrugh reported that they had considered proposals of Edw. Tufnell and Strong, masons, and Hues and Billinghurst, bricklayers, referred to them by the Committee, and that they had therefrom drawn two other proposals, one for mason's work and the other for bricklayer's, in East Greenwich church, and proposed that they be called in and shown same, and asked whether they would do the work specified at rates therein proposed. Done accordingly, and they severally agreed.
8. Tufnell offered to find scaffolding at £100, and Strong at £110; after which the artificers were again called in and asked whether, if any should subsequently undertake to build any of the fifty new churches at a cheaper rate and make their work of equal goodness, they would agree to abate their prices accordingly; to which they severally agreed.
9. Tufnell and Strong to be jointly employed in mason's work, Greenwich church.
10. Hues and Billinghurst to be jointly employed in the bricklayer's work there.
11. Committee empowered to finish contracts with said masons and bricklayers and to proceed to do all other things necessary for forwarding building of the church.
12. Committee to be further empowered to agree and contract for such sites for churches, etc., as they think fit.
13,14. About obtaining chambers in Lincoln's Inn for the Commission.
15. Committee to meet at Secretary's house on Friday next at 4 p.m.
16. Hawksmoor to submit to the Committee the forms of proper contracts to be made with masons and bricklayers for East Greenwich church.

24. [p. 55] 17 Sep. 1712, at Secretary's house in Doctors' Commons
1. Earth dug in making foundations of Greenwich church to be laid in the body of the church, or where else necessary, at bricklayers' charge.
2. Resolution of 26 August to be communicated to Lady Mordaunt and Sir John Bennet.

3. All papers or models that shall be in future be delivered to Commissioners or Committee and approved by either of them shall be kept by Secretary, and not redelivered without order.
4. Secretary to read the minutes every day to Commissioners or Committee before they rise; Chairman to sign them before he depart.
5. No person in future to be employed by the Commissioners till he has stood proposed a week at least.
6,7. About proposed site in Red Lion Street, Spitalfields.
8. Nelson and Jennings to agree with Mr Brewer for his chambers in Lincoln's Inn Great Square for one year at £30, and to direct alterations for the Commissioners' reception.
9. Consideration of site in Whitecross Street, Cripplegate, deferred until Ironmongers' Company give in their proposals.
10. Committee to meet here on 24 September.

25. [p. 57] 28 Oct. 1712, at the Banqueting House, Whitehall
1. Read petition of John James.
2,3. Agreed with Committee to accept Wise's demand for £400 for a site of two and a half acres at Deptford for a church etc. Crop on the ground to be valued.
4. Committee appointed by former Commissioners to be continued; Sir Nat. Lloyd, Marriott, Child, Bettesworth, King and Halley to be added; all Commissioners attending to have votes.
5. Committee to meet next Friday at Lincoln's Inn at 4 p.m.

26. [p. 59] 12 Nov. 1712, at Lincoln's Inn
1. Agreed with the Committee in their resolution of 7 November (**509**), to give the three proprietors £1,260 for ground proposed for a church, etc. in Red Lion Street, in Spitalfields, if their titles be approved.
2. Secretary to sign counterpart of minute relating to purchase of site if vendors require it.
3,4. Secretary stated he had received two bills from Mr Lowther for passing the two Commissions for building churches. Marriott to report if they are reasonable.
5. Committee to consider what salaries to be given to the officers, and what officers ought to be employed.
6. Committee to meet every Monday at 4 p.m.; advertisement to be put in *Gazette, Postman, Post Boy, Spectator* and *Daily Courant*.
7. Agreed with Committee's resolution of 22 August, that Hawksmoor finish model for East Greenwich new church in all its parts, in order to have an exact plan drawn therefrom to be annexed to agreements with the several artificers. Hawksmoor to finish model with all expedition.
8. Hawksmoor to measure foundation of Greenwich church, Archer supervising.
9. Referred to Committee to consider what further conveniences necessary in this place.

27. [p. 61] 26 Nov. 1712
1,2. Marriott reported he had examined the bills for passing the Commissions, which were reasonable; the bills to be paid.

3,4. Gratuity of £5. 5*s*. to be paid Brooks as Doorkeeper.
5,6. Nelson, Bulstrode and Hawksmoor to view site in Hatton Garden.
7. Hawksmoor to lay Greenwich church designs before Committee on Monday.
8. Agreed with Committee in following resolution, that:

(1) £200 p.a. be allowed Rous as Secretary, commencing 21 Sept. 1711.

(2) £30 p.a. be allowed Thos. Crocker as Messenger and Doorkeeper, from Michaelmas 1711.

(3) £100 p.a. to be allowed Skeat as Agent and Solicitor, from time aforesaid.

(4) Whatever has been already paid to be taken as part of salaries.

12 [*sic*]. None of the salaried officers to be allowed any perquisites or rewards but what first allowed by the Commissioners.
13. A balloting box to be provided. All questions arising at this Board to be determined by balloting, if demanded by any of the Commissioners.
14. Concerning burial ground for St Olave Southwark.

28. [p. 63] 10 Dec. 1712
1. Concerning St George's, Ormond Street.
2,3. Pardon church yard, in St James Clerkenwell parish.
4,5. Agreed with Committee that Hawksmoor and Dickinson be allowed £200 p.a. each as Deputy Surveyors and Clerks of the Works under this Commission, including all incidentals except charges of making wooden models, opening of ground, and travelling (if required) beyond parishes where any of the new churches are to be built. To commence from Michaelmas 1711, and what already paid them to be deducted from salaries.
6,7. Read Committee minutes of 1 December (**514**) relating to mason's petition for sheds for sheltering their workmen employed on East Greenwich church. Masons to provide sheds at their own charge; and to be allowed £25 for use thereof.
8. Commissioners to meet on 22 December to apply to Lord Treasurer for issue of money.

29. [p. 65] 22 Dec. 1712
1. Letter to Governors of the Charterhouse.
2,3. Application to Lord Treasurer for issue of £5,000.
4. All models proposed for any of the fifty new churches to be delivered to Secretary by 14 January, to be that day considered; notice to be given in summons.

30. [p. 67] 14 Jan. 1712/13
1,2. Dickinson submitted two models of churches, and Archer three.
3. Three more weeks to be allowed for bringing in models.
4. The models submitted to continue in this room to be viewed only by Commissioners, or such as they bring with them.
5. Doorkeeper to attend here to show them every day from 10 to 3, till further order.

31. [p. 68] 4 Feb. 1712/13
1. Agreed with Committee that Bishop of Chester and Lord Rochester make application to Queen for leave to build a church for the use of the inhabitants of St Mary le Strand at the Maypole in the Strand.
2. Commissioners and Committee to have use of the great room they now meet in and all other rooms on the same floor, except the little closet backwards, and also have a room below stairs for their servants, and a vault for coals, for £40 p.a., payable quarterly, from Michaelmas 1712; payments to be made by Treasurer without further application to Commissioners.
3. Hawksmoor delivered four models.
4. Committee to settle forms of warrant for payments ordered by Commissioners.

32. [p. 70] 11 Feb. 1712/13
1. Warrant signed for paying salaries.
2–4. Considered Beckley's bill as Solicitor. Buckley to have £80 p.a. for all solicitor's business save drawing and engrossing conveyances.
5. Annesley delivered drafts of agreements with masons and bricklayers employed in Greenwich church, which were formerly read and agreed to with some few amendments he had made by the Committee's direction.
6,7. Title to Manor of Stockwell, and conveyance of site.
8. Hawksmoor to draw particular plan of site for annexing to conveyance.
9,10. Bishop of Chester reported the Queen required to be informed of her interest in site before she could answer their request about the Maypole in the Strand. Inquiry to be made.

33. [p. 72] 25 Feb. 1712/13
1. Agreed with Committee to accept proposal of trustees of Ormond Street chapel to sell pews for £1,500.
2. Beckley to engross all writings ordered to be engrossed by this Commission.
3,4. Concerning Smith's site, Westminster.
5. Masons and bricklayers employed in Greenwich church to deliver estimates of arcades or breaks in south and north sides to Committee on Monday.
6. About valuation of crops on Deptford church site.
7. Secretary to pay Mrs Clarke £6 in full of her bill for printing summons for the Commissioners delivered this day.
8. Secretary to give notice to smiths who have proposals to offer to attend the Committee on Thursday 5 March.

34. [p. 74] 11 Mar. 1712/13
1. £70 to be paid for crops on Deptford church site.
2,3. Further about Smith's site, Westminster.
4. About Mercers' Company site, Shadwell.
5. St Olave Southwark to be considered at next meeting.
6. The workmen at Greenwich church to go on with arcades on north and south sides, as formerly proposed by Hawksmoor.

Read minutes of Committee of 5 March (**529**). Resolved that:
7–9. John Graysbrook be employed to do plumber's work of Greenwich church, giving £1,000 security for performing it in workmanlike manner; should he fail of due performance, then whatever price the Commissioners have to give any other plumber to perfect the work over and above the prices now contracted for shall be deducted out of monies due to Graysbrook for work he may have done. A convenient place to be assigned him wherein to lay his lead. The Commissioners not to be answerable for any lead stolen from him.
10. East Greenwich church to be covered with milled lead.
11. Read Committee's minutes of 9 March (**530**). Resolved that James be employed to do carpenter's work of East Greenwich church. James being called in desired that Jeffs might be joined with him, which was granted, Jeffs contracting to work at James's prices.
12. Skeat's proposal for smith's work of Greenwich church was returned to him, to consider whether he can abate his prices.
13. Consideration of what person shall be employed to do smith's work of that church deferred till Monday next.

35. [p. 77] 16 Mar. 1712/13
1. John Skeat to be employed to do smith's work of East Greenwich church.
2,3. Norton Folgate site agreed for at £1,550.
4,5. Jennings reported that Beckley had drafted a conveyance for Wise's site at Deptford, which had been approved by Solicitor General; conveyance to be engrossed.
6,7. Concerning proposal for a site in Burr Street, St Botolph Aldgate.

36. [p. 79] 25 Mar. 1713
1. About conveyance of Deptford site.
2. Notice to be given to Hawksmoor that Commissioners and Committee expect him to attend every time they meet.
3. £400 to be advanced to bricklayers for Greenwich church.

37. [p. 80] 15 Apr. 1713
1. Agree to Ironmongers' Company's proposal for a site in St Giles Cripplegate parish, provided Company contract for building a street leading thereto before 25 March 1714; otherwise, Company's earlier proposal to be accepted.
2. Thos Green jnr to be paid £6. 7*s*. 4*d*. for work done in Commissioners' rooms at Lincoln's Inn.
3. Notice to be given in *Gazette* next Saturday that Committee will sit every Thursday at 9 a.m. from 23 April.
4. About possible arrangements in Aldgate.
5. Agreed with Committee to give Wise £240 for four houses to be pulled down to make avenue to site already purchased for a church at Deptford.
6. Thos Crocker, messenger, discharged from attendance to look after the models.
7,8. Conveyance of Deptford site; Treasurer to pay Wise £640.
9,10. Site proposed near Hatton Garden.

38. [p. 82] 23 Apr. 1713
1,2. Proposed site in St Andrew Holborn parish.
3. Solicitor to see Attorney General about Limehouse site, and prepare conveyance if satisfactory.
4. Old iron belonging to East Greenwich church to be weighed by parish officers, and delivered to Skeat on his receipt.
5. Agreement about crops and trees on Deptford site.
6. Signed warrant for rent for Lincoln's Inn chambers.

39. [p. 84] 30 Apr. 1713
1. The model of the church with four towers proposed by Archer is proper to be built on site purchased of Smith within St Margaret Westminster parish.
2. Archer and Medlicott to view site proposed by Lord Scarborough in St Martin in the Fields parish, and report at next meeting.
3. Resolved to fix upon the model of the church to be built upon Wise's site, Deptford, on Thursday next.

40. [p. 85] 7 May 1713
1. Graysbrook, plumber, to attend with his security.
2. Notice to be given in *Gazette* next Saturday for receiving proposals from masons, carpenters and bricklayers for building new churches in parishes of Deptford and St Margaret Westminster, at the Commissioners' office, 6 Lincoln's Inn Great Square; this is published as an encouragement to workmen in the country as well as town to give in proposals, time being allowed to 4 June for that purpose.
3,4. Considered, the models for the new churches in Deptford and St Margaret Westminster parishes; Archer to bring an estimate for building them according to the models proposed by him, as soon as convenient.
5. Warrant for incidentals.

41. [p. 87] 14 May 1713
1. Bills referred to Jennings and Nelson.
2,3. Gibbs submitted several draughts for churches; to make two models from the draughts.
4,5. Hawksmoor to prepare site plan for conveyance of Ormond Street chapel, and for Jefferys' site, Tower Hill.
6. Hawksmoor to measure mason's work done at Greenwich church as soon as convenient.

42. [p. 88] 21 May 1713
1,2. Graysbrook, plumber at Greenwich church, proposed Mr Alsop at the Angel in Bishopgate Street as his security; Beckley to execute bond accordingly.
3. Concerning site at the Maypole in the Strand.
4. Rearrangement of St Giles Cripplegate and St Alphage parishes to be further considered on 11 June.
5. Memorial to Treasury for issuing £10,000; warrants signed.

6. Mason and bricklayers employed in East Greenwich new church to attend on 4 June to execute their articles.

43. [p. 90] 4 June 1713
1,2. Petition to the queen about site near the Maypole in the Strand, asking leave to introduce a bill.
3. About Spitalfields site.
4. Graysbrook's security to be investigated.
5. Deptford site to be walled.
6. Sir C. Wren and Mr Wren, attended by Surveyors, to view ground purchased of Smith in St Margaret Westminster parish, and report what foundation will be necessary on Thursday next.
7. Concerning a minister's house for Ormond Street chapel.
8. Warrants signed for paying workmen for Greenwich church.
9. Masons, carpenters and bricklayers who attended with their proposals for building the new churches in St Margaret Westminster and Deptford to attend on Thursday 18 June.

44. [p. 92] 11 June 1713
1. Reported that the Queen will give leave for a bill concerning the Maypole site.
2. Alsop satisfactory as Graysbrook's security.
3. Warrants signed for payments.
4. Concerning Trinity Chapel, St Martin in the Fields.
5,6. Deferred to Thursday next consideration of Hudson's proposal for coping with stone the wall to be erected about Wise's ground, Deptford.

45. [p. 94] 18 June 1713
1. Referred to next meeting consideration of purchasing the pews in St George's chapel, Ormond Street.
2. Lucas to be employed to do bricklayer's work of Deptford new church, at following prices: for every rod of brickwork, reduced to a brick and a half: for foundation, £5; for every rod above water table, £5. 2*s*. 6*d*., scaffolding included. He is to use 200 of lime and two load of best Fytham (*sic*) sand to each rod of brickwork.

46. [p. 95] 20 June 1713
1. Hawksmoor to draw a plan of district agreed to by the Commissioners for parish of St George's, Ormond Street, for next meeting.
2. New church in Deptford to be of Portland stone.
3. Lucas to be allowed 4*d*. per yard for digging the foundation of said church.
4. Several masons (Tufnell, Strong, Townsend, Hodson, Humphreys, Copson, and Higget) delivered proposals for mason's work of new churches in St Margaret's Westminster and Deptford.
5. Surveyors to peruse masons' proposals, to make a table of their prices, and to report which is cheapest and how near it is to prices of the masons employed on East Greenwich church; to lay their report before Sir C. Wren, and Messrs Wren, Archer and Vanbrugh at Wren's house on Wednesday next at 10 a.m.

6. Beckley to prepare conveyance for site proposed for new church on Tower Hill in St Botolph Aldgate parish.
7. Sir C. Wren, Mr Wren and Vanbrugh to be desired to view Mr Smith's ground in St Margaret's Westminster, and consider what foundation necessary, and report to Commissioners on Thursday next. Surveyors to attend them

47. [p. 97] 25 June 1713
1. £600 to be paid to Dr Proctor for three acres in St Pancras for a church yard for new parish of St George's, Ormond Street, and any other parishes that the Commissioners shall direct.
2. Secretary to make out a warrant accordingly.
3. Sir C. Wren, Mr Vanbrugh and Mr Wren to be desired to view Mr Smith's ground in St Margaret's Westminster and consider what foundation necessary, and report to the Commissioners on Thursday next; Surveyors and workmen to be employed on the church to attend them.
4. Capt. Tufnell and Strong to be employed for mason's work in Deptford new church, and that to be erected on Smith's ground in St Margaret's Westminster, at prices proposed by them to the Commissioners at their last meeting.
5. Hues and William Tufnell to be employed for bricklayer's work in new church in St Margaret's Westminster, at following prices: £5 per rod, reduced to a brick and a half thick for the foundation; £5. 2*s*. 6*d*. per rod above water table, scaffolding included. To use 200 pecks of lime and 2 loads of best Fulham sand to each rod of brickwork.
6. Hawksmoor to make a plan of three acres in St Pancras purchased of Proctor, to be annexed to the conveyance to be drawn by Beckley.
7. Proposals of carpenters (Tho. Denning, Wm Baker, James Grove senr, Rob. Jeffs, and Jas Grove jnr) opened and referred to Surveyors, to peruse and make a table of prices therein, showing which is cheapest, and how near they are to those of carpenters employed in East Greenwich church, to lay before Sir C. Wren, and Messrs Wren, Archer and Vanbrugh on Wed. next at 10 a.m., to report their opinions to the Commissioners at their next meeting.
8. A statue of Queen Anne, 'made by the best hands', to be set up 'in the most conspicuous and convenient part' of each new church.
9. Mr Bird and Mr Gibbons to be desired to provide designs and estimates for such statues.
10. Warrants signed for salaries to last midsummer.

48. [p. 100] 2 July 1713
1. Archer delivered new proposal for roof and foundation for new church on Smith's ground, Westminster.
2. Copies thereof to be delivered to the carpenters who sent in proposals, to set down their prices for articles mentioned in new design, and deliver them to Dickinson, who is to make a schedule for Sir C. Wren and Messrs Archer, Wren and Vanbrugh to report upon on Thursday next.
3. Consideration of carpenters' proposals for new churches in Westminster and Deptford adjourned to Thursday next.

4. Skeat to be employed for any smith's work in new churches in Westminster and Deptford if such necessary before a smith is chosen, at his rates for East Greenwich.
5. Capt Masters delivered a proposal for a site for a church, church yard and minister's house at St Mary Whitechapel.
6. Box and Bulstrode, who have viewed the site, to be desired to report thereupon on Thursday next.
7. No counterpart of conveyances of ground purchased by this Commission to be made, unless by special direction.
8. Secretary to pay T. Crocker £5 for extraordinary attendances to show models, etc.

49. [p. 102] 9 July 1713
1. Bulstrode and Box to be desired to view site proposed in Whitechapel parish, attended by Dickinson, and report as soon as convenient.
2. Grove to be employed for carpenter's work in Deptford new church, at prices he proposed today.
3. Jeffs and James to be employed for carpenter's work in new church in St Margaret's Westminster, at prices they proposed today.
4. Surveyors to view Lambeth site proposed by Sir John Thornicroft and consult Mr Angell and other inhabitants whether there may be a more convenient site belonging to Thornicroft.

50. [p. 104] 16 July 1713
1. Hawksmoor or Dickinson to stake out ground purchased of Humphrys, Michell and others in Spitalfields Hamlet, and make a plan to be annexed to the conveyance.
2. Bishop of Hereford, Lord Willoughby De Broke and Earl of Rochester to be desired to invite Mr Walker to lay his title deeds to waste ground near the Maypole in the Strand, and his demand for the same, before the Commissioners.
3. Besides the Queen's statue in a conspicuous part of each of new churches, following inscription shall be put under every statue: 'That such church is one of the New Churches built by virtue of an Act of Parliament passed in the ninth Year of the Reign of Her Majesty Queen Anne'.
4. Carpenters employed in new church in St Margaret Westminster to prepare timber and other suitable materials for foundations.
5. Skeat delivered two proposals, from Mr Raleigh and Mr Slackhouse, for two houses adjoining site commonly called Green Dragon Inn, St Giles in the Fields.
6. Surveyors to make a plan of inn and houses, and King and Stanley to be desired to view them.
7. Hawksmoor or his servant to attend Archer upon his setting out foundation of Deptford new church.
8. Hawksmoor and Dickinson to take Archer's directions in all matters relating to building of the new churches in Deptford and Westminster, particularly in setting out foundations.

9. Accepted Mr Hastings' proposal for £1,000 for a site for a church, etc. in St Paul, Shadwell.
10. Thompson to make abstract of Hastings's title to lay before Webb.

51. [p. 106] 23 July 1713
1. Walker to be desired to lay his title deeds to waste ground near the Maypole in the Strand before Webb by this day week.
2. Beckley to inquire at Duchy Office in Grays Inn what application was made by Walker or others claiming a right to the waste ground about building a shed where fish is now sold, and report on Wednesday next.
[3.] Archer to be desired to obtain leave from Dean and Chapter to dig near Westminster Abbey to find what its foundation stands on.

52. [p. 107] 29 July 1713
1. Beckley laid a copy of a petition of the inhabitants of St Mary Le Savoy to King William, relating to watch-house near the Maypole in the Strand.
2. Annesley and Jennings to be desired to consult attorney-general how to proceed with building of new church near the Maypole, pursuant to act lately passed for that purpose, with respect to clause relating to Walker's pretended interest in site.
3. Surveyors, masons and bricklayers employed on new church in St Margaret Westminster to put in writing the report they have made today relating to the foundation on Smith's ground, and Archer desired to sign it. The workmen to proceed forthwith on foundation.
4. Bulstrode to be desired to treat with proprietors of site at Hatton Garden Chapel, attended by Buckley.
5. Dean of St Asaph or Mr Hoare to be desired to treat with proprietors of the Green Dragon with Three Cups Inn, in St Giles and St Andrew Holborn parishes, and report their lowest demands.

53. [p. 109] 5 Aug. 1713
1,2. Walker's title deeds to the waste ground in the Strand.
3. Report on foundation of new church in St Margaret Westminster to be perfected this day week, specifying manner and nature of brick and wood work, and prices of each sort of work.
4. Secretary to write to Archer, acquainting him that Vanbrugh will wait on him before Wednesday next to settle foundations of new church in St Margaret Westminster, and that he and Vanbrugh be desired to be at next meeting of the Commissioners.
5. Referred to Sir Thomas Crosse and Mr Bertie to consult Smith about drain to be made on site lately purchased of him.
6. Secretary to write to Mr Lionel Wafer that difficulties attending purchase of the houses necessary to make his site in Hatton Garden convenient for a new church, etc. are so great that the Commissioners have not at present any thought of proceeding further.
7. Read petition of Paul Mucklebray, for £25 for a year's attendance to look after the works at new church, East Greenwich.
8. An allowance of 12*d*. per day to be made to Mucklebray for time he has already attended; and he is to continue at same rate until further orders.

54. [p. 111] 13 Aug. 1713
1. Instrument ascertaining bounds of new parish of St George the Martyr was executed.
2. Hawksmoor to make two counterparts of plans annexed to the instrument, to be lodged with enrollment to be made in Chancery.
3. Two acres for church yard for St George the Martyr parish to be enclosed with brick wall like that at Deptford.
4. Hues and Wm Tufnell to build the walls.
5. Hawksmoor to report what fence may be proper for the church yard.
6. Dickinson desired leave to resign his Surveyorship, having accepted an employment which would leave him insufficient time to serve the Commission.
7. Dickinson to deliver all his plans and papers made as Surveyor to this Commission to Secretary.
8. Secretary to compute Dickinson's salary to this day and make out warrant.
9. Mr Wren delivered a letter from Lord Bingley and another from Dr Arbuthnot, recommending John [*sic*] Gibbs to succeed Dickinson.
10. Resolved to appoint at next meeting a time to consider choice of successor to Dickinson.
11. Hawksmoor to compute sums due to masons and bricklayers employed on East Greenwich church against Wednesday next, and Secretary to prepare warrants.
12. Commissioners to meet this day week to sign warrants.
13. Commissioners not to meet thereafter till 7 October.

55. [p. 114] 19 Aug. 1713
1. Medlicott delivered certificate from Sir C. Wren on behalf of Gibbs who petitions to succeed Dickinson.
2. Hawksmoor delivered an estimate of work done by masons and bricklayers at East Greenwich church.
3. Warrants for paying £500 to Tho. Hues and Rich. Billinghurst; £2,000 to Strong and Tufnell.

56. [p. 115] 7 Oct. 1713
1–3. Details about church yard for St George the Martyr.
4. James petitioned for the Surveyor's place.
5. Resolved to choose a Surveyor in place of Dickinson on this day fortnight; notice to be given in summons for the meeting.
6. Mr Dacres delivered a proposal for a site, etc. in St Giles in the Fields parish.
7. Hawksmoor to report on the site.
8. Empty smith's shop and adjoining houses at east end of church yard of Deptford new church to be pulled down, and materials used in covering the work from weather this winter.
9. Hawksmoor to measure Lucas's work at Deptford and report on manner of performance.
10. Lead for Greenwich new church to be 9 lb on flat and 10 lb per foot in gutters, and 2ft 3ins wide between seam and seam.

11. Read petition of Jeffs and James for payment for carpenter's work at new churches in Deptford and St Margaret Westminster.
12. Hawksmoor to report thereon.

57. [p. 117] 14 Oct. 1713
1. Gibbs delivered petition praying to be Surveyor.
2. Read recommendation for Walter Thomas to be watchman at Deptford new church, signed by Mr Loader and other inhabitants.
3. Hawksmoor to measure and report on church yard wall for St George the Martyr.
4,5. Hawksmoor reported that £800 might be safely impressed to Lucas on account of his brickwork at Deptford; and £800 to Jeffs and James for carpenter's work.
6. Secretary to prepare warrants accordingly.
7. Hawksmoor to estimate charge of foundation of new church in St Margaret Westminster under heads of digging, bricklayer, mason and carpenter.
8. Secretary to prepare memorial to Lord High Treasurer to receive into Exchequer £10,000 upon the credit of Coal Duty from any willing to make such loan.
9. Beckley to inquire of Webb what he has done about Walker's interest in site at the Maypole in the Strand, and report at next meeting.
10. Notice to be given in *Gazette* that Commissioners ready to receive proposals for painter's work for East Greenwich new church on 28 Oct. 1713.

58. [p. 119] 21 Oct. 1713
1. Read Gibbs's petition praying to be Surveyor, and letters from Lord Bingley and Dr Arbuthnot, and Sir C. Wren's certificate.
2. Read James's petition for the same place.
3. Choice of a Surveyor adjourned to this day month; notice to be given in summons for that day.
4. Read, a petition from several inhabitants of St Mary Rotherhithe and a demand of £200 for a site for church, etc.
5. Mr Wren and Child to be desired to view site mentioned in the petition; Hawksmoor to attend them.
6. Hawksmoor to survey and report what is due to Hues and Tufnell for walling church yard of St George the Martyr, computed at prices allowed Lucas for building Deptford church yard wall.
7. Hawksmoor delivered estimate for foundation of new church at Westminster.

59. [p. 121] 28 Oct. 1713
1. Painters' proposals for East Greenwich new church delivered by Preedy, Pickering, Bennet and Thompson.
2. Hawksmoor to draw a blank schedule of required painter's work, and deliver copies to applicants, so they may give in their prices next week.
3. Warrants for house rent, and for £1,260 to Michell, Heath and others for site at Spitalfields.

4. Signed memorial to Lord Treasurer.
5. Signed further memorial to Lord Treasurer for £5,000 to be imprested to Treasurer.
6. Resolved to consider this day fortnight a method to procure endowments for the fifty new churches.

60. [p. 123] 4 Nov. 1713
1. Hawksmoor to estimate cost of building west end of Deptford new church with one steeple; with two steeples and a portico; and with two steeples without a portico.
2. Thompson, Preedy and Bennet delivered proposals for painter's work.
3. The painters to be desired to reduce the painting of ironwork to yard measure and make their proposals accordingly next week.
4. Ordered warrants for Hues and Tufnell.

61. [p. 124] 11 Nov. 1713
Read letter from Thos Cole, complaining of badness of bricks used in foundation of the new church at Westminster.
2. Secretary to invite Cole to attend on Wednesday next to give Commissioners information about the bricks used in foundation of new church now building near Mill Bank, in St Margaret Westminster.
3. Cross and Bulstrode to be desired to view the bricks used about foundation and church, and report on Wednesday next.
4. Hawksmoor to report on painters' proposals (Thompson and Preedy) next week.
5. Considered how to proceed to procure endowments for the fifty new churches; adjourned to this day fortnight.
6. Secretary to invite Walker to speak to Commissioners about the Maypole site in the Strand this day fortnight.

62. [p. 126] 18 Nov. 1713
1. Elected by ballot Gibbs as Surveyor in room of Dickinson.
2. Scott to be employed for painter's work at East Greenwich at following rates: 8*d.* per yard of plain colour done four times with good white lead and linseed oil, after the best manner, upon the woodwork, inside and outside; 1*s.* per yard upon iron work, reduced to superficial measure.
3. Crosse and Bulstrode to be desired to view the bricks used about near Mill Bank.
4. Resolved to consider method of providing better bricks next week.
5. Lucas, bricklayer at Deptford new church, to attend next week.

63. [p. 128] 25 Nov. 1713
1. Examined Lucas about bricks he used in Deptford new church.
2. Secretary to ask Mr Hobson of Eltham for his proposal in writing, for his interest in a site for church, etc. in Horsley Down for St Olave's parish, Southwark.
3. Agreed to Walker's demand for £200 for his interest in site at the Maypole in the Strand.

4. Consideration of a method of providing endowments adjourned to next week.

64. [p. 129] 3 Dec. 1713
1. Surveyors to view Greenwich and Deptford churches tomorrow and report in writing on lead used to cover East Greenwich church and bricks used in Deptford new church.
2. Gibbs to have a copy of proposal formerly made by Hawksmoor and Dickinson.
3. Hawksmoor to see that gates for St George the Martyr church yard be hung up as soon as possible.
4. Bricklayers at Deptford and Westminster new churches to proceed no further until directed to do so by the Commissioners.
5. Consideration of a method of providing endowments adjourned to next week.
6. Beckley's bill for work done as Solicitor referred to Messrs Annesley, Jennings and Box, or any two of them, to report as soon as convenient.

65. [p. 131] 9 Dec. 1713
1. Surveyors reported on work done in and about new churches erecting at Deptford and Greenwich.
2. Surveyors to report in writing on work done in and about new church at Westminster.
3. Surveyors in future to make monthly written report of progress and state of every work carrying on; specifying days when they viewed same; and deliver their report at first meeting in every month.
4. Consideration of a method of providing endowments adjourned to next week; Dean of Ely to have notice thereof; and at the same time consider endowment of St George the Martyr, Ormond Street.
5. Settlement of Treasurer's salary to be considered at first meeting after Christmas; notice to be given in summons.
6. Bills for all models that have been made for use of the Commissioners to be brought in at second meeting after Christmas.
7. Surveyors to draw designs on paper for new church to be built in the Strand.

66. [p. 133] 16 Dec. 1713
1. Consideration of a method of providing endowments adjourned to first meeting after Christmas; Dean of Ely to have notice thereof; and at same time to consider endowment of St George Ormond Street.
2. Surveyors to prepare proposals for brickmakers as follows:
   1. How much per thousand for bricks without Spanish delivered at the waterside in London.
   2. How much per thousand at the clamp.
   3. How much per thousand if they use six loads of Spanish to 100,000 bricks.

67. [p. 134] 30 Dec. 1713
1. Gibbs delivered report signed by himself and Hawksmoor relating to bricks; consideration deferred to next meeting.

2. Consideration of endowment of the fifty new churches adjourned to the same time.
3. Read memorial delivered by John Jefferys about an acre at lower end of Minories, Aldgate parish.
4. King and Archer to be desired to discuss the site with the Earl of Northampton, and enquire whether it be within Liberties of the Tower.
5. The Officers' salaries to be paid to Christmas last; warrant signed.

68. [p. 135] 13 Jan. 1713/14
1. Resolved that Henry Smith, Esq., Treasurer to the Commission, receive £300 p.a. for salary and all expenses except fees at Exchequer and Treasury on issues, and on passing accounts with auditor of Imprest. Warrant to be made out.
2. Treasurer to lay account of his receipts and payments to Christmas last before first meeting in February.
3. Read a letter from Governors of the Charterhouse—Resolved:
4. That Surveyors make exact measurement desired, and report as soon as convenient.
5. Considered endowment of the fifty new churches—Resolved:
6. That a committee be appointed to consider further of method of endowing the churches, to meet every Monday at 4 p.m.; all Commissioners to be of the committee, three being a quorum.

69. [p. 137] 20 Jan. 1713/14
1. Resolved that the several Officers employed by this Commission (except Treasurer) be elected annually, and that his and their salaries be appointed every year the first meeting after Lady Day.
2. Resolved that the committee to consider method of endowment be dissolved and the subject be considered on Wednesday next by the Commissioners.
3. Secretary to inform Dickinson that the Commissioners expect his attendance on Wednesday next, with all plans and papers drawn by their orders during his Surveyorship.
4. Surveyors to certify what is due to John Graysbrook, plumber employed in covering Greenwich church, and a blank warrant to be drawn.
5. Surveyors to examine books of Lucas, bricklayer employed on Deptford new church and report thereon before Lucas proceeds further.

70. [p. 138] 27 Jan. 1713/14
1. £600 to be imprested to Graysbrook on account for Greenwich church.
2. One Surveyor to see Mr Lowndes about taking a plan of a site proposed in St James's parish, Westminster.
3. Gibbs delivered a plan of the Charterhouse's Pardon church yard, in St James's parish, Clerkenwell.
[4.] Skeat delivered a proposal for a site in St Saviour's parish, Southwark, which is to be made complete.

71. [p. 139] 3 Feb. 1713/14
1. Nelson and Jennings to review proposals for a site in St Giles in the Fields parish, and report.
2. Rogers and Neale, brickmakers, and Hues, bricklayer, to be given notice to attend next Tuesday.
3. Method of endowing new churches to be considered on 17 February.

72. [p. 140] 9 Feb. 1713/14
1. Skeat to inquire about a house in Leicester Street belonging to Mr Vanhalse.
2. Rogers, brickmaker, to make 100,000 of bricks at 16*s*. per thousand, no Spanish to be used; and to attend on Wednesday week.

73. [p. 141] 17 Feb. 1713/14
1. Skeat reported on house in Leicester Street.
2. Read representation from several inhabitants of Spitalfields, for a church to be built in the hamlet.
3. Resolved to proceed forthwith to build a church on the ground purchased there; Hawksmoor to make a plan, with an estimate.
4. Beckley reported that Lord Hatton desired to know what district would be made for new church to be built in Hatton Garden before making any proposal, as he fears that poor rate will be increased.
5. Bulstrode to be desired to wait on Lord Hatton and inform him that division of the parish will not affect the poor rate.
6. Dickinson delivered up all maps and plans (except two specified in a schedule) made as Surveyor.
7. Gibbs delivered a measurement of ground belonging to the Governors of the Charterhouse.
8. Gibbs to make a plan specifying how much of the ground will be sufficient for a church and minister's house for St James's parish, Clerkenwell.
9. Warrant for Greenwich church watchman.
10. Skeat to collect rent of house bought in Spitalfields.
11. Consideration of method of endowing new churches adjourned to next week.

74. [p. 143] 24 Feb. 1713/14
1. Bulstrode reported having seen Lord Hatton.
2. Sir R. Hoare and Bulstrode to view Pardon church yard and ascertain how much it would be necessary to purchase.
3. Gibbs to make a plan of Lady Russell's garden in Bloomsbury, and ground plat of a church to be built there.
4. Read Mr Johnson's proposal for a site for church, etc. for Wapping hamlet, Stepney.
5. Hawksmoor to report whether it will admit of a good foundation.
6. Two cases for maps and draughts to be made for Surveyors, the Secretary to have a key to each.
7. Warrant for Mucklebray, watchman at Greenwich, ordered.
8. Hawksmoor to report who is employed to look after materials at Westminster, and what pay he expects.

75. [p. 144a] 3 Mar. 1713/14
1. Skeat to return Sir Wm Wyndham's proposal for a site in St James's Westminster.
2. Signed Mucklebray's warrant.
3. Mucklebray to be discharged from attending the works at Greenwich. The workmen employed on building churches to take care of the works and tools themselves in future.
4. Gibbs delivered a plan of Lady Russell's ground in Bloomsbury, with ground platt of a church to be built there.
5. Messrs Nelson, Jennings and Hoskins to be desired to wait on Lady Russell to know her lowest demand for said site.
6. Bricklayers employed to build new churches of Deptford and Westminster to attend the next meeting.

76. [p. 145] 17 Mar. 1713/14
1. Jennings and Nelson reported that Lady Russell is willing to take £1,000 for her ground in Bloomsbury, but hopes Mr Burscough (who will lose benefit of a chapel in Russell Street) may be first minister.
2–4. Agreed to Lady Russell's demands; Nelson and Jennings to inform her so.
5. Resolved to meet, during this session of Parliament, at 9 a.m.
6. Beckley to prepare conveyance of Watts's site in Upper Wapping, Webb having approved title. Beckley to deposit with Secretary now and in future all approbations of title by counsel of purchases by the Commission.
7. Beckley to ensure that all purchases in County of Middlesex be registered, according to the act.
8. Surveyors to measure masons' and bricklayers' works of new churches of Greenwich, Deptford and Westminster by next meeting, in order to pay workmen.
9. Brickmakers and bricklayers to attend next meeting in order to enter into articles with penalties, one to furnish, the other to lay, only bricks fit for the Commissioners' use.

77. [p. 147] 31 Mar. 1714
Adjourned to 5 April, only five Commissioners being present.

78. [p. 148] 5 Apr. 1714
1. Agreed with Mr S. Brewster to have use of their rooms as in his brother Samuel Brewster's time, for £40 p.a.
2. Agreed with bricklayers of new churches of Deptford and Westminster that the Commissioners should supply their bricks, paying £2. 2*s*. for lime, sand and workmanship per rod of brickwork, reckoning 4,500 bricks to the rod. If, upon measuring, a less quantity shall be found to have been used, a proportionable allowance to be made to the bricklayers of 14*s*. per thousand.
3. Price of bricks discussed with brickmakers; some progress being made, adjourned to next meeting.

79. [p. 150] 9 Apr. 1714
1. Resolved to meet, during this session of Parliament, at Mr Smith's, the Treasurer's, in Old Palace Yard.
2. Mr Talman to be desired to send from Italy one statue of the Queen in metal, with its price; to be furnished with a medal of the Queen and a print for that purpose.
3. Sherlock to be desired to draw up memorial to the Queen, representing Lady Russell's request about Mr Burscough.
4,5. Hawksmoor presented a design for new church for Spitalfields, to be considered at next meeting.
6. Bricklayers employed on the new churches of Deptford and Westminster to pick out the best bricks already laid in, carry off the bad ones, and resume work.
7. Notice to be given to the brickmakers treated with, each to bring 100,000 bricks picked as proposed to Deptford and Westminster, as directed by Surveyors.
8. The whole work now set at Deptford and Westminster to be measured and computed, for next meeting.
9. Skeat delivered proposal for a site belonging to Sir Thos Davall in St Botolph Aldgate.
10. Cox delivered a proposal for a site in Bermondsey.
11. Surveyors to measure the two sites.

80. [p. 162] 15 Apr. 1714, at Henry Smith's House, Old Palace Yard
1,2. Nelson delivered a memorial from Sherlock to be laid before the Queen relating to Burscough, to be presented by Archbishop of York and Bishop of London.
3. Sir Jas Bateman presented petition from Vestry of St Botolph Bishopsgate; referred to next meeting.
4. Resolved to consider designs for a church to be erected at the Maypole in the Strand at next meeting.
5. Four pillars to be added for a portico at west end of Deptford new church, according to Archer's design.
6. Resolved to consider design for church to be erected at Spitalfields at next meeting.
7. Sir T. Davall's site to be considered at next meeting.
8. The bricklayers to wait upon Archer, to settle prices for lime, sand and workmanship per rod of brickwork at Deptford and Westminster new churches, and also for work done with the bricks already laid in.

81. [p. 154] 22 Apr. 1714
1. Hawksmoor's design for Spitalfields new church, estimated at £9,129. 16*s*., approved.
2. Agreed to a proposal from Hues and Tufnell, bricklayers employed on Westminster new church; Lucas, bricklayer at Deptford, agreed to the same.
3. Surveyors to draw schedule of bricklayer's work, pursuant to the proposal, to fix the agreement.

4. Method of endowing the new churches to be considered at next meeting, and notice to be given in summons.
5. Gibbs delivered plan of Cox's ground in Bermondsey; Gibbs to examine foundation and report.
6. Advertisement to be put in *Gazette* for proposals for painter's work for East Greenwich church.
7. Surveyors to deliver specification for vaulting Greenwich church, with prices of work.
8. Surveyors to buy two sets of weights and scales, to weigh lead, iron, etc.
9. Secretary to invite Michell to attend this day fortnight about his proposal to supply stone.
10. All churches built by the Commission to be vaulted under the pavements.
11. The old houses purchased at Deptford to be valued by Hawksmoor, and materials to be sold.
12. Surveyors to give in a separate account of work done in each church; a distinct measurement of each kind of work, prices of materials, and total of each particular work, in separate columns.

82. [p. 156] 29 Apr. 1714
1. Reported that the Queen gave a favourable answer concerning Burscough.
2. An address to be presented to the Queen, praying her to recommend to Parliament to find out some method for endowment of the new churches, to be applied to each when ready for use. Dean of Ely and Master of the Temple to draw up such address.
3. Warrant for Beckley's bill.
4. Mr Archer and Mr Wren, with Hawksmoor, to view Johnson's ground in Wapping.
5. Instead of statues to be put in the fifty new churches, a steeple in form of a pillar to be built at west end of the church near the Maypole in the Strand, with the Queen's statue on top, with bases for inscriptions to perpetuate the memory of the building of the fifty new churches.
6. Surveyors to submit designs of such a steeple.
7. The church to be built near the Maypole to Archer's design.
8. Surveyors to lay before next meeting such matters as they were this day directed.

83. [p. 158] 6 May 1714
1. Robt Wetherell and Chrysostom Wilkins, plasterers, delivered proposals for work at East Greenwich new church.
2. Surveyors to prepare a specification for the plasterers to make their proposals at next meeting, and to inquire into their characters.
3. The business this day appointed to be laid before the Commissioners to be adjourned to next week.
4. Afterwards, before the above minutes were signed or the Commissioners all retired, Dean of Ely coming with an address to the Queen, Board reassumed to consider the address, that it might be presented this week, to have the effect of this session of Parliament. Address agreed to,

with some amendments, and Archbishop of York and Bishop of London desired to present it to Her Majesty.

84. [p. 160] 13 May 1714
1. Read a representation of Company of Tylers and Bricklayers.
2. Hawksmoor delivered specification for vaulting Greenwich church.
3. Hawksmoor to make an exact plan of site proposed by Lady Davall.
4. Secretary to make out warrant for £400 payable to John West for his ground at Limehouse.
5. A similar warrant for £400 payable to Bridge Watts for his ground in Upper Wapping.
6. King, Nelson and Hoare to be desired to visit sites proposed by Hayes and Dacres in St Giles in the Fields, attended by Hawksmoor.
7. Bishop of London to treat with Charterhouse about Pardon church yard.
8. To inquire whether houses could be bought to make an approach to Cox's ground in Bermondsey.
9. Secretary to make schedule of sites purchased.
10. Price of ironwork at Westminster new church to be considered at next meeting.
11. Secretary to prepare warrants for paying tradesmen.
12. Proposals for plasterer's work to be considered at next meeting.
13. Business concerning St Alphage and St Giles Cripplegate to be considered in three weeks time.

85. [p. 163] 27 May 1714
1. Read memorial from the Lord Treasurer concerning Aylesbury chapel in St James Clerkenwell parish.
2. King, Mr Wren and Jennings to view it, attended by Hawksmoor, see Dr Kerr, and report.
3. Hawksmoor reported that the following sums were due to tradesmen: Lucas, £723. 19*s*. 7*d*.; Hues and Tufnell £1,007. 16*s*.; £500 and £800 to be impressed to them respectively.
4,6,8. Warrants for masons, etc.
5. Reported that the queen had promised to consider address concerning an endowment for the new churches.
7. Plasterers' proposals referred to Vanbrugh, to report as soon as convenient.

86. [p. 165] 3 June 1714
1. Warrants.
2,3. Letting of house and grazing at St George Ormond Street cemetery.
4. Consideration of adding part of parish of St Giles Cripplegate to St Alphage parish to be resumed Thursday next; parties to be informed.
5. Beckley to take Annesley's directions about drawing conveyance for site near the Maypole in the Strand.
6. Notice to be given in *Gazette* for proposals for bricklayer's and mason's work for new church near the Maypole; such tradesmen to obtain from the Secretary particulars to be prepared by the Surveyors.

7. Archer to direct fencing of church to be built near the Maypole, and digging its foundations; and fencing of Westminster new church; and to make agreement with persons to perform same.
8. Resolved to give Mr Gostwick Cox £900 for his ground in Bermondsey, provided he make a foot passage through the Hatchet Ground; Cox to have old materials of houses purchased of him, except bricks, and to receive the rents until Commissioners need the site.

87. [p. 167] 10 June 1714
1,2. Enlargement of St Alphage parish deferred until new churches built.
3. Hawksmoor reported that Johnson's ground, Wapping, would admit of a good foundation.
4,5. Read petitions from Upper Wapping and Limehouse for speedy erection of new churches on sites purchased; adjourned to next meeting.
6. Owners of sites to be asked for their title deeds.
7. Pardon church yard to be considered first at next meeting.
8. Hawksmoor to send Hurst a blank plasterer's proposal, for him to set his prices to the articles for next meeting.
9. Archer to lay plan and estimate for new church near the Maypole in the Strand before next meeting.
10. Notice to be given in *Gazette* for proposals for glazier's work for East Greenwich new church to be submitted next Thursday.
11. Masons' and bricklayers' proposals for new church near the Maypole to be considered at next meeting.

88. [p. 169] 17 June 1714
1. Surveyors to prepare draughts for two churches to be erected on sites purchased of Watts in Upper Wapping and West in Limehouse for next week.
2. Ground purchased of Mr Humphreys, Mrs Heath and others in Spitalfields to be enclosed with a brick wall, and foundations dug, under direction of Hawksmoor, who is to prepare a model of a minister's house for new parish.
3. Hawksmoor to direct enclosing with a brick wall the road leading from the Common Road to cemetery for new parish of St George the Martyr.
4. King, assisted by Gibbs, to treat with tenants of houses standing on Pardon church yard, and receive their lowest demands; 23 years' purchase to be offered to Governors of the Charterhouse for £19. 10*s*. p.a. ground rent for said houses, provided Commissioners can agree with the tenants.
5. Archer reported Johnson's ground, Wapping Stepney, would admit of a good foundation.
6. Title deeds required from Hastings and Johnson.

89. [p. 171] 24 June 1714
1. Bishop of Winchester, Dean of Canterbury, Halley, Mr Wren and Surveyors to review site proposed by Capt Cox in Bermondsey.

2. Wm Ransome delivered pattern of glasswork and proposal for glazier's work in East Greenwich new church.
3. Ransome to make a new pattern of common Newcastle glass to satisfaction of Surveyors; and then Commissioners will agree to give him 7*d*. per foot, and 6*d*. for pinning in each casement.
4. Surveyors to consider how waterpipes underlying foundation of intended new church near the Maypole may be removed without damage to City water works.
5. Hy Hester and Fra. Withers to be employed to do bricklayer's work of new church near the Maypole, at the prices in their proposal delivered this day; bricks to be as good, in Surveyor's judgment, as any now used in Westminster new church.
6. Hues and Townsend to be employed to do mason's work of said church, according to their proposal delivered this day.
7. Notice to be given in *Gazette* for proposals from masons and bricklayers for Spitalfields new church, to be received next week.

90. [p. 173] 1 July 1714
1. Surveyors to estimate for turning City waterpipes round church to be erected in the Strand, and also for an arch over them.
2. Hawksmoor submitted draughts for two churches to be erected on sites purchased of Watts in Upper Wapping and West in Limehouse, which were left on the table for Commissioners' consideration.
3. Jas Ellis and Jas Hands to be employed to do plasterer's work in East Greenwich new church, at prices proposed by them this day.
4. Bishop of Hereford, Lord Bingley, Sir C. Wren, Archer, Vanbrugh, Arbuthnot, Halley and Mr Wren to consider of a model of a pillar to be erected in the Strand.
5. Consideration of Cox's site at Bermondsey adjourned to next meeting.
6. £30 to be paid Mr Lev for obtaining perfect title to site proposed by Sclater in Bethnal Green.

91. [p. 175] 8 July 1714
1. Bishop of Hereford and Arbuthnot to wait upon Queen with plan of ground near the Maypole in the Strand and design of a pillar to be erected there.
2. Surveyors to prepare specification for masons' proposals for the pillar.
3. Thos Slemaker and Ric. Goodchild to be employed to do bricklayer's work for Spitalfields new church, according to their proposal delivered this day.
4. Mr Sadler, Lord Salisbury's steward, delivered a proposal for a site for a church, etc. in Bermondsey, at £500.
5. King and Halley and Surveyors to view site.
6. Consideration of enclosing more ground near the Maypole for workmen to lay in their materials adjourned to next week.
7. Adjournment for six weeks to be considered at next meeting.
8. Hawksmoor to take care that after foundation of Spitalfields new church is laid, a drain be made to carry off water into main sewer.

9. Resolved that there be two tiers of galleries in new church in Spitalfields.

92. [p. 177] 15 July 1714
1. Bishop of Hereford, Lord Bingley, Sir C. Wren, Vanbrugh, Arbuthnot, Halley, Mr Wren and Archer to confer together about design for church to be erected near the Maypole.
2. Bishop of Hereford reported that he and Arbuthnot had waited upon the Queen, who thought pillar intended to be erected in the Strand ought to be 50 ft from the church and not directly against Somerset House Gate.
3. Above-mentioned committee to direct laying of the pillar's foundation; Tufnell and Strong, masons, to attend them with proposals.
4. Halley and King reported on Lord Salisbury's Bermondsey site.
5. Surveyors to measure Jeffery's Minories site.
6. Archer to speak to Sir C. Wren to know whether the Commissioners can be accommodated with the Office Room in Whitehall, or any other room.

93. [p. 179] 21 July 1714
1. Before any site for a church is agreed to, Surveyors to bring a plan, and a perpendicular section, with a scale, and the nature of the sorts of earth down to lowest part of the foundation.
2. Hawksmoor to provide an auger for boring.
3. Hawksmoor to submit at next meeting a plan of the ground in Spitalfields, with a perpendicular section and scale, and report nature of the soils.
4. The gravel excavated from the foundation of new church in the Strand, except what Bishop of London requires at Somerset House, to be carted to new church in Westminster.
5. Jennings, Archer and Alderman Child to be desired to treat with proprietors and inhabitants of Great Square, Lincoln's Inn, to obtain their consent to building a new church there.
6. Foundation of new church in the Strand to be brought level with ground as soon as convenient.
7. Strong and Tufnell, masons, to be employed to lay foundation of the pillar to be erected in the Strand.
8. Surveyors to employ Skeat for what cramps they want, till further order.
9. Hawksmoor to inquire for stones for steps for inside new church at East Greenwich.

94. [p. 181] 29 July 1714, at Lincoln's Inn
1,2. Read a letter from Talman, that he is providing a statue to cost £340, which he wishes remitted to Leghorn; payment ordered.
3. Surveyors to view site proposed by Hay and Hunter in Russell court, Drury Lane, St Martin in the Fields.
4. Warrants ordered.
5. Watts' ground, Upper Wapping, and West's, Limehouse, to be enclosed.

6. Hawksmoor to go forthwith to give directions for laying foundation of new church in the Strand.
7. £250 to be allowed for planking foundation for Spitalfields new church.
8. The masons employed to build new church in the Strand to prepare their stones ready for setting before they bring them on site.
9. Thos Dunn to be employed to do mason's work of Spitalfields new church at prices delivered by him this day.
10. New churches for Upper Wapping and Limehouse to be built to designs this day delivered by Hawksmoor; Slemaker and Goodchild, bricklayers, to be employed to lay foundations of the churches at prices they agreed to for brickwork of new church in Spitalfields.
11. Warrants for paying £400 to Jas Grove, carpenter, Deptford; £900 to Hues and Tufnell, bricklayers, Westminster; and £130 to Geo. Norris, digging foundations, Westminster.

95. [p. 184] 5 Aug. 1714
1. Surveyors reported on site proposed in Russell Court, Drury Lane, which was rejected as impracticable.
2. The bricks and stones now lying on south side of ground enclosed in the Strand to be removed to the west, and nothing to lie there to incommode passage; all rubbish to be cleared as soon as possible.
3. No more stone to be laid in for foundation of the pillar intended to be erected in the Strand until further notice.

96. [p. 185] 12 Aug. 1714
Read memorial by Townsend the mason; resolved that he have leave to lodge and work his stone within the enclosure in the Strand, and as far westward of enclosure as convenient for his purpose, with as little inconvenience as possible to inhabitants. Adjourned to 26 August.

97. [p. 186] 30 Sep. 1714
1. Secretary to write to members of the committee appointed on 15 July last to confer on design for new church in the Strand, to report as soon as convenient.
2. Notice to be given in *Gazette* for masons' proposals for the two new churches in Limehouse and Upper Wapping to be delivered this day fortnight.
3,4. Surveyors to view sites proposed, belonging to Widow Terry in St Saviour Southwark and Thos Halls, Grays Inn Lane, St Andrew Holborn.
5,6. Surveyors to report what inside finishing necessary for East Greenwich church, and to submit designs for, with estimate for each item except pewing. Plasterer to perform ornamental work according to proposal made by Surveyor this day.
7. Works of new churches now carrying on to be covered, to preserve them from the weather.

98. [p. 188] 14 Oct. 1714
1. Read memorial from several inhabitants of the Strand, complaining of

the water courses being stopped; Surveyors to seek to rectify the inconvenience.
2,3. Proposal from Strong and Tufnell for mason's work at Limehouse and Upper Wapping churches referred to Hawksmoor to compare with their former prices.
4. Warrants to pay £400 to Hester and Wither, bricklayers, Strand church.
5. Surveyors to measure brickwork in foundations, Limehouse and Wapping new churches.

99. [p. 190] 28 October 1714
1. Read representation from Hawksmoor and Gibbs concerning canals in the Strand.
2. Crosse and Bertie to be desired to view the canals and give directions for remedying inconveniences.
3. Committee to confer on designs for Strand church to meet on Tuesday next at Smith's, the Treasurer's, at 11 a.m., and report to next meeting.
4. Legal complication about payment of £200 to Mrs Walker.
5. Strong and Tufnell to be employed as masons for Limehouse and Wapping new churches at same rates as for Westminster.
6. Surveyors to report what is due to Strong and Tufnell for masonry work at churches they are engaged in.

100. [p. 191a] 4 Nov. 1714
1,2. Memorial to Treasury for £2,000 to be impressed.
Warrants for paying Slemaker and Goodchild, bricklayers: £800 for Spitalfields, £650 for Wapping, £550 for Limehouse.
3. Read memorial from Lucas, bricklayer, Deptford church, for £700 to be impressed to him.
4. Surveyors to measure all brickwork there and report what is due to Lucas.
5,6. On consideration of report of committee meeting on 2 November (**536**) on design of new church in the Strand, resolved that it be built to Gibbs's design.
7. Treasurer to lay account before next meeting of sums in his hands and in the Exchequer.
8. Beckley and Surveyors to state what demands are likely to be made shortly, either for sites or work.

101. [p. 193] 10 Nov. 1714
1. Warrants for paying Slemaker and Goodchild not to be signed until they have signed their agreements for Limehouse and Upper Wapping churches.
2. Signed memorial to the Lords of the Treasury for a further £10,000 to be taken into the Exchequer upon the loan on coals.

102. [p. 194] 17 Nov. 1714
1. Surveyors to view ground proposed by Ironmongers Company.
2. Warrants submitted for Sleemakers and Goodchild, who had signed their contracts.

103. [p. 195] 24 Nov. 1714
1. Read report from Gibbs on Ironmongers' Company ground in St Giles Cripplegate parish.
2. Signed memorial desiring Lords of the Treasury to imprest £14,000 to Hy Smith, Esq., Treasurer to this Commission.

104. [p. 196] 1 Dec. 1714
Surveyors to view and make plan of Three Cups Inn, Holborn.

105. [p. 197] 8 Dec. 1714
1. Gibbs reported on Three Cups Inn.
2. Beckley and Hawksmoor reported what sums were likely to be demanded of the Commissioners.
3. Warrants to be made out for: Tufnell and Strong, £1,000 for Greenwich, £2,000 for Deptford, £2,000 for Westminster; Hues and Billinghurst, £500 for Greenwich; Tufnell and Hues, £400 for wall inclosing St George's cemetery; Lucas, £800 for Deptford; Grove £400 for Spitalfields, £50 for St George's cemetery, £50 for Wapping; Benj. Coker, £70 for digging foundation, Limehouse; Geo. Norris, £100 for digging foundation for Strand and £100 for Spitalfields; John Clark, £40 for digging foundation, Wapping; Geo. Vaughan, £70 for making road to St George's cemetery; Robt Record Hastings, £1,000 for ground and six houses in St Paul's Shadwell.

106. [p. 199] 15 Dec. 1714
1. Warrants signed.
2. Surveyors to report on memorial of James and Jeffs, carpenters, East Greenwich church.

107. [p. 200] 12 Jan. 1714/15
1. Secretary to write to churchwardens of East Greenwich about their enlarging churchyard for security of the fabric.
2. A letter from Treasury referring to the Commissioners security offered by the Commissioner's Treasurer.
3. Resolved that £5,000 mentioned is sufficient if Robt Cotton, Esq., is bound with Treasurer in the whole sum.
4. Secretary to prepare warrants for James and Jeffs and for Grazebrook, plumber, Greenwich church.

108. [p. 201] 19 Jan. 1714/15
1. Warrants filled up and signed for paying James and Jeffs, carpenters, £200 for Greenwich, £100 for Westminster, £50 for Limehouse, and £50 for Strand churches; Graysbrook, plumber, £200 for Greenwich; Brewster £20 for half-year's rent.

109. [p. 202] 26 Jan. 1714/15
1. Bishop of London to be requested to consecrate church yard of St George the Martyr.
2. All persons who have made models for Commissioners' use to bring in their bills.

3. Warrant ordered for rent.

Secretary read Brewster's letter of 13 June last; consideration referred to Jennings and Hy Hoare.

110. [p. 203] 16 Feb. 1714/15
1,2. Commissioners will not treat further with Ironmongers' Co. about site at present.
3. Barker's proposal about Three Cups Inn referred to next meeting.
4. Vanbrugh and Mr Wren to view Johnson's ground, Wapping, with Surveyors, and report on foundation.
5. The workmen at the several new churches to proceed as soon as proper.

111. [p. 204] 23 Feb. 1714/15
1. Cross, Annesley, Jennings and Mr Wren to view Three Cups Inn and examine value of ground.
2. Surveyors to make a plan of the ground purchased of Lady Russell, if one not already made, and submit designs for a church for that site.

112. [p. 205] 9 Mar. 1714/15
1. Secretary to make out warrant for Treasurer to pay Sir Edw. Gould £351. 10*s*. to answer £340 at Florence to Talman, for statue of Queen Anne in brass.
2. Surveyors to make plan of site proposed by inhabitants of Bermondsey, reported on by King and Halley, 15 July last.
3. Bishop of London to be desired to consult Dr Sacheverell about transferring parish charity now charged on Three Cups Inn.
4. Surveyors to open ground at site proposed by Mr White in St Giles Cripplegate, and attend Sir Thos Crosse and Mr Wren to view it.

113. [p. 206] 16 Mar. 1714/15
1–3. Accepted offer of free site in St Martin in the Fields parish from Lord Scarborough. Surveyors to take copy of plan.
4. Gibbs reported on White's ground in St Giles Cripplegate.
5. Surveyors to examine whether ground will admit of a good foundation, taking such workmen as they need.
6. Secretary to prepare warrants for paying Geo. Vaughan £30 for digging at the two cemeteries purchased in St Pancras; Hester and Withers £400 for Strand church.
7. Bridges Watts petitioned to be paid £30 retained by Beckley out of £400 for a site in Upper Wapping until Watts obtained copies of writings relating to the site, owner of the writings refusing to give copies.
8,9. Beckley's bill of £59. 16*s*. 8*d*. referred to Annesley and Jennings.

114. [p. 208] 23 Mar. 1714/15, at Treasurer Smith's house
1. Surveyors to proceed to finish East Greenwich church so far only as the acts oblige the Commissioners to do it; and to give parishioners notice to prepare for pewing church and making it ready for public service.
2. Secretary to write to minister and churchwardens of Greenwich that

the Commissioners are informed that there have been several burials within new church, contrary to the acts, and that in future they forbear burying there.
3,4. Upon the Surveyors' complaint, resolved that Slemaker and Goodchild, bricklayers employed in new churches of Limehouse, Spitalfields and Upper Wapping, be discharged from any further service under this Commission.
5. Surveyors to submit to next meeting proposals for getting better bricks.
6. Surveyors to stake out ground for new church to be erected at Stockwell in Lambeth parish next Tuesday, and notify Sir John Thornicroft, Mr Angel and some other parishioners.
7,8. Proposal from Dacres for site in St Giles in the Fields referred to next meeting.

115. [p. 210] 6 Apr. 1715
1. Petition from Slemaker and Goodchild referred to next meeting.
2. Read memorial from Gibbs proposing a method to procure good bricks.
3. Warrants to be made out for Dowager Duchess of Bedford and Lady Russell for the site in St Giles in the Fields parish; for R. Webb, Esq., 33 guineas fee for inspecting title deeds of purchases.

116. [p. 211] 27 Apr. 1715
1. Read petition from Slemaker and Goodchild.
2. Slemaker and Goodchild to proceed on their works at new churches, making an allowance for bad bricks already used by them; in future not to suffer any bad bricks to be brought on site on pain of permanent discharge.
3. Secretary to send copy of above resolution to every bricklayer employed under the Commission.
4. Beckley to refer Sclater's title deeds for site in Bethnal Green to Webb.
5. Notice to be given in *Gazette* for masons', carpenters' and bricklayers' proposals for a new church in Bloomsbury to be brought on Tuesday 10 May.
7. Masons employed at Limehouse and Upper Wapping churches to execute their contracts as soon as Hawksmoor has explained them.
8. Dickinson brought remainder of the maps in his custody to Secretary; Commissioners signed warrant for £28. 18*s*. 6*d*., for his salary as Surveyor.

117. [p. 213] 10 May 1715
1. Notice to be given in *Gazette* for workmen to bring proposals for building church in Bloomsbury this day fortnight.
2. Secretary's accounts to be referred to Dean of Canterbury and Sherlock.
3,4. Surveyors to inquire into value of ground proposed, in plan of Three

Cups Inn, Holborn, for next meeting, when Commissioners will give proprietors an answer.
5. Vanbrugh, and Messrs Wren, Archer and Hoare, to view Johnson's site in Wapping, attended by Surveyors.
6. Beckley to pay Watts the reserved £30, being now satisfied by Webb's opinion.
7. Secretary to prepare warrant for paying Jas Ellis and Jas Hands, plasterers, East Greenwich church, £150.
8. Dacres to be offered £1,400 for his site in High Holborn.

118. [p. 215] 17 May 1715
1. Surveyors to inquire value of Three Cups Inn site for next meeting.
2. Church on Lady Russell's ground in Bloomsbury to be built to Vanbrugh's design; and built north and south, as it cannot conveniently be built any other way.
3,4. An application to be made to the King to recommend to Parliament endowment of the fifty new churches; to be considered by Dean of Canterbury, Moss and Sherlock, or any two of them.
5. Box to be added to the Commissioners to view Johnson's ground, Wapping; and any two of them to make the view.
6. Hawksmoor to give orders for walling at east end of Deptford new church, and making gates as soon as convenient.
7. Messenger to give notice in next Thursday's summons that Commissioners will then consider form of application to the King for an endowment, and choice of officers.
8. To consider an order about plans and estimates for building churches next Thursday.

119. [p. 217] 19 May 1715
1. Elected the following officers for the year ensuing at salaries stated: Hy Smith, Esq., Treasurer, £300 p.a.; Thos Rous, Secretary, £200; N. Hawksmoor and Jas Gibbs, Surveyors, £200; Simon Beckley, Solicitor, £80; John Skeat, Agent, £100; Thos Crocker, Messenger, £30.
2. No church to be begun until a plan, with model, and estimate be made; when such plan or model agreed upon, it shall not be altered without direction of the Board, and an agreement made for the charge of such alteration.
3. Referred to Lord Bingley, Bromley, Bertie, Crosse, Sir C. Wren, Archer, Mr Wren, Vanbrugh, Bishop of Hereford, Foley, Newton, Arbuthnot, Halley, Child, and Bateman, or any three of them, to consider rules for bringing in plans and estimates; Vanbrugh to submit an estimate for Bloomsbury new church.
4. Appointed a committee of Bishops of London, Bristol, Hereford, and Chester, Stanhope, Crosse, Jennings, Bertie, Annesley, Raymond, Hoare, Mr Wren, Arbuthnot and King, or any five of them, to consider the maintenance to be applied for the ministers of the fifty new churches; all other Commissioners that attend to have votes.

120. [p. 219] 24 May 1715
Agreed upon address to the King to recommend provision of a maintenance for the ministers of the fifty new churches to Parliament.

121. [p. 220] 31 May 1715
1. Bishop of London reported King's gracious answer to address presented by Archbishop of York and others; Secretary to enter it in Book of Muniments.
2. Letter from Talman about Queen's statue referred to next meeting.
3. Secretary to prepare warrants for smith's work at Deptford, £600; Westminster, £300; Spitalfields, £100.

122. [p. 221] 14 June 1715
1. Surveyors to report on site called Pewter Platter Inn, St James parish Clerkenwell.
2. Gibbs to make a plan of Sclater's ground, Bethnal Green, for next meeting.
3. Gibbs to view Lord Salisbury's ground, Bermondsey, and report what other ground will be required there.
4. Box and Mr Wren to treat with Johnson about price of ground wanting to make his site complete.
5. Barker to have £1,900 for Three Cups Inn, Holborn, he clearing the ground.
6. Talman to finish Queen's statue at £800, remitting the remainder of the sum at £50 per month.
7. Secretary stated he had disbursed more money than had been imprested to him, and that Dean of Canterbury and Sherlock had approved his accounts: resolved that a further £100 be imprested to him.

123. [p. 223] 28 June 1715
1. Surveyors to lay report of progress on churches this day fortnight; and a similar report at first meeting in every month.
2. Hawksmoor to submit plan or model of Limehouse and Upper Wapping churches at next meeting.
3. Strong and Tufnell allowed to dispose of stone belonging to them lying near the Maypole in the Strand.
4. Gibbs to make a plan for a church, 'the most convenient that can stand East and West', for ground already bought of Johnson in Lower Wapping; and another, supposing additional ground purchased.
5. Gibbs to report at next meeting on sites at Pewter Platter Inn (St James, Clerkenwell), Sclater's ground (Bethnal Green), and Lord Salisbury's (Bermondsey).
6. Accepted Barker's demand of £1,900 for site at Three Cups Inn, Holborn; deeds to be laid before Webb.
7. Abstract of debt on new churches account submitted by Surveyors referred to Crosse, Annesley, Jennings and Bertie, or any two, to report what further sum should be taken into Exchequer.

124. [p. 225] 5 July 1715
1. Secretary to prepare memorial to Treasury for taking a further £11,000 into Exchequer upon loan on coal duty; done accordingly, and signed.
2. Secretary, Treasurer and Surveyor to report what cemeteries bought and agreed for; progress made in each church; how Exchequer issues have been spent; and what demands are now made.
3. Notice to be given in *Gazette* for proposals for plumber's work, Deptford new church.
4. Mr Wren and Box to report on Sir Thos Davall's site near Burr Street, St Botolph Aldgate.
5. Agreed to give Johnson £200 for additional pieces of ground.
6. Read a letter from Major Godfrey; Secretary to inform him that the masons are ordered to proceed at Limehouse church with all expedition.

125. [p. 227] 12 July 1715
1. The three papers prepared by the Secretary, Treasurer, and Surveyors, pursuant to order, be entered in Secretary's books.
2. Gibbs delivered reports on Sclater's ground (Bethnal Green) and Pewter Platter Inn (St James, Clerkenwell).
3. Resolved, not at present to build a church in Clerkenwell; Gardner at liberty to dispose of his ground.

126. [p. 228] 5 Aug. 1715
1,2. Secretary to prepare warrants for payments of £10,862. 6*s*. 10*d*. in Surveyors' schedule, £800 to J. Townsend, mason for Strand church, and £700 to Bastwick Johnson, Esq. for ground at Lower Wapping.
3. Notice to be given in *Gazette* for receiving proposals for plumber's work, Deptford new church, on Thursday next.
4. Secretary to prepare warrants for Solicitor's bill and salaries.
5. Surveyors to make plan for a church to be erected on Thornicroft's ground [Lambeth].
6. Memorial presented to Queen Anne respecting Burscough to be laid before the King.
7. Kemp's title deeds for site for minister's house, Bow, to be laid before Solicitor.
8. Halley and Box, attended by Surveyor, to view Davall's ground, Aldgate.

127. [p. 230] 11 Aug. 1715
1. Warrants signed.
2. Treasurer to submit report at next meeting of monies in his hands.
3. Bishop of Bristol and Jennings to treat with Lord Salisbury about his Bermondsey site.

128. [p. 231] 18 Aug. 1715
1. Hawksmoor to inform Sadler, Lord Salisbury's steward, how much ground Commissioners require at Bermondsey, and report to next meeting his price.

2. Blank warrant for Dunn, mason, Spitalfields church, filled up at £400.
3. Signed warrant for transmitting £460 at £50 per month to Talman for brass statue.
4. Hawksmoor to report next week on plumbers' proposals for Deptford church.

129. [p. 232] 1 Sep. 1715
1. Geo. Osmond to be employed for plumber's work at Deptford church at the following prices: for milled lead, carriage and labour, 11*s*. 9*d*. per cwt.; for workmanship and solder of rainwater pipes, 9*d*. per foot running; for rainwater cisterns, 15*s*. each.

[Pages 233–6 blank]

130. [p. 237] 5 Jan. 1715/16, at St Paul's Chapter House
The commission under Broad Seal dated 2 Dec. 1715 was read and accepted.
1. John Leacroft, Esq., presented a royal commission dated 9 Dec. 1715 appointing him Treasurer to the Commissioners.
2. The Commissioners elected following officers: Jenkin Thos Phillips, Secretary; Nich. Hawksmoor and John James, Surveyors; Vigerus Edwards, Solicitor; John Skeat, Agent; Wm Waters, Messenger.
3. The commission and acts of parliament relating to the fifty new churches to be printed, with abstracts in margin.
4. Messenger to enquire whether lease of chambers in Lincoln's Inn has expired.

131. [p. 239] 10 Jan. 1715/16
1–3. Rous, Smith and Gibbs to attend next meeting and deliver up all books, papers and draughts, with schedules of them.

132. [p. 241] 14 Jan. 1715/16
1. Dean of Chichester reported that Smith, late Treasurer, was ready to supply a copy of all his accounts, but could not part with originals, which have not yet been passed by Exchequer.
2. Smith to submit a signed copy with all convenient speed.
3. Nottingham, clerk to Rous, late Secretary, called in; all Rous's books and papers relating to the late Commission would be delivered at next meeting, and he was preparing a schedule of them.
4. Gibbs called in; said he would in a week's time deliver all designs, models, sites, etc. and all books and papers relating to the late Commission in his custody in a month's time.
5,6. Read letter from Gibbs; to give detailed account of his demands for next meeting.

133. [p. 243] 19 Jan. 1715/16
1. Smith to attend with copy of all his accounts at next meeting.
2. Gibbs to attend next meeting with all draughts, plans, maps, etc. in his custody.

3. Secretary to ask Archbishop of Canterbury to appoint time and place for next meeting.
4. Nottingham brought books and papers with schedule; Secretary to examine, and give receipt if they agree.
5. Rous to deliver what other books and papers he has relating to the Commission.

133A. [p. 244] 27 Jan. 1715/16, at the Banqueting House, Whitehall
1,2. Agreed to Gibbs's request to be allowed to finish Strand church, and that no one be allowed to take a copy of his design, he intending to engrave it for his own use; and that all models made by him for the last Commission be paid for, and he receive his salary and travelling charges.
3. Brewster attending made proposals concerning his chambers in Lincoln's Inn, hired by the late Commissioners.
4. If Brewster cannot dispose of his chambers by Lady Day, rent to be paid him to Midsummer.
5. Beckley to deliver all his papers and deeds, with a schedule thereof.
6. Secretary and Solicitor to examine minutes of last Commission in order to submit report on state of affairs as soon as convenient.
7. Hy Smith to provide accounts.

134. [p. 246] 4 Feb. 1715/16
1. Committee appointed to examine Gibbs' account: Cannon, Sherlock, Hare, Phillips, Newton, Clayton, Naylor, Ellis, and any other attending.
2. Certificate that John Leacroft, appointed Treasurer by His Majesty, has given security in office of Remembrancer of Exchequer, 4 Jan. 1715/16.
3. Agreed the committee should draw up representation to Treasury regarding Smith; which was done, read and agreed to. Clayton to lay it before Lords of the Treasury.
4. Committee to report salaries of all officers of late Commission.
5. Committee to report all accounts of late Commission.
6. Beckley, Solicitor to late Commission, attended; willing to deliver deeds and writings, but not till Thursday next; and prayed direction about Lady Russell's deeds of sale, executed by her, the money not being paid according thereto.
7. Beckley to deliver the deeds to Barcroft, her agent now present, to have them re-executed on payment of purchase money.
8. Surveyors to measure and make out bills for work in the new churches.
9. Agreed to Gibbs' request for use of models of church in the Strand, in order to perfect the church.
10. Notice to be given to Brewster that the Commissioners will use his chambers in Lincoln's Inn till Midsummer next.
11. Furniture belonging to the Commissioners at Smith's house to be removed to Brewster's chambers in Lincoln's Inn.
12. Application to Treasury to take money into Exchequer on loan on coals to be submitted at next meeting.

135. [p. 249] 14 Feb. 1715/16, at Lincoln's Inn
1. Allowed Gibbs' account, £221. 19*s*., for trying the ground, making wooden models, and salary to Christmas last.
2. Committee to report on all accounts from last Commission.
3. Site in St Giles Cripplegate parish referred to committee.
4. Reported, Beckley had agreed with Edwards on a schedule of all deeds and papers in his possession.
5. Consideration of Beckley's bill referred to committee.
6. Committee to consider form of application to Treasury to direct Receipt of Exchequer to take in money on loan on coals. Committee to meet here on Monday at 5 p.m.
7. Lord Scarborough wishes a church to be speedily erected on site he gave.
8. Commissioners not yet ready to build new church on the ground mentioned in Lord Scarborough's letter.
9. Dean of Chichester to request Archer to continue his care of Westminster new church.

136. [p. 252] 24 Feb. 1715/16
1. Minutes of last meeting of Commissioners and committee read.
2. Treasury to be asked to take in £25,000 upon the loan on coal duty.
3. Ironmongers' Company's site, St Giles Cripplegate parish, not convenient, 'being in the extream parts'.
4. Agreed with committee that Beckley's bill, £35. 16*s*., be allowed.

137. [p. 254] 29 Feb. 1715/16
1,2. Medlicott proposed a site near Devonshire House.
3,4. Lord Scarborough's ground not a convenient site.
5. Committee appointed to consider report to king and parliament: Archbishop of Canterbury, Bishop of London, Kennet, Sherlock, Cannon, Waddington, Butler, Waugh, Gooch, Ellis, Naylor, Farrer, Meller and Peck.
6. Treasury require to know why £25,000 applied for.

138. [p. 256] 5 Mar. 1715/16
1. Considered heads of a report to be laid before the King and Parliament.
2. Resolved to consider first a report on method of endowing the new churches.
3. Secretary and Surveyors to update report laid before Parliament on 8 July last, and report where new churches are intended.

139. [p. 257] 8 Mar. 1715/16
1. Secretary submitted report of state of the churches and an account of sites and funds.
2. None of the churches being finished, Commissioners unable to act to provide a maintenance for their ministers.

140. [p. 259] 12 Mar. 1715/16
1,2. Secretary read draft reports to King. Report amended and to be engrossed for next meeting.
3. Treasurer reported that Treasury will direct officers at Receipt of Exchequer to take in £25,000 on the loan of coals.

141. [p. 260] 19 Mar. 1715/16
1. Secretary submitted a general account and state of the new churches, together with a report and duplicates to be presented to King and both houses of Parliament, which was read and signed.
2–5. Report and account to be entered in Secretary's books; to be carried to the Archbishops and Bishops Commissioners for signing and to be laid before King and House of Lords by Archbishop of Canterbury, and before House of Commons by Mr Farrer.
6. Barker requested perfecting of conveyance of Three Cups Inn ground.
7. Commission will confirm the agreement; Barker to take title deeds to Edwards for laying before Webb.
8. Surveyors to direct workmen to proceed as soon as they judge it convenient.
9,10. Treasury require to know what interest is to be paid on the £25,000 loan. Rate to be left to Treasury to decide.
11. Secretary to prepare blank warrants for paying workmen.
Both Surveyors to submit design for church to be erected in St Mary Woolnoth parish, with estimate.

142. [p. 263] 26 Mar. 1716
1. Filling up warrants deferred to next meeting.
2. James to consult proper workmen about best method of taking down St Mary Woolnoth church.
3. Referred to another meeting a memorial from James about roofing Westminster new church.
4. As only £1,500 brought in at 5 per cent, Commissioners want 6 per cent to be offered on their loan, as given on Land Tax, etc.
5. Agreement with Dacres for site in St Giles in the Fields confirmed, if title good.

143. [p. 265] 9 Apr. 1716
1,2. Reports laid before King and Parliament.
3,4. Read petition from East Greenwich for completion of church; parish required to procure a sufficient graveyard first.
5. Sclater's ground, Bethnal Green, referred to Webb for approval of title.
6. Secretary submitted application to Treasury for impresting £12,000 to Treasurer.
7. Notice to be given in next Saturday's *Gazette* for proposals for carpenter's work for the roof of Westminster church and plasterer's work at Deptford.

144. [p. 267] 16 Apr. 1716
Minister and churchwardens of East Greenwich delivered Vestry order of 15 April. Commissioners expect a penal bond as security that no grave shall be made within six feet of the church. Half-acre mentioned in vestry order to be purchased before Commissioners will proceed further.

Edwards reported he had obtained Sclater's title deeds for Bethnal Green site from Webb, and was instructed to return them for his approbation.

Treasurer reported he had obtained a Treasury order for £12,000 and lodged it with Mr Clayton. Secretary submitted warrant to pay £1,000 to Lady Russell for her site in St Giles in Fields parish, to be lodged with Mr Edwards until she executes the conveyance.

Warrants ordered for half the £23,133. 15*s*. 7*d*. due to workmen.

Read letter from minister of St Giles Cripplegate about a site; consideration adjourned to next meeting.

Hawksmoor to attend with a plan and design of the church to be erected on ground purchased of Lady Russell [Bloomsbury].

145. [p. 269] 19 Apr. 1716
1. Treasurer reported he had received £12,000 at Exchequer.
2. Warrants signed for paying workmen.
3. Hawksmoor and James to act jointly in all their official business, and report to next meeting what is due to each workman.
4. Surveyors and Skeat to report on site in St Martin in Fields parish proposed by Medlicott.
5. Surveyors to report on site proposed by the minister of Windsor [*sic*], in St Giles Cripplegate.
6. Mr Whitfield, minister of St Giles Cripplegate, asking for a new church to be built there speedily, was told one should be as soon as a convenient site could be found.
7. Consideration deferred of Hawksmoor's design for Bloomsbury church.

146. [p. 271] 23 Apr. 1716
1. Skeat reported that site in St Martin in the Fields parish proposed by Medlicott was too small, being only 30 ft north-south.
2. Denning delivered proposal for taking down church of St Mary Woolnoth, which was read.
3. James submitted design for a church to be erected in Lombard Street, St Mary Woolnoth parish.
4,5. Proposal for leasing Smith's house, Old Palace Yard, at £70 p.a.
6. Surveyors to confer on design for roof of Westminster new church, and report at next meeting.
7. Archbishop of Canterbury to renew application to King respecting Burscough.
8. Surveyors to give notice to masons employed on Westminster new church not to prepare any stones for the towers until further order.

147. [p. 273] 30 April 1716
1. Reported that King gave gracious answer about Burscough.

2. Treasurer had agreed to take Smith's house at £75 p.a. from Midsummer.
3. Treasurer and Solicitor to find out what term remains of Smith's lease, and the conditions required of the Commission.
4. Treasurer to produce his vouchers for payments to workmen at next meeting.
5,6. Further suggestions from Medlicott for a site in St Martin in the Fields parish; Skeat to view.
7,8. Inhabitants of St Mary Woolnoth request Commissioners to take down their church, but are willing themselves to inspect the workmen; props that now support church to be returned to them.
9. Notice to be given in Saturday's *Gazette* for proposals for taking down St Mary Woolnoth church.
10. Treasury memorialised for a further issue of £13,000.

148. [p. 275] 9 May 1716
1,2. Agreement to be drawn up with East Greenwich parish not to bury within 6 ft of church walls.
3. Surveyors to prepare patterns of wainscot for Greenwich church.
4. Treasurer produced vouchers for payment to workmen, which were examined.
5. Resolved to give Treasurer £75 p.a. for Smith's house, by him taken for the use of the Commission. Committee appointed to inspect Smith's house and report what rooms are most convenient for meetings and the accommodation of the officers: Bishops of Gloucester, Bristol, St Asaph, Dean of Chichester, Cannon, Gooch, Phillips and Meller.
6. Hawksmoor and James to submit as detailed an estimate as possible of cost of Hawksmoor's design for Bloomsbury new church.
7,8. Proposals from Grove, Ford, Whitton, Townsend, Hester, Withers and Denning for taking down St Mary Woolnoth church referred to Surveyors.

149. [p. 277] 16 May 1716
1. James reported that patterns of wainscot for Greenwich new church were not yet completed.
2. James delivered estimate for building new church in Great Russell Street amounting to £9,790. 17*s*. 4*d*., exclusive of pewing.
3. James to write to workmen to ask the most they will give severally for old materials of St Mary Woolnoth church.
4. Archer to be invited to next meeting to discuss Westminster new church.
5. Solicitor to draw instrument obliging Treasurer to discharge all parish taxes, repairs etc. on house in Old Palace Yard.
6. Treasurer to have office on first floor [of Smith's house] and sole use of parlour and other first floor rooms when Commissioners not sitting.
7. Secretary and Solicitor each to have an office up one pair of stairs, and Secretary to have lodging up two pair.
8. Agreed that inhabitants of St Mary Woolnoth have two weeks notice before demolition of church begun, to remove monuments, etc.

9. Edward to lay draft of indenture between Commissioners and Rector and Churchwardens of Greenwich before Melmoth; if approved, copy to be sent to Greenwich.
10. Surveyors forthwith to adjust to Christmas last the accounts of workmen to whom warrants have not been issued.
11. Plasterers' proposals for Deptford church and carpenters' for Westminster referred to Surveyors.

150. [p. 279] 23 May 1716
1–4. James brought patterns for pews for East Greenwich church, but decision deferred for fuller report.
5. Notice to be given in Saturday's *Gazette* for proposals for pewing East Greenwich church according to patterns to be seen at 6 Lincoln's Inn [Great Square] from 8 a.m. to 8 p.m.
6. Jas Ellis and Jas Hands to be employed as plasterers at Deptford.
7. Secretary to inform Directors of Greenwich Hospital that Commissioners will finish church as soon as possible.
8. Rich. Goodchild to take down St Mary Woolnoth church, allowing £250 for old materials, and £50 more if employed to build the new church.
9. Solicitor to examine contracts drawn between the Commissioners and workmen.
10. Surveyors to submit design for St Mary Woolnoth at next meeting.
Commissioners will settle salaries at next meeting.

151. [p. 281] 30 May 1716
1. James reported on pewing for East Greenwich church.
2. Resolved to pew the church, and that the pews be double-seated.
3. Archer attending presented a model of tower of Deptford church and a model of the four towers for Westminster new church and reported he thought foundation would bear proposed towers.
4. Inhabitants of St Mary Woolnoth presented paper about monuments, etc.
5. Goodchild proposed that some of old materials might be used for fencing church, leaving the Commissioners to offer Seager, the carpenter, what they think fit for their use.
6,7. Resolved that all salaries be settled for one year only from opening of this Commission.
8. Treasurer to have £300 p.a.
9. Secretary to have £200 p.a.
10. Further consideration deferred to next meeting.

152. [p. 283] 6 June 1716
1. Archer to proceed with the four towers for Westminster new church only so far as is necessary for the roof.
2,3. Hawksmoor and James to have £200 p.a.
4–6. Edwards to have £80 p.a. as Solicitor, with further allowance for conveyancing, etc.
7. Skeat to have £100 p.a., and Messenger £40.
8. Read a memorial from inhabitants of Bermondsey about site pro-

posed for a new church; Skeat and Hawksmoor to treat with Lord Salisbury's steward, Stephens.
9. Resolved to build Bloomsbury new church on Lady Russell's ground according to Hawksmoor's model.
10. Read representation from some inhabitants of St James Clerkenwell for converting Aylesbury chapel into a church.
11. Notice to be given in Saturday's *Gazette* for bricklayers' and masons' proposals for laying foundations of Bloomsbury church.
12. Commissioners will complete agreement with Lady Davall only according to the first plan delivered to them.

153. [p. 285] 13 June 1716
1. Edwards' books referred to another meeting, he not being present.
2. Skeat and Hawksmoor reported meeting with Lord Salisbury's steward about Bermondsey site; Hawksmoor to enquire further.
3,4. Referred to Surveyors proposals for doing the brickwork at Bloomsbury church from Hy Hester, Fra. Withers, Edw. Boswell, Geo. Collins and John Ford.
5. Surveyors to give blank articles of work to masons who wish to tender for Bloomsbury new church.
6. No one attending for Lady Davall, consideration of her proposal deferred to next meeting.
7. Martha Styler to have £10. 10*s*. for cleaning the chambers.
8. Commissioners will pay Brewster a year and a half's rent at Midsummer, and 50*s*. for 'the shelves with the ironwork upon which the models stand'.
9,10. Referred to Surveyors proposals for pewing Greenwich new church (from John Fosset, John Simons, John Gilham, and John Smallwell); and for roofing Westminster church (from John Grove and Thos Denning); to report at next meeting.
11. Surveyors to report on request of parishioners of St Mary Woolnoth that bodies buried near the walls may be conveniently disposed of when the foundation is removed.

154. [p. 287] 20 June 1716, at their office in Old Palace-yard.
1. Agreed to Edwards' proposal to keep one book in which he should enter all abstracts of title, etc.
2. Hawksmoor reported that Lord Salisbury's steward stated nothing was to be done about Bermondsey site until his lordship came to town.
3. Read petition of Philip Clement relating to his watercourse; referred to Surveyors, to report at next meeting.
4. Goodchild attended to answer complaint of his using bad bricks at Spitalfields; Surveyors to examine bricks he uses in other churches, and estimate what damage the work may sustain from bad bricks already used, reporting to next meeting.
5. Surveyors recommended Ford and Boswell to be employed as bricklayers for Bloomsbury church; contract to be made.
6. Mr Wright, for Lady Davall, asks for materials of old houses on proposed site; Surveyors and Skeat to report value.

7. John Mist selected from diggers tendering for Bloomsbury church.
8. Surveyors to direct workmen to start on Bloomsbury church.
9. Gilham and Smallwell being 'considerably more reasonable', appointed to pew Greenwich church.
10. John Grove's the lowest tender for roofing Westminster new church.

155. [p. 290] 27 June 1716
1. Sambrook and St John discharged from their agreement of 16 March 1712 about a site in case Mr Tillard be purchaser.
2. Hawksmoor reported that his report on Clement's water-course was not ready.
3. Boswell and Ford to attend next meeting.
4. Surveyors to consider ways to keep bricklayers to letter of contract.
5,6. Wright, empowered by Lady Davall, requested the Commissioners would allow her old materials of four houses, etc., supposed by her to have been left out of contract; agreed. Solicitor to prepare conveyances.
7. Surveyors reported on disposing of bodies in St Mary Woolnoth; further consideration referred to their care.
8,9. Signed warrants for one and a half year's rent to Mr Brewster and 50*s*. for shelf that supported the models; and £10. 10*s*. to M. Stapler.

156. [p. 292] 4 July 1716
1. Hawksmoor further to consider Clement's case and report what damage his water-course may sustain.
2. Boswell and Ford, bricklayers for Bloomsbury church, promised to stand to letter of their contract.
3. Bill for expenditure by Secretary, Nottingham and Waters for the Commission's service to be submitted to next meeting.
4. Waters to take in three chardrons of coal.
5. James to see whether Ironmongers' Company will stand to their proposal to accommodate the Commissioners with another site [Cripplegate].

157. [p. 293] 18 July 1716
1. Hawksmoor reported that Clement's water-course may have sustained damage from building Spitalfields church; to inquire further.
2. Allowed bills for expenditure (4 July, minute 3), and £6. 6*s*. 10*d*. for painting the chambers in Lincoln's Inn.
3. Smart, for Dacres, stated that he was willing to build six feet further back from Bloomsbury church than originally intended.
4. Ironmongers' Company delivered a proposal for a new site in Clerkenwell [Cripplegate] for £1,000.
5. Referred to Surveyors proposals from Edw. Tufnell and John Townsend for mason's work at Bloomsbury church.
6. Rejected memorial of Jas Anger, rector of St Mary Woolnoth, in relation to his parsonage house, endangered by taking down steeple.
7. Read memorial of Strong, Tufnell and Townsend, masons, for measurement of their respective works.

8. Referred to Surveyors proposal by Grove for roofing new church in the Strand according to model delivered by him this day.
9,10. Signed warrants for salaries to Midsummer last, and for impresting £30 to Secretary for paying bills and incidentals.

158. [p. 295] 25 July 1716
1. Hawksmoor reported that damage Clement's watercourse may have sustained is not very great; consideration deferred.
2. Dacres is not able to convey his site in St Giles in the Fields parish because a highway forms part of it; Commissioners consider agreement at an end.
3. Consideration of Ironmongers' Company's site in St Giles Cripplegate, offered for £900, was adjourned.
[4.] Skeat and Surveyors to view site proposed by Kemp for Bow.

159. [p. 297] 10 Aug. 1716
1,2. Agreed to give Ironmongers' Company £900 for their site in St Giles Cripplegate parish.
3,4. Surveyors report that Clements sustained some damage in his watercourse by building of Spitalfields church; £20 to be allowed to make good, on conditions.
3 [*sic*]. Mr Burgess, for Mr Bows, requested that his watercourse and lights should not be prejudiced by rebuilding of St Mary Woolnoth; agreed; new church not to be built beyond old foundation.
4. Read memorial of Goodchild to be allowed to lay foundation of St Mary Woolnoth.
5. Surveyors to ask masons for their proposals for St Mary Woolnoth.
6. Goodchild to advance work of the churches under his care to such level as Surveyors direct, so works may be measured.
7,8. Tufnell and Strong appointed masons for Bloomsbury new church as the most reasonable tenderers.
9. Notice to be given in *Gazette* for carpenters' proposals for the three new churches in Stepney.

160. [p. 299] 17 Aug. 1716
1. Secretary to send officers copies of all minutes relating to them.
2. Carpenters to obtain designs and scantlings of Stepney churches from Surveyors.
3. Accepted Thos Dunn's proposal for rubble work in foundation of St Mary Woolnoth, on Surveyors' recommendation.
5. Referred to another meeting Dr Bolter's renewed proposal for a site on Artillery Ground, in St Olave's Southwark; Secretary to consult minute book.
[6.] Blank application to Treasury to be prepared, for taking in money on the loan of coals.
[7.] Agreed to treat with Kemp for additional piece of ground at Bow.

161. [p. 301] 24 Aug. 1716
1. Skeat and James to inspect Artillery Ground, St Olave's Southwark, Secretary having found no reference in the minute book thereto.

2. Treasury requested to take in £10,000 upon coal tax.
3. Blank warrants to be prepared for paying workmen part of what is due to them.
4. Referred to James carpenters' proposals for the three Stepney churches from Grove and Leger.
5. Agreed to Kemp's demand of £140 for Bow site, reduced from £160.
6. Skeat to view Bermondsey site, Mr Middleton having suggested an addition to site proposed by Lord Salisbury.
7. Skeat [smith] to prepare copper finishing upon Deptford church steeple according to design now submitted.

162. [p. 303] 7 Sep. 1716
1. Skeat and James report Artillery Ground, St Olave's Southwark, convenient for new church.
2. As soon as Treasury give order for taking in the £10,000 applied for, Treasurer to ascertain Archbishop of Canterbury's pleasure when the Commissioners are to meet next.
3. Denning submitted proposal for carpenter's work in Stepney churches.
4. Grove to be employed to roof Limehouse church, subject to such deductions from his tender as Surveyors think reasonable because his timber is not die square.

163. [p. 304] 18 Sep. 1716, at the lobby of the House of Lords
1. Signed application to Treasury to imprest £10,000 to Treasurer.
2. Turner to be employed in painting and gilding vase and fane on stone spire of Deptford new church; James to make agreement.

164. [p. 305] 1 Oct. 1716, at the office in Old Palace Yard
1. Secretary submitted warrants for paying the workmen on account; being examined and approved by James, they were signed.
2. Secretary to ascertain Archbishop of Canterbury's pleasure about next meeting.

165. [p. 306] 30 Nov. 1716
1,2. Skeat reported on additional ground for Bermondsey site. Bishop of Winchester to treat with Lord Salisbury.
3. Notice to be given in Saturday's *Gazette* for glaziers' and painters' proposals for Deptford church, and plasterers' for Strand church.
4. Secretary to desire Vaughan to attend next meeting, that the Board may know on what terms he holds the cemetery near St George's chapel.
5. Read letter from Dean of Canterbury on behalf of Commings for doing glazier's work at Deptford.
6,7. Complaint being made against Jas Hands for delay in plasterer's work at Deptford church, ordered his co-contractor Jas Ellis to attend next meeting.
8. Treasurer to obtain certificate from Exchequer of how much lies there to the Commissioners' credit.
9,10. On request of inhabitants of St Mary Woolnoth parish to indemnify Mr Anger, their minister, whose house was damaged by demolition of the

church, agreed that damage shall be made good, provided parish secure the house to minister and his successors and remove part of it from the church.

11. Masons to bring proposals for paving Greenwich new church at next meeting.

166. [p. 309] 7 Dec. 1716

1. Read letter from Dean of Canterbury recommending Commings for glazier's and Turner for painter's work at Deptford new church.
2. Read proposals for glazier's work at Deptford new church from Chas Scriven, Thos Commings, Jos. Goodchild, Wm Ransom.
3. Read proposals for plasterer's work at Strand new church from Geo. Osmond, Hy Savage, Wm Knight, Rob. Evans.
4. Received instrument from inhabitants of St Mary Woolnoth parish securing house to incumbent.
5. Vaughan acknowledged he held cemetery near St George's chapel by permission of the Commissioners in consideration of damage he sustained in fencing cemetery.
6. Ellis promised to finish plastering Deptford new church with all possible speed.

7,8. Johnson applied for £100 due for purchase of several pieces of ground in Stepney; Edwards to inquire whether sufficient security given to indemnify Commissioners.

9. Surveyors, having perused plasterers' proposals, found Osmond's and Evans's the same and lowest.
10. Osmond to be employed to do plasterer's work in Strand new church; Solicitor to make contract.
11. Evans to be employed to do plasterer's work in Westminster new church; Solicitor to make contract.
12. Surveyors to report on glaziers' proposals at next meeting.

13,14. Treasurer delivering certificate that £2,475. 16*s*. 7*d*. in Exchequer due to Commissioners, application signed for that sum.

15. Secretary to prepare memorial to Treasury to take in £20,000 on coal duty.
16. Surveyors to report on masons' proposals for paving Greenwich church at next meeting.
17. Accepted Marples's proposal for cramping lead for the masons.

167. [p. 313] 10 Dec. 1716

1. Signed memorial to Teasury for £20,000 loan.

2,3. Strong and Tufnell to be employed to pave Greenwich church.

4,5. Commings to be employed for glazing Deptford new church with crown glass, with lead of 9 inches to the ounce.

6. Dr Marshall to enjoy cemetery ground now in possession of Geo. Vaughan, for £4 p.a., during the Commissioners' pleasure, on conditions.

168. [p. 315] 22 Dec. 1716

1. Secretary to take from James names of workmen to whom money due, and prepare warrants for next meeting.

2. Surveyors to prepare annual accounts for all work done under this Commission and the last, to end of December 1716, according to forms submitted this day by James.
3. Secretary to ascertain Archbishop of Canterbury's pleasure about time of next meeting.
4. Smith, late Treasurer, to pay over Johnson's £100 to Leacroft.

169. [p. 316] 4 Jan. 1716/17
1. Application made to Treasury to pay £20,000 to Treasurer.
2. Signed warrants for salaries.
3. James and Skeat to obtain Tillard's proposals for site in Norton Folgate; James to make plan.
5 [*sic*]. Surveyors empowered to settle rates of all works in the workmen's bills.
6. Mary Moor to be allowed £5 p.a. for cleaning the Commission's rooms.
7. Secretary to ascertain Archbishop of Canterbury's pleasure about date of next meeting.

170. [p. 318] 8 Mar. 1716/17
1. Tillard delivered proposal for a site in Norton Folgate, and James a plan; referred to next meeting.
2–4. Read petition from inhabitants that chapel in Hatton Garden be converted into a parish church; Surveyors to report.
5. Marshall's representation about state of St George's chapel [Ormond Street] referred to next meeting.

171. [p. 320] 21 Mar. 1716/17
1. Agreed to petition of minister and trustees for measuring, surveying and paving St George's chapel in order to make it a parish church; Surveyors to report at next meeting.
2,3. Concerning obtaining Johnson's money from Smith.
4. Signed warrant for impresting £10 to Secretary for incidentals.
5,6. Sir H. Masters and Gooch to view site in St Olave's Southwark for which Dr Bolton asks £600.
7. Agreed that Surveyors should rate run mouldings prepared by Townsend but not contracted for.
8. Dunn to have such allowance as is usual for carriage of stones for building Spitalfields church.
9,10. Surveyors reported on Hatton Garden chapel; to inquire whether nearby houses could be purchased.

172. [p. 322] 28 Mar. 1717
1. Masters and Gooch reported in favour of site in St Olave's Southwark.
2. Dr Bolton, in the trustees' name, promised that a small house adjoining the site should be removed.
3. Consideration of Hatton Garden chapel to be resumed at next meeting.
4. Notice to be given in *Gazette* for proposals for joiner's work at Deptford new church.

5. Surveyors to measure plasterer's work at Deptford.
6. Secretary to pay four guineas upon conditions to City authorities for liberty to erect hoard at St Mary Woolnoth church.
7. Skeat the smith to be allowed additional sum in proportion to the rate that iron shall be above £18 per ton, from Lady Day 1717.
8. Secretary to prepare blank warrants for paying workmen.
9. Ric. Evans to have one guinea for putting up hangings in Banqueting House for reception of the Commissioners.
10. Edwards reported on title of Sir Thos Davall to proposed site in St Botolph Aldgate; consideration deferred.

173. [p. 324] 4 Apr. 1717
1. Surveyors reported that £300 might be safely advanced on plasterer's work at Deptford church.
2. Surveyors to submit new method of keeping workmen's accounts by next meeting.
3. Notice to be given in next Saturday's *Gazette* for proposals for carpenter's work at Spitalfields new church.
4. Lady Davall to make a good title to her site, or Commissioners will not treat further.
5,6. Read, Mist's proposal for paving area before St George's Ormond Street. Commissioners will allow £180 for paving.
7. Repeated complaints being made against Ric. Goodchild of using bad bricks, resolved not to employ him unless he performs his contract and employs workmen approved by Surveyors.
8. Skeat to go ahead with iron work for windows of new church in the Strand, according to patterns submitted formerly.
9. Leacroft reported he had received of Smith £100, residue of £700 for purchase of Johnson's land.

174. [p. 327] 11 Apr. 1717
1. Agreed to imprest additional £100 to Ellis and Hands, plasterers at Deptford church when accounts have been adjusted between them.
2. Reported that a petition to parliament is preparing for the rebuilding of ten ruinous City churches as part of the fifty new churches; resolved that, this being against the intention of the acts, Bishop of Bristol and John Ellis, Esq., seek the Speaker's support, and Sir Harcourt Masters and Drs Bradford, Gooch and Waugh acquaint Lord Mayor with Board's views.
3. Pews to be erected in Deptford new church to be all single pews; Surveyors to report on joiners' proposals for pews, and carpenters' for Spitalfields new church.
4. Approved the method for keeping workmen's accounts this day proposed by Surveyors, being that used at Greenwich Hospital; accounts to be made out twice yearly, at Midsummer and Christmas.
5. £100 in Treasurer's hands to be paid to Johnson.

175. [p. 329] 16 Apr. 1717
1. Ellis reported that the Speaker had promised his favour respecting ten old churches petition.

2. Reported that Lord Mayor told Board's deputation that he would stop his proceedings, but hoped the Commissioners would assist him in the proper time and way.
3. Surveyors to obtain Archer's directions about a parsonage house for minister of Deptford new church.
4. Dr Bennet was granted permission to peruse plans and papers in Secretary's custody about parish of Cripplegate.
1 [*sic*]. John Gilham and John Smallwell to be employed as joiners at Deptford new church.
2. A plan for St Mary Woolnoth church to be submitted at next meeting, and notice given in *Gazette* for masons', bricklayers' and carpenters' proposals.

Notice to be given in *Gazette* for proposals for home made pew hinges, iron locks for pews and iron squares to stiffen the pews, for Greenwich new church.

Grove petitioned for money; £500 to be imprested.

Surveyors and Treasurer to prepare everything necessary for the Commissioners appointing payment of tradesmen at next meeting.

176. [p. 332] 2 May 1717
1. Secretary to prepare warrants.
2. Committee appointed to examine method for keeping workmen's accounts delivered in by Surveyors, and Solicitor to attend Monday next (Deans of Peterborough and Worcester, Drs Linford and Cannon, Sir John Phillips, Edward Peck, Esq., and any others who wish).
3. Surveyors submitted plan of St Mary Woolnoth church; estimate to be laid before next meeting.
4. Notice to be given in next *Gazette* for masons', bricklayers' and carpenters' proposals for Lombard Street church [St Mary Woolnoth] by Thursday next.
5. Zachary Gisborn to be employed to make hinges, etc., for pews at Greenwich church.
6. Joiners to submit proposals for pewing Strand new church; pews to be single.

177. [p. 334] 9 May 1717
1. Agree with committee that workmen's accounts 'as stated in the books delivered in by the Surveyors' be approved.
2. Warrants signed for paying workmen.
3. Gisborn, ironmonger, to attend next meeting.
4,5. Objections being made to the number of pillars in Hawksmoor's model for St Mary Woolnoth church, James to inform Hawksmoor; Surveyors to submit another plan 'as they two shall think fit'.
6–8. Title to Ironmongers' Company's site [Cripplegate] approved by Webb; Surveyors to prepare plan of site and a design for church.

178. [p. 336] 16 May 1717
1. Warrant signed for paying Grove £500.
2. Hy Smith's petition for half-year's salary and two and a quarter year's house rent referred to next meeting.

3. Surveyors to consider further the number of pillars in Lombard Street church and report to next meeting.
4,5. Dunn and John Townsend delivered proposals for mason's work at St Mary Woolnoth; Dunn to be employed as more reasonable.
6. Hester to be employed as bricklayer at aforesaid church; Solicitor to make contract.
7. Simmons to be employed for joiner's work in Strand church.
8. Gibbs' plan for pewing Strand church approved, except that aisle be ten feet wide.
9. Secretary to inquire how much money remitted to Talman for the Queen's statue, and report to next meeting.
10. Notice to be given in next Saturday's *Gazette* for glaziers' and plasterers' proposals for Strand church.
11. Surveyors reporting that item of carriage in mason's bill for Spitalfields church of £53. 15*s*. 6*d*. had been omitted, warrant of 9 May cancelled and a new one signed.

179. [p. 339] 23 May 1717
1. Surveyors submitted new design setting out disposition and number of pillars in Lombard Street church, which was allowed.
2,3. Hy Smith to be paid £136. 17*s*. for salary from Midsummer to 9 December 1715; committee to examine his claims.
4. Petition from Wapping referred to next meeting.
5. Letters from Directors of Greenwich Hospital referred to next meeting.

180. [p. 341] 31 May 1717
1. Talman attending reported he had spent £340 at Florence towards making the Queen's statue.
2,3. Talman to be desired to attend next Thursday and give particular account of his expenditure, Smith to attend to give account of the £460 he received to transmit to Florence.
4–6. Read petition for church to be speedily built on Johnson's site, Wapping; Surveyors to prepare plan and estimate; resolved to build there with all possible speed.
7. Surveyors to submit plan of boundaries of new parish intended at Bow.
8. Waugh, Waddington, Sir Harcourt Masters and Peck to view site proposed by Mr Tillard with Surveyors and report to next meeting.
9. Chas Scriven to be employed as glazier at Strand church.
10. Surveyors to report on plasterers' proposals for Strand church and carpenters' for Spitalfields.
11. Committee to consider Smith's affair to meet on Monday next.

181. [p. 343] 8 June 1717
1. Smith allowed £100 for use of his house for meetings of the late Commissioners, £10 for coals for two winters and his bill of fees, £89. 17*s*.
2. Leacroft to discuss with Auditors of Imprest their annual fee of £40 for passing Commission's accounts.

3,4. Marshall and trustees of St George's chapel [Ormond Street] representing its state, Surveyors to report what sum sufficient for its repair.
5. Secretary to make out warrant paying Hawksmoor £275. 5*s*. 9*d*. for models made by several artificers.
6. Notice to be given in next Saturday's *Gazette* for plumbers' proposals for Upper Wapping new church.
7. Consideration of Talman's particular account of his expenditure on the Queen's statue referred to another meeting.
8. Smith to submit all letters sent him from Talman about the statue.

182. [p. 345] 20 June 1717
1. Leacroft reported that Auditors of Imprest insisted on payment of fee. Leacroft to see the Auditor himself and report to next meeting.
2. Marshall petitioned for repair of roof of St George's chapel [Ormond Street], now very ruinous. Surveyors to view and report to next meeting.
3. Surveyors to survey Bow and Old Ford, set out boundaries, and consider condition of Bow chapel.
4. Secretary to select any proper person as his clerk.

183. [p. 347] 11 July 1717
1. Leacroft reported that Mr Auditor Foley insisted on his fee.
2,3. Surveyors reported that £500 would repair St George's chapel fit for worship. Surveyor to search proceedings of late and present Commissions to discover true state of what has been done. Solicitor to report on past proceedings about chapel, and ascertain what Marshall and trustees desire of the Commissioners.
72. Sir Fisher Tench attended about Hatton Garden; Lord Hatton will treat about some houses.
5. Surveyors submitted a map of Bow hamlet; Solicitor and Surveyors to make the hamlet parochial by ascertaining its boundaries.
6,7. Geo. Osmond to be employed for plumber's work for Wapping new church, his good, substantial work under the Commission being approved of, and his prices the same as Rob. Evans.
Surveyors to determine what every work done since last Christmas severally mounts to, for paying sums on account.
7 [*sic*]. Commissioners ready to comply with request of Directors of Greenwich Hospital as soon as Attorney-General states that this Board 'is empowered to meddle with the moneys appropriated towards the finishing of Greenwich Hospital'.
8. Surveyors and Agent to report on Shadwell site.

184. [p. 350] 18 July 1717
1–3. Secretary reported what had been done to make St George's chapel [Ormond Street] parochial; necessary repairs to be made; Surveyors to view the area before the chapel.
4. Consideration of Hatton Garden to be continued at next meeting.
5. Secretary to prepare memorial to Treasury for taking in £11,000 on coal dues.

6,7. Surveyors submitted model and design for Lower Wapping new church; church to be built accordingly.
8,9. Read petition of Rob. Burgess for satisfaction for damage to house sustained by demolition of St Mary Woolnoth; Surveyors to view.

185. [p. 352] 25 July 1717
1. Signed application to Treasury to take in £11,000 loan.
2. A debate arising upon the fifth article of the Ironmongers' Company's proposals [for Cripplegate site], resolved that no houses should be nearer than 25 ft to churchyard wall, and no buildings nearer than ten feet.
3. Greenwich church altar 'neech' to be painted in plain panels.
4. Warrants for Auditors' fees.
5. Hatton Garden question referred to next meeting.

186. [p. 353a] 5 Aug. 1717
1. Signed application to Treasury for loan.
2. Warrants signed.
3. Ric. Goodchild to pay Treasurer £250 for old materials of St Mary Woolnoth.
4. Auditors of Imprest certify that £11. 10*s*. intended as commission for Sir Edw. Gould's transmitting money to Talman.
5. Sir Fisher Tench delivered more papers about Hatton Garden.
6. Secretary to make out general warrant for workmen.
7. Agreed Ironmongers' Company might built houses on east or west sides of site [Old Street, Cripplegate] either facing or away from it.

187. [p. 356] 15 Aug. 1717
Warrant signed for paying £10,750 to the workmen.
1 [*sic*]. Ironmongers' Company agree about site; Solicitor to proceed.
2. Surveyors to submit plan or design for church for that site.
3. Solicitor to prepare instrument for ascertaining bounds of hamlet of Bow.
4,5. Solicitor to ascertain rent of houses to be sold near Hatton Garden chapel; Surveyors to estimate their value if a new church built there.
6. Surveyors to view site formerly proposed at north end of Hatton Garden.
7. Deptford parsonage house to be put in hand according to Archer's design.

188. [p. 358] 12 Sep. 1717
1. James to bring design of a church for the Ironmongers' Company's site in St Giles Cripplegate parish by next meeting; masonry between the compartments of windows to be range work of rag stone; Surveyors to call on masons employed in the churches to give estimates for rag stone.
2. Hatton Garden to be considered at next meeting (minutes 4 and 5 of 15 August).
3. The workmen having been guilty of great disorders at Strand church upon finishing of tower, master mason and other master workmen to attend at next meeting.

There being no plan left in the office for the intended parsonage house at Deptford, Surveyors to stop the work till a particular plan and estimate be submitted.

4. Memorandum. Minute 7 of 15 August stating that there was a plan for Deptford parsonage house delivered by Archer was a mistake, only a general plan of the church being produced and Archer not present.

189. [p. 360] 10 Oct. 1717

1. James submitted design of church for Ironmongers' Company's site, St Giles Cripplegate.
2. The said plan approved; James to bring two estimates to next meeting: one built with ashlar, the other with rag stone.
3. James and Edwards reported enquiry about value of Hatton Garden houses; proprietors of the seven houses to be informed that Commissioners willing to treat with them.
4. Townsend attending was asked to explain disorders at the finishing of tower of Strand church, and charged to try to prevent such disorders in future.

190. [p. 362] 17 Oct. 1717

1. Johnson, of whom site in Lower Wapping was purchased, reported death of Mrs Caley alias Bodelow in Jamaica; to bring a certificate from minister and churchwardens of Kingston in Jamaica attested by a public notary, in order to obtain his securities.
2. James submitted two estimates for church in St Giles Cripplegate for ashlar and rag stone. South front to be built in Portland stone in the Ionic order, according to design now given in; north front and east and west ends of rag stone; coins, windows and entablatures to be of Portland.
3. Nothing having been done in relation to minute of 11 July last about Hastings's ground, Shadwell, the Surveyors and Agent to inspect ground, and Edwards to examine the agreement.
4. Whitton asked £850 for six houses and a coach house in Hatton Garden, but no one appeared for Alridge, proprietor of the seventh house.
5. Notice to be given in *Gazette* for plumbers' proposals for Limehouse church this day fortnight.
6. Groves to make a shed at Spitalfields church for the engines, the place where they now are being spoilt by the new works.

191. [p. 365] 31 Oct. 1717

1. James submitted a plan for ascertaining bounds of Bow.
2. Edwards reported conveyance with plan of Hastings's site, Shadwell. Site to be separated from adjoining ground by line of stakes; Skeat to enquire for a tenant.
3. Edwards to make best agreement he can with Alridge's executor for house on south side of Hatton Garden chapel.
4. Fresh notice to be given in next *Gazette* for plumbers' proposals for covering Limehouse church, Evans' and Osmond's proposals being advanced in each article.

192. [p. 367] 14 Nov. 1717
1. Skeat reported that Hastings's site was separated from adjoining ground by a line of stakes. Edwards to submit conveyance at next meeting; Secretary to write out all Minutes relating to it; and open side to be walled in brick work.
2. Evans' and Osmond's proposals for plumber's work at Limehouse church being considered, resolved that Osmond be employed.
3. Read petition of minister and inhabitants of East Greenwich; Surveyors to make estimate for repairing tower, enclosing burial ground and paving about church.
4. Signed application to Treasury for impresting £1,122. 12*s*. 11*d*.

193. [p. 369] 28 Nov. 1717
1. Edwards submitted conveyance of Hastings's site; does not appear that Mrs Hastings has any right to fruit trees, etc.
2. Edwards to prepare an article to oblige Alridge and Whitton to convey their Hatton Garden interests for £850 and £440 respectively [*sic*], on passing of an act of parliament for appropriating site of Hatton Garden chapel for a new church.
3. Hy Hester and Fra. Withers delivered their proposal for making good bricks.
4. Notice to be given in Saturday's *Gazette* for bricklayers' proposals for new church in Old Street, 'with the best hard burnt bricks, free from sammel or under burnt bricks'.
5,6. Bow and Old Ford: parish marks for fixing the boundaries to be erected in proper places.
7. Edwards to inform Bishop of Ely that Commissioners have resolved to build a new church in room of Hatton Garden chapel; a draught of a bill for appropriating the site for a new church, the bishop consenting, to be prepared by Solicitor.

[One folio, numbered 371–2, has been cut out of the book]

194. [p. 373] 9 Jan. 1717/18
1. Edwards reported that Bishop of Ely approved draught of Hatton Garden bill.
2. Bishop of Norwich had given Duke of Montagu a copy of the bill: he had said he would consider it.
3. Pursuant to a resolution of the last meeting, the Commissioners elected their officers for year ensuing: Secretary: Jenkin Thomas Philipps.
4. Taking into consideration the behaviour of Philipps to the Board at last meeting, resolved that he should acknowledge his fault before the Commissioners then present, and ask pardon of Dr Cannon next time he appears. Philipps asked pardon of the Board accordingly. He was then admonished to take care that his entries in the book be made in the very words signed in the minutes.
5. Re-elected Hawksmoor and James as Surveyors; Edwards as Solicitor; Skeat as Agent; and Waters as Messenger for the year ensuing.

6. The Board will elect their officers at the first meeting in January every year; notice to be given in the summons.
Board will consider salaries at next meeting.
7. Solicitor to report at next meeting names of Treasurer's securities, and whether they be yet living.

195. [p. 375] 23 Jan. 1717/18
1. Same salaries as formerly to be continued. In future, salaries to be taken into consideration before election of officers.
2. Read proposal for making good hard bricks from Mr Scot, brickmaker.
3. Notice to be given in *Gazette* for receiving bricklayers' and brickmakers' proposals for Old Street church this day fortnight.
4. Surveyors to consider what use an Under-Surveyor may be in inspecting the works, and to report on best means of providing the best bricks.
5. Secretary to prepare warrants for salaries to last Christmas.
6. Provision for ministers of the new churches to be considered at next meeting.
7. The great expense in building the new churches to be considered at next meeting.
8. Joiners to be limited to a certain time for finishing their work, under penalty.
9. Secretary to look out papers on proposal for a site in St James's parish, Westminster.
10. Warrant for paying £140 to Abraham Kemp for site for a minister's house at Bow.
11. If act passed for vesting in the Commissioners ground in Hatton Garden belonging to See of Ely, Commissioners will pay Sam. Whitton £850 for his 6 houses, entry in Gt. and Little Kirby Street, and Thos Abridge [Alridge] £440 for his house adjoining the chapel if a good title made out.

196. [p. 378] 6 Feb. 1717/18
1. Warrants signed for paying salaries, and £140 for site of minister's house at Bow.
2. Leave having been given to bring a bill into the House of Commons to enable the parish church of St Giles in the Fields to be rebuilt instead of one of the fifty new churches, and the Commissioners being unanimously of opinion that this is against the intention of the acts for building fifty new churches, desire Bishop of Bristol and John Ellis, Esq., to seek Speaker's support. Secretary to desire assistance of all Commissioners who are MPs.
3. Notice to be given in *Gazette* for painters' proposals for ironwork in Millbank and Strand churches.
4. Brickmakers' and bricklayers' proposals opened and referred to Surveyors for report.
5. Hawksmoor to inform Archer of Board's opinion that the towers of the church near Millbank be carried no higher till further consideration.

197. [p. 380] 13 Feb. 1717/18
1. Bishop of Bristol and Mr Ellis reported that Speaker promised to do what service he can, advising that a petition should be presented to the House; a petition drawn up accordingly, read and signed.
2. Painters' proposals for Millbank and Strand churches referred to next meeting.
3,4. Surveyors reported on brickmakers' proposals; referred to next meeting. Wilson, as most reasonable of the bricklayers' proposals, appointed for Old Street church.
5. Secretary to make out warrant for half-year's rent to Christmas last.
6. Hawksmoor to view Mr Lowndes's site in St James Westminster parish.

198. [p. 382] 20 Feb. 1717/18
1. Read petition of Thos Carter, Esq., trustee for children of John Walker, Esq., deceased; £200 and interest to be paid.
2. Signed warrant, £37. 10*s*. for half-year's rent.
3. Pursuant to order of 9 December 1713, Surveyors shall in future make a monthly detailed report on all works in progress at first meeting in each month; Secretary to read the order at every such meeting.
4. Reynolds to paint iron work and Breedy the wood work of Millbank church.
5. John and Thos Waxham to make good, hard, well-burnt bricks for Old Street church.

199. [p. 384] 27 Feb. 1717/18
1. Notice to be given in *Gazette* for proposals for digging foundations of Old Street church by this day fortnight.
2. Reynolds the painter agreed to paint the iron work at Millbank church thus: first with red lead and white lead; second, a light second prime; third, a light lead colour; fourth, a dark lead colour.
3. Warrant ordered for paying Wm Lee £30 according to minute of 1 July 1714.
4. Committee reported in favour of allowing Secretary's bill for incidentals.
5. James's report on an Assistant Surveyor deferred to next meeting.

200. [p. 386] 6 Mar. 1717/18
1. Signed warrant for paying £30 to Wm Lee.
2. James's particular report on the progress of works referred to next meeting.
3. Warrant ordered for paying £600 for a site to Governors of Free School of St Olave Southwark, in pursuance of Chancery order.
4. Warrant for paying £900 to Ironmongers' Company for site [Old Street].
5. Secretary to copy out minutes and get ready other papers relating to Poplar chapel for consideration at next meeting.
6. Referred to Surveyors petition of Thos Hollins, apothecary, Drury Lane.

201. [p. 388] 13 Mar. 1717/18
1. Warrants signed for paying £900 to Ironmongers' Company, £600 to governors of Free School, St Olave, Southwark.
2. James reported that Hollins's house had suffered inconvenience by the turning of a watercourse belonging to Strand new church.
3. Mist's the most reasonable proposals for diggers at Old Street church.
4. Edwards to inform himself of fit persons for officers and vestrymen of new parish of Stratford Bow; Sir H. Masters and Peck to assist him in forming a list to lay before the Board.
5. Secretary to ascertain from Archer how the pavings within and without Deptford church are to be finished.
6. Osmond to attend next meeting.
7. James to consider whether Poplar chapel is fit to be a parochial church; Edwards and Dr Landon to attend East India Company committee about it.

202. [p. 390] 20 Mar. 1717/18
1. Hollins told that inconvenience to his house would be removed as soon as possible; any damage would be taken into consideration.
2. Form of contract with workmen for Old Street church to be considered at next meeting.
3. Sir H. Masters promised a list of fit officers for Stratford Bow at the next meeting.
4. Secretary reported that Archer promised to prepare several designs for paving at Deptford church.
5. Osmond attending, and complaints being made that parts of his lead in covering of Limehouse church were faulty, he offered that what was faulty should be changed for good, and that he would give security on the Board's terms to mend all defects for 20 years.
6. James reported that Poplar chapel required repairs to roof, stone windows, paving, pewing and galleries, 'besides that it has no tower at the West End which perhaps will be thought necessary if it be made parochial'.
7. Surveyors to submit plan and estimate for church on Free School site, Southwark, at next meeting.
8. John Skeat and partner to make iron fence, 3 ft 6 in high, for Strand church, at 3½*d*. a lb, besides the extraordinary allowance of iron above £18 per ton.
9,10. Approved answer (being approved by Mr Talbot, counsel) to bill in Chancery of Betty Clark Walker and her sisters; Solicitor to put in the said answer.

MINUTES OF THE COMMISSIONERS, 1718–27

Lambeth MS 2691

203. [p. 1] 3 Apr. 1718
1. Secretary to attend Archer about paving at Deptford (minute 5, 13 March 1718).
2. Dr Landon petitioned about converting chapel at Poplar into a parish church. Consideration deferred.
3. Surveyors to submit plan and estimate for church to be built in St Olave Southwark.
4. Surveyors to attend Sir H. Masters and Peck in viewing site purchased of Hastings in St Paul Shadwell, that purchased of Johnson in Lower Wapping, and the new church in Wapping, and report to next meeting what should be done.
5. Read Act for finishing the tower of St Michael Cornhill. Resolved to finish it in the most expeditious manner. Advertisement ordered for workmen to submit proposals.
6. James delivered monthly progress report; consideration referred to next meeting.
7,8. Agreed, subject to consent of Bishop of London, to list submitted at last meeting by the Solicitor, assisted by Sir H. Masters and Peck, of officers and vestrymen for the new parish of Stratford Bow, viz., church-wardens: Abraham Wilmer, William Fletcher; surveyors of highways: William Van Luth, Richard Remnant; overseers of the poor: William Blackmor, William Ellis; vestry: Rev. Dr Henry Lamb and the minister for the time being, Robt Hardesty, John Round, Metford, Ambrose Page, Thos Wilson, Esquires; Abraham Wilmer, gent. Messrs Daniel Selman, Jonathan Sandford (grocer), Hy Tilbury (baker), Nich. Greenslate, Thos Kynneston (silk dyer), and the church wardens for the time being.
9. Workmen who have not yet sealed their contracts to do so within a fortnight; and none hereafter to begin any work until he shall have sealed his contract.

204. [p. 5] 17 Apr. 1718
1. Minute 4, 3 Apr. 1718, relating to Johnson's site in Lower Wapping etc. be adjourned to next meeting.
2. Resolved that no model of any parsonage house be received where estimate exceeds £1,000. The estimate of the proposed house at Deptford greatly exceeding that sum, Archer be desired to make another. If he do not submit such a model in a fortnight, Hawksmoor and James to prepare one.

3. Advertisement ordered for joiners, painters and plasterers to submit proposals for Limehouse and Wapping churches by the next meeting.
4. Bricklayers and plumbers at St George's chapel to put roof and gutters in good repair.
5. Solicitor to prepare contract with Grove for carpenter's work, Spitalfields, according to his proposal.
6. Strong delivered proposal for mason's work, St Michael Cornhill; referred to Surveyors to report to next meeting.
7. Bishop of London's letter to be considered at next meeting.
8. Minister of Stratford Bow to have pew assigned for him and his family.
9. Secretary to prepare memorial to Treasury for Exchequer to take in £25,000 on the credit of the loan upon coals.
10. Skeat to inquire into value of land belonging to Michell, Wood and Le Keux, in order to buy it to add to Spitalfields cemetery.
11. Leacroft memorialised Commissioners to certify his having paid John Graysbrook, decd, £21. 1*s.* 7*d.*; supported by three affidavits. Resolved to sign same at next meeting.

205. [p. 8] 24 Apr. 1718
1. Read, letter from Archer about Deptford parsonage house. Surveyors to prepare another draught and estimate for next meeting.
2. Referred to Surveyors to report to next meeting, proposals from joiners, painters and plasterers.
3. Solicitor to prepare contract for mason's work at tower of St Michael Cornhill according to Strong's proposal.
4. Secretary submitted memorial to Treasury (minute 9, 17 Apr. 1718); signed by Commissioners.
5. Skeat reported that proprietors of ground proposed to be added to Spitalfields cemetery desired a fortnight to make their answer.
6. Signed, a certificate delivered by Leacroft (minute 11, 17 Apr. 1718).
7. Dr Bolter and others from St Olave Southwark were admitted to see plan of new church, and desired that foundation might be laid with all possible speed.
8. The work to be put in hand according to the plan brought in by the Surveyors; advertisement ordered for diggers, bricklayers and masons to submit proposals by next meeting.
9. Rector and parishioners of St Michael Cornhill admitted to see design for tower; they were satisfied with it. Work to be put in hand with all possible expedition.
10. Blank warrant to be prepared by next meeting for impresting money to Secretary for incidental expenses.
11. Surveyors' report on Greenwich church to be considered at next meeting.
12. Petition from Mr Kemp relating to list of vestrymen for Stratford Bow to be considered at next meeting, and Masters and Peck to have copies.

206. [p. 11] 1 May 1718
1. Surveyors submitted draught for Deptford parsonage house (minute

1, 24 Apr. 1718); consideration deferred; the plan to lie on the table for Commissioners' perusal.
2. Solicitor to dispatch form of contract with Strong for mason's work at St Michael Cornhill as soon as possible.
3. Treasurer reported progress relating to memorial to Treasury; able to give fuller account at next meeting.
4. Referred to Surveyors to report at next meeting, proposals from diggers, bricklayers and masons for new church in St Olave's Southwark.
5. Signed, warrant for impresting £50 to Secretary (minute 10, 24 Apr. 1718).
6. Read petition against some persons appointed to vestry of Stratford Bow. The minister and other inhabitants satisfied Commissioners that alleged facts were untrue, and Mr Van Luth, one of the signatories, being unable to substantiate the allegations, the list of vestrymen already appointed, consented to by Bishop of London, was confirmed. Masters and Peck thanked.
7. Site purchased for minister's house for Stratford Bow to be walled in, and Surveyors to prepare plan and estimate for house.
[8.] Surveyors reported on Greenwich church. Surveyors to wall in new burying ground at not more than £200; and to build wall at west end of church with piers and gates to separate old burying ground from the access and entry to the church, at not more than £200; and to pave the two sides of the church at not more than £170. Consideration of repairing the old steeple deferred. Before Surveyors proceed with works, inhabitants to give security that pavement shall never be broken up or removed for burying the dead or any other use. Minister and principal inhabitants were called in and agreed. Solicitor to draw up form of security.

Surveyors reported on Johnson's ground, Wapping; consideration deferred.
9. Wingfield and Mahew to be employed for joiner's work at Limehouse, and Solicitor to prepare contract.
10. Gilham to be employed for joiner's work at Wapping, and Solicitor to prepare contract.
11. Wilkins and Hands to be employed for plasterer's work at Limehouse and Wapping, and Solicitor to prepare contract.
12. Leacroft to pay £244. 11*s*. 1*d*., according to Chancery decree for principal and interest for purchase of part of site on new church in the Strand from Walker, decd. Warrant to be prepared for next meeting.
13. Treasurer to receive rent of £4 p.a. from Marshall for piece of ground adjoining St George's chapel.

207. [p. 16] 8 May 1718
1. Solicitor reported that Strong's contract for mason's work at St Michael Cornhill will be executed by next meeting.
2. Treasurer reported that upon application to Treasury for taking in £25,000, they declined to proceed further. Letter to be written to Mr Lowndes, Secretary to the Treasury, to urge the matter.
3. Painters' proposals deferred.
4. Nathaniel Miller to be employed as bricklayer on new church in St

Olave Southwark, Commissioners finding their own bricks. Solicitor to prepare contract.
5. John Mist to be employed there as digger; Solicitor to prepare contract.
6. Edward Tufnell to be employed there as mason; Solicitor to prepare contract.
7. Solicitor to draw instrument containing agreed list of vestrymen and parish officers for Stratford Bow, inserting Abraham Kemp *vice* Thos Wilson, decd.
8. Lucas to be employed to build wall to enclose ground purchased of Kemp for site for parsonage house.
8 [*sic*]. Upon letter from Archer and report from Dean of Canterbury that the triangular figure of a parsonage house for Deptford first projected will be convenient according to foundations already laid,
9. Ordered Surveyors to proceed in erecting the house at an expense not exceeding £1,000, according to the letter and promise of Archer that it shall be finished for that or a less sum.
10. John Smallwell, joiner at Greenwich, reproved for dilatoriness and ordered to finish before 1 August next.
11. Dean of Canterbury moved that want of pewing in Deptford church was inconvenient. Agreed to proceed therein, and that a time limit of one year be inserted in the joiner's contract.
12. Cemetery for Deptford new church to be walled in.

208. [p. 19] 16 May 1718
1. Treasurer reported he had delivered Commissioners' letter to Lowndes, who had not yet had the opportunity to deliver it to the Lords of the Treasury.
2. John Reynolds to be employed as painter at Wapping; Solicitor to prepare contract.
3. Samuel Showell to be employed as painter at Limehouse; Solicitor to prepare contract.
4. Solicitor reported that contract with Strong for St Michael Cornhill was executed.
5. Dean of the Arches and Peck, accompanied by Surveyors, to view ground proposed by Stephen Bateman, Blunt and others in Bermondsey.
6. Advertisement ordered for smiths' proposals for iron work in the new churches; Surveyors to specify the several works.
7. Surveyors to view iron work prepared for the corner of the Strand church by Skeat, and to direct him to proceed no further until further orders.
8. Agreed, that in advertisements for work to be done for the Commission, a fortnight's notice be given, and that the notice be twice repeated and that no proposals be received after the day limited. All proposals to be sealed, and no one to be allowed to lower price after delivery.

209. [p. 21] 26 May 1718
1. Treasurer reported that upon application to Mr Clayton at the

Treasury he was told no money could be advanced till a loan now depending for £250,000 be completed.
2. Dean of the Arches and Peck reported that site proposed by Bateman, etc. in Bermondsey was the most proper yet offered.
3. Skeat to inquire for proprietors' lowest terms, and whether any more convenient sites may be had.
4. Surveyors to estimate value of materials of buildings on site for church in Shadwell, and sell them to best advantage; receipts to be paid to the Secretary.
5. Surveyors to view site bought of Hastings [Shadwell] and report whether reasonable to comply with Mrs Campbell's request about opening a door.
6. Surveyors to report on smiths' proposals at next meeting.

210. [p. 23] 5 June 1718
1. Treasurer to renew application to Lowndes to use his good offices with the Lords of the Treasury by representing Commissioners' pressing necessity for money to pay workmen for what was due to them before Christmas last.
2. Skeat reported he could not find a more convenient site in Bermondsey at a reasonable rate; Bateman insists on his former demand of £200, but Taleton willing to take £180, Blunt £125, Carter £50 and Grantham £90.
3. Skeat to perfect agreement on these terms if he cannot obtain better.
4. James reported that the highest bidder offered £8 for the old materials of buildings on the Shadwell site; he recommended that the bricks should be used to wall in the ground, and the rest disposed of to best advantage. The Board agreed.
5. Commissioners refuse Mrs Campbell's request for opening a door from her garden to their ground.
6. Messenger to attend Dr Lamb and the officers of the parish of Stratford Bow with the instruments of their appointments.
7. Messenger to attend Bishop of London to obtain his signature to appointment of the vestry of Bow.
8. Skeat to finish iron fencing around Strand church, Robins to be employed for the iron work at St Mary Woolnoth, and Cleaves that at Bloomsbury church.
9. James to report on proposals from the two Mr Blinckoes for plasterer's work.
10. Goodchild not to proceed with Spitalfields church until he provide such bricks as James approves of.

211. [p. 26] 2 Oct. 1718
1. Treasurer reported that on application to the Lords of the Treasury he had obtained their warrant for the taking in of £25,000.
2. James reported that the bricks of the old house adjoining the churchyard of Wapping were used in repairing the churchyard wall, and the other materials sold at price agreed by Hawksmoor.
3. Skeat to report on purchase of ground in Bermondsey.

4. Waters (Messenger) reported he had complied with orders of 5 June (minute 7).
5. Upon reading the petition of minister and inhabitants of Greenwich in vestry, 22 Sept. 1718, about obstruction given to erecting a seat for the service of His Majesty, it is unanimous opinion of the Board not to proceed any farther with the church until obstruction be removed.
6. Inhabitants of St Mary le Strand were called in to petition for removing wooden fencing about the church.
Signed, a memorial to Treasury for £25,000, and warrants for half year's salary due to the officers at Midsummer and for office rent.

212. [p. 28] 23 Oct. 1718
1. James to report at next meeting on smiths' proposals for the tower of St Michael Cornhill.
2. Smallwell and Gilham to be summoned by the messenger to attend the next meeting.
3. Skeat reported that he had agreed with the several proprietors for their interests in the site proposed for a new church in Bermondsey. Skeat to deliver the papers to Solicitor, and title deeds to be referred to counsel.
4. Warrant to be prepared for next meeting for paying workmen according to James's estimate.

213. [p. 30] 30 Oct. 1718
1. Cleave to be employed as smith for St Michael Cornhill; Solicitor to prepare contract.
2. Smallwell having neglected to sign his contract for joiner's work at Deptford for more than six months, and not appearing this day to explain why, Gilham alone to be employed to perform all the joiner's work there, to be completed by Michaelmas, 1719.
3. Signed, two warrants to pay workmen according to James's estimates.
4. Surveyors to report on memorial from Grove.
5. Books of accounts to pay the workmen to 31 Dec. 1717 to be examined at next meeting.
6. Abstract to be drawn of the several demands of the workmen, and the several abatements made on them, to be kept by Secretary and entered on the books.

214. [p. 32] 6 Nov. 1718
1. Examined and signed books of accounts.
2. Master and wardens of Ironmongers' Company petitioned for further time to clear ground bought from them.
3. To be allowed till 1 March next.

215. [p. 33] 13 Nov. 1718
Adjourned to 20 Nov.

216. [p. 34] 27 Nov. 1718
1. Proposals for glazier's work at the churches now building received from: Joseph Goodchild, Chas Scriven, R. Ransom, Thos Commings, and John Tracy.

2. Goodchild, being the lowest, to be employed at Limehouse and Wapping; to use best London crown glass wrought in strong lead $8\frac{1}{2}$ ins running to the oz, according to the proposal and pattern delivered, to complete within two months of the plastering being finished; Solicitor to draw contract.
3. £20 directed to be paid to Philip Clement (minutes 3, 4, 10 Aug. 1716) to be paid to executrix, and warrant to be prepared.
4. Adjourned consideration of glazier's work for Westminster and plasterer's for Limehouse, Wapping, and Westminster.
5. Signed application to Treasury for £20,000.

217. [p. 36] 4 Dec. 1718
1. Scriven to be employed for glazier's work for Westminster; solicitor to prepare contract.
2. Read order of committee of House of Commons to inquire into expenditure on new churches and sites.
3. Treasurer, Secretary, Surveyors, Solicitor and Agent to submit to a committee of this Board such particulars as may enable Board to respond.
4. Advertisement ordered for smiths' proposals for locks and hinges for Strand and Deptford churches to be made by Thursday week.
5. Isaac Mansfield to be employed as plasterer at Westminster; Solicitor to prepare contract.
6. Archer to submit estimate for finishing churches at Westminster and Deptford before committee on Monday next; Secretary to write to him.
7. Commissioners now present or any three of them to meet as committee on Monday next to receive officers' report.

218. [p. 38] 10 Dec. 1718
1. Approved Officers' report of churches in building. Surveyors to attend House of Commons committee therewith, and with Commissioners' answer to their precept.
2. Warrant for £5,000 payable to workmen to be prepared for next meeting.

219. [p. 39] 15 Dec. 1718
1. Commissioners drew up and signed answer to precept of House of Commons committee dated 11th inst.

220. [p. 40] 18 Dec. 1718
1. Commissioners drew up and signed answer to precept of House of Commons committee dated 16th inst.

221. [p. 41] 29 Jan. 1718/19
1. On petition from St Mary le Strand, Secretary to write to Simmons the joiner to hasten finishing of the pewing.
2. Advertisement ordered for proposals from brick makers for bricks for new church in St Olave's Southwark, to be delivered this day fortnight.

3. John Meard, carpenter, to be employed at Bloomsbury and St Mary Woolnoth as lowest bidder; Solicitor to draw up contract.
4. Smith's final bill of fees laid: £50. 12*s*. 9*d*. Allowed except last article of £4. 2*s*. 7*d*.
5. Arthur Nash, smith, to be employed to make hinges, locks and keys, Is and Ls for the pews at Deptford and Strand churches; Solicitor to draw contract.
6. Signed warrant for paying £20 to Mrs Clement.
7. George Devall to be employed on plumber's work at Spitalfields church; Solicitor to draw contract.

222. [p. 44] 19 Feb. 1718/19
1. Warrant for £46. 10*s*. 2*d*. payable to Henry Smith to be prepared.
2. Advertisement ordered for brick makers to bring proposals for supplying bricks for the new church in St Olave's Southwark on Thursday next.
3. Hawksmoor to report on condition of steeple of St Mary Woolnoth, what inconvenience Mr Dodson may have suffered, and how it may be remedied.
4. Petition of James Wilson about one of the houses to be demolished on Ironmongers' Company's site to be complied with.
5. Chicheley and Wade, carvers, who offered their services for Deptford church to attend on Thurs. next with James, bringing their proposals.
6. Sir John Philipps and William Farrer to be desired to move House of Commons to insert in bill brought in last Thurs. clause to enable Commissioners to build churches of rubble, brick, or brick coined with stone where they shall think proper.
7. Solicitor to draw up such a clause.

[Ten numbers have been omitted in the pagination, which runs from 45 (recto) to 56 (verso)]

223. [p. 57] 26 Feb. 1718/19
1. Smith's warrant signed.
2. Warrants ordered for paying salaries for half year to Christmas last and for house rent.
3. Read petition of John Webster, carver, for employment in Strand or any other church; to bring in his proposals for next meeting.
4. No more new churches to be begun until we find ourselves in condition to discharge contracts for churches already begun.
5. Open committee appointed to meet next Monday to consider how maintenance may be provided out of the duties granted by Act of first of George I for ministers of the new churches.

224. [p. 58] 5 Mar. 1718/19
1. Bishop of Bristol reported that the committee had approved, with amendments, Dean of Canterbury's proposals for providing a maintenance for the ministers and their assistants.
2. Approved the report after some additions and further amendments;

to be prepared with duplicates for both Houses of Parliament, to be signed at next meeting.
3. Signed two warrants for salaries and house rent.
4. James reported that the proposals of Wade and Chicheley, carvers, were lower than those of Webster. Wade and Chicheley to be employed at Deptford if James thinks prices as low as those paid at Greenwich.

225. [p. 60] 9 Mar. 1718/19
1. Treasurer's bill of fees allowed; warrant ordered for £85. 5*s*.
2. Walter Younger's petition referred to James to report what damage he had sustained.

226. [p. 61] 12 Mar. 1718/19
1. Representation to King for providing maintenance for ministers, with duplicates for both Houses of Parliament, read, signed and sealed. Secretary to attend bishops of the Commission for their signatures.
2. Waugh to be asked to request Archbishop of Canterbury to present representation to the King and a duplicate to House of Lords; and Secretary to ask Farrer to present that to House of Commons.
3. Petition from St Giles in the Fields further considered; petitioners told Commissioners not yet ready to answer them, but would have a church rebuilt for them in convenient time as obliged by Act of Parliament.
4. Signed warrant for Treasurer's bill.
5. Satisfied by Hawksmoor's report that Dodson has sustained no damage from steeple of St Mary Woolnoth.
6. Surveyors to measure work already done and make up accounts to Christmas last.
7. Labourer to be employed, at Hawksmoor's request, to secure lead of Spitalfields church.
8. Advertisement ordered for carvers' proposals for ornaments of joiner's work at Strand church.
9. Solicitor presented his bill; to be considered at next meeting.
10. Hawksmoor and James to direct roofing and ceiling of west portico of Deptford church and see it done as soon and cheaply as possible.
11. Surveyors likewise to contract with Grove to finish roof and other carpenter's work still wanting in parsonage house, Deptford.
12. Enclosing ground for minister's house and the churchyard on east and west to be done according to plan now submitted, as cheaply as possible.
13. James reported that Wade and Chicheley's prices for carving at Deptford were cheaper than those for Greenwich. Wade and Chicheley to be employed.
14. On Dr Bennet's request, Surveyors to give orders for clearing ground in order to begin work on church in Old Street. James to prepare a plan and estimate for building in brick.

227. [p. 65] 19 Mar. 1718/19
1. Waugh reported waiting on Archbishop of Canterbury. Secretary reported that archbishop stated he had presented report on ministers'

maintenance to the king, and he wished another bishop to lay duplicate before the Lords.
2. Solicitor's bill referred to committee to meet in fortnight's time. Meller and Melmoth desired to attend.
3. James to submit plan for parsonage house for Bow to next meeting.
4. Solicitor ordered to prosecute Peter Patrick and Robt Brumfield, who were reported to have stolen iron and lead from St Mary Woolnoth.
5. Several inhabitants of Stratford le Bow petitioned about difficulties in executing their offices as appointed by this Board, and the uncertainty of the chapel's ever having been consecrated. Bishop of London agreed, to settle matter, to consecrate chapel in a week's time.
6. Parish officers to be appointed at first meeting after consecration.
7. Before Gibbs direct any further carver's or painter's work for finishing Strand church, design and estimate to be laid before Board so that agreements may be made with artificers before they are put in hand. Copy to Gibbs.

228. [p. 68] 2 Apr. 1719
1. Vestrymen and officers appointed for Stratford le Bow and Old Ford: churchwardens: Mr Abraham Wilmer, Mr Wm Fletcher; overseers: Thos Mitchell, Isaac le Hob; surveyors of highways: Wm Van Leut, Rich. Remnant. Vestrymen: Rev. Dr Robt Warren, Ambrose Page, Robt Hardesty, John Mitford, Abr. Wilmer, and Daniel Selman, Esquires; Jonathan Sanford, Hy Tilbury, Nich. Greenslade, Thos Kinnaston, Abr. Kemp, Wm Andrewes, John Warner, and churchwardens.
2. Solicitor to wait on Bishop of London with list of vestry.

229. [p. 70] 23 Apr. 1719
1. Read opinion of counsel on workmen's representation for hastening their payment.
2. Surveyors to measure works and make up accounts from Christmas 1717 to Lady Day 1719 with all possible speed.
3. Read representation of minister and trustees of St George's chapel: consideration deferred.
4. Waddington and Masters to view Mrs Futrel's ground: Surveyors to examine its nature.

230. [p. 71] 30 Apr. 1719
1. Waddington reported that he and Masters thought the ground in St Giles Cripplegate a convenient site for a church.
2. Surveyors to open the ground to see if it will admit good foundation and report to next meeting.
3. Representation of St George's chapel to be considered at next meeting, with all original papers.
4. Warrant to be prepared for £645 for site in Bermondsey.
5. Secretary to write to Surveyors (being absent) to attend next meeting to suggest how grievances complained of by Sir Gilbert Heathcote and Mr Craggs about church in Lombard Street may be removed.
6. Dodson's representation to be considered at next meeting.

231. [p. 73] 6 May 1719
1. Last order (minute 2, 30 Apr. 1719) on opening Futrel's ground to be renewed; Surveyors to employ some other labourer than the person contracted with for digging in that parish.
2. Surveyors to attend Dr Marshall and trustees of St George's chapel to report to next meeting on state of pews.
3. Signed warrant for £645 for Bermondsey site.
4. Surveyors reported that the grievances complained of at St Mary Woolnoth might be removed at little cost; this to be done.
In consideration of Dodson's representation, agreed that the projection of the cornice on west of steeple be made as small as possible.

232. [p. 75] 28 May 1719
1. Waddington reported that he and Masters had viewed Futrel's ground since it was opened in three places; it would not admit of good foundation.
2. Further consideration of repairs of St George's chapel to be deferred until after next sitting of Parliament.
3. Surveyors to adjust workmen's accounts to Lady Day last, entering prices agreeable to contract; those not contracted with to be referred to Commissioners' consideration at next meeting.
4. Surveyors to prepare plan and estimate of church proper to be built in Bermondsey.
4. Instruments of appointment of officers of new parish of Bow to be prepared for next meeting.

233. [p. 77] 5 June 1719
1. Surveyors submitted account of moneys due to workmen to Lady Day last.
2. Treasurer and Secretary to request Archbishop of Canterbury to speak to Lord Sunderland, chief commissioner of the Treasury, about issue of tallies to pay workmen.
3. Signed application to Treasury for issue of tallies for £45,000.
4. Secretary to remind Archer that Commissioners expect answer to their reply to his undertaking to finish Deptford parsonage house for not more than £1,000.

234. [p. 79] 19 Nov. 1719
1. Read petition of the workmen. Treasurer to obtain Attorney-General's opinion on case before him about the tallies of loan to be issued to discharge debts due to workmen; if it is delayed for want of a reference from the Treasury, then he is to desire chancellor of the Exchequer to obtain such an order.
2. Marples to be allowed 10*s*. 6*d*. for lead, instead of 11*s*. charged in his bill.
3. Strong to be allowed 12*d*. per ton for double hoisting at Limehouse.
4. Solicitor's bill referred to Meller or Hiccocks.
5. Read letter from Dean of Canterbury; Surveyors to take Archer's directions for covering in Deptford parsonage house.
6. Workmen's accounts to be stated at next meeting.

235. [p. 80] 26 Nov. 1719
1. Secretary reported that Attorney-General had promised to give his opinion in two or three days.
2. Examined and signed books of works done from 1 Jan. 1717/18 to 25 Mar. 1719.
3. Secretary to make 10 or 12 fair copies of representation to the King respecting the maintenance of ministers.
4. Read petition of workmen for opening a loan.
5. Further consideration of St George's chapel deferred to next meeting.

236. [p. 82] 3 Dec. 1719
1. Secretary reported that Attorney-General had not yet given his opinion.
2. Secretary submitted 12 copies of representation respecting maintenance of ministers.
3. Secretary to pay five guineas to Lucas Ken, clerk who attended House of Commons committee, for his service in examining the accounts of the churches in last session of Parliament.
4. Secretary to memorialize Treasury to direct Exchequer to take in sum of [blank] on loan on coals.
5. Gilham, joiner at Greenwich church, to finish vestry room and remove his materials; remaining part of the locks to be set on pews where they are wanting.

237. [p. 83] 10 Dec. 1719
1. Signed memorial to Treasury.
2. Solicitor to wait on Bishop of London about constituting Bow vestry.
3. Surveyors to deliver Dr Warren the key of enclosed ground at Bow.

238. [p. 84] 17 Dec. 1719
1. Solicitor to take counsel's advice about constituting Bow vestry.
2. Surveyors to report to next meeting on disposition of scaffolds and fence in Shernburn lane.

239. [p. 85] 7 Jan. 1719/20
1. Meller reported that he had settled Solicitor's bill at £216. 5*s*. 4*d*.; warrant ordered to be prepared.
2. Solicitor reported he had taken counsel's opinion about Bow vestry; the deed for the purpose was executed.
3. New application to be made to Treasury for £46,000, which is ready to be advanced as soon as the loan is opened. Treasurer to desire Mr Charles Stanhope's favour.
4. Secretary to make out warrant for year's salary for officers to Christmas last.
5. Notice to be given in next summons for the annual election of officers at next meeting.

240. [p. 86] 14 Jan. 1719/20
1. Read report from Treasury signed by Lowndes; Secretary to enter it into the books; application pursuant to it signed.

2. Signed two warrants for salaries and Solicitor's bill.
3. Agreed that same salaries be continued to the officers for ensuing year.
4. J. T. Philipps to be continued Secretary for ensuing year; James to be one of Surveyors, the election of the other to be postponed to next meeting; Edwards to be continued as Solicitor, Skeat as Agent and Waters as Messenger.

241. [p. 88] 21 Jan. 1719/20
1. Repairs of St George's chapel having been done in an expensive manner, far exceeding the estimate, it is made a standing order that Surveyors shall not at any time execute a design without presenting a plan and estimate and obtaining Board's express direction.
2. Hawksmoor to be Surveyor for year ensuing.
3. Affairs of Mr Johnson to be referred to a committee of any three members, to meet an hour before Board on Sat. next.
4. Farrer submitted draft bill for providing a maintenance for ministers of the new churches, to be considered at next meeting.

242. [p. 89] 23 Jan. 1719/20
1. Commissioners agreed with report of committee on Johnson's security.
2. Draft bill read, discussed and referred to Hiccocks, Meller and Farrer.

243. [p. 90] 28 Jan 1719/20
1. Solicitor reported that Johnson would not comply with terms proposed for changing his security.
2. On Dr Bennet's application, Waugh and Waddington desired to review Mrs Futrel's ground, attended by Surveyors.
3. Draft of maintenance bill brought in today by Meller and Farrer to be put into Mr Yorke's hands by Solicitor.
4. Dean of Ely, Farrer and Meller desired to wait on Speaker with a copy of representation on providing a maintenance for the ministers.

244. [p. 91] 4 Feb. 1719/20
1. Dean of Ely reported that Speaker had promised to assist in promoting intended bill.
2. Simmons, joiner at Strand church, to attend next meeting.
3. Read Grantham's proposals for supplying bricks; he is to bring specimens to the next meeting.

245. [p. 92] 11 Feb. 1719/20
1. Solicitor to proceed with business of intended bill for maintenance, and report to next meeting what progress Yorke has made.
2. Surveyors to make estimate of joiner's work brought into Strand church and report to next meeting.
3. On report and plan of Mrs Futrel's ground from Waugh and the Surveyors, ordered estimate of planking and making good faulty part of the foundation.

4. Surveyors to report on Grantham's proposal at next meeting.
5. Warrant to be prepared for paying one year's rent to Christmas last.

246. [p. 94] 25 Feb. 1719/20
1. Read Surveyors' report on Futrel's ground.
2. Consideration deferred of petition and plan of parish from St Mary le Strand.
3. Signed warrant for paying year's rent.

247. [p. 95] 10 Mar. 1719/20
1. Resolved to accept Mrs Futrel's ground if the two Surveyors at next meeting adhere to their first estimate of charge of making good foundations.
2. Solicitor to search First Fruits Office in respect of St Mary le Strand.
3. Surveyors to view works on steeple of St Michael Cornhill and report on remedying grievances stated in inhabitants' petition.
4. Sir Gilbert Heathcote presented petition from parishioners of St Mary Woolnoth about scaffolding in Lombard Street. Surveyors to consider best way of removing scaffolding and proceed forthwith.
5. Cannon and Ellis, accompanied by Hawksmoor (James being sick), to examine nature of ground near Hanover Square proposed for a new church, and report to next meeting. If a good account given, and convenient places for cemetery and minister's house can be had reasonably, Commissioners will build one of the fifty new churches on the site as soon as they are in a condition to go forward with it.

248. [p. 97] 11 Mar. 1719/20
1. Cannon, Ellis and Hawksmoor reported on proposed site near Hanover Square. Resolved that according to the resolution of yesterday (minute 5), one of the fifty new churches to be built there, if it can be given gratis.
2. Solicitor to write urgently to Mr Yorke for the papers that were put into his hands.

249. [p. 98] 17 Mar. 1719/20
1. Solicitor reported having received the papers from Yorke, who had not leisure to settle them and was on circuit; Solicitor to lay them before Mr Ward.
2. The two Surveyors to report to next meeting whether they adhere to the first estimate for making good the foundation of Futrel's ground.
3. Warrant to be prepared for Simmons, joiner at Strand church.
4. Read petition from St Michael Cornhill and proposal of Strong. Resolved that the first money the Commissioners shall have to dispose of after the debt of £46,000 be discharged shall be applied to finishing tower.
5. Read letter from Mr Barlow concerning parsonage house and cemetery for church near Hanover Square.

250. [p. 99] 24 Mar. 1719/20
1. Solicitor reported that he had put the writings into Ward's hands.

2. Hawksmoor delivered report signed by himself and James adhering to first estimate for making good foundation for Futrel's ground, £600; if piling necessary, an additional £100–£150.
2 [*sic*]. Agreed to purchase Mrs Futrel's ground if she abide by her price of £350 (minute, 28 Mar. 1719). Solicitor to lay her title before counsel.
3. Dr Bennet's printed proposal read; to be considered at next meeting.
4. Dr Prat's petition adjourned to next meeting.
5. Lambeth petition referred to next meeting.

251. [p. 100] 31 Mar. 1720
1. Bennet's printed case referred to a committee (Dean of Canterbury, Waugh, Dean of the Arches, Ellis and any members), to meet next Thurs.
2. Nobody attending about Prat's petition, it was referred to next meeting.
3. Read petition from Lambeth. Skeat instructed to look for a more convenient site between South Lambeth and Fox Hall, and consult minister and churchwardens.
4. Read memorial from Gilham and letter from James, stating that no part of joiner's work at Deptford, amounting to upwards of £1,500, has yet been paid for. Agreed that Gilham have a proportionable payment out of £23,000 now advanced upon loan, though measurement of his work has not yet been formally returned.
5. Treasurer to lay balance of accounts before the next meeting.
Mr Gibbs to submit model of pulpit and reading desk for Strand church, which may be finished for less than £150.
6. Solicitor to meet Gen. Steuart's agent to have site near Hanover Square legally conveyed.
7. Hawksmoor's memorial deferred to next meeting.
8. Hawksmoor to view the ground Mrs Hastings complains of.

252. [p. 102] 7 Apr. 1720
1. Dean of Canterbury reported from the committee on Bennet's printed case that, there being no likelihood of the bill for the maintenance of ministers being brought into Parliament this session, they thought it unnecessary to consider such a clause as he desired; but will recommend other expedients to encourage his design.
2. Skeat to view ground near Harticock, between South Lambeth and Fox Hall, and report to next meeting.
3. All minutes relating to the Queen's statue and moneys disbursed on that account to be transcribed for next meeting.
4. Treasurer submitted balance of his account, with £6,768. 2*s*. 6¾*d*. in hand.
5. Treasurer and Surveyors to submit to next meeting the state of debts due to workmen, that just distribution may be made.
6. Hawksmoor read memorial by himself and James with account of works necessary for security of churches in hand; referred to next meeting.
7. On application of St Mary Woolnoth parish, Hawksmoor to

endeavour to remove grievances by carrying up wall to full height on Lombard Street so that scaffolds may be removed, and to consider remedy in respect of vault and burials.

253. [p. 104] 28 Apr. 1720
1. Read all minutes respecting the Queen's statue.
2. Treasurer to inquire of Sir E. Gould to whom £460 paid to him by Treasurer, 18 Aug. 1715, was transmitted.
3. Secretary submitted two warrants for money to be paid by Treasurer to workmen: £8,626. 6*s*. 6*d*. for clearing accounts for 1717; and £14,359 by way of imprest.
4. Surveyors to put in hand works mentioned in their memorial, laying an estimate of each before next meeting.
5. Their memorial to be entered after the Minutes.
6. Skeat to let ground in Bermondsey and that in Shadwell bought of Hastings, reserving power of resumption, and restraining tenants from planting or digging within 5 ft of the walls.
7. Solicitor to examine Johnson's agreement in respect of his claim of enjoying the profits of the ground until a church is built on it.
8. Skeat to see that fence to Bermondsey ground be made good and the charge paid out of the rent.
9. Skeat to require satisfaction for a tree cut down in the ground by Grantham.
10. Peter Christian to be allowed to make drain into sewer of Strand church at his own cost in manner Surveyors think proper and under such conditions as those near St Paul's are allowed to make drains into the common sewer.

[p. 105] The Surveyors' Memorial

Several works are necessary in the new churches, without which they will suffer damage:

'1. The porch at Deptford Church is finished all except the lead, for want of which the rain rots the timber and boards, and destroys the stone work, the porch also wants paving with rough Purbeck, and the gate to the church ground ought to be finished.

We beg that the plumber may have orders to lay lead upon the said porch, to hinder the damage.

2. The new house at Deptford built for the minster is in extreme want of the roof and tiling, the walls are up and finished.

3. The new church in Spittlefields has all its walls up to their proper heights, and the two side ails covered with lead but in the middle of the church, although the walls are up and the timbers of the roof prepared, yet the carpenter has not bin able to compleat the said roof for want of money, having a great debt, at this church and in other parishes, due to him, of above £2,000.

We humbly pray that the carpenter have such encouragement by way of imprest as may enable him to lay on this roof and an order may be given to the plumber to prepare his lead to cover it.

4. It will be advisable also to turn the vaults of this church, and then

the fabrick will be secured from damage of weather and other accidents.

5. If the out walls of St Mary Woolnoth in Lombard Street could be finished, which want not more than seven or eight feet height, the scaffolds might after that be entirely struck and taken away.

We desire some expedient may be found to enable the mason to carry up the said walls; otherwise we must take away the scaffolds to quiet the inhabitants.

6. We desire leave to mention to this Board that the porches of St Michael's Cornhill adjoining to the north and south sides of the tower, and some parts of the church on the east side of the tower, have been damaged by taking down the old steeple, and erecting the new one. The south porch is also much abused and injured by a wild building raised upon it by the parish for a tenement and by making shops for trade, in the very porch. We doubt not but the estimate of £6,000 which was formerly made by Sir Christopher Wren and now lately given by Parliament for finishing this tower, was always intended to include the charge of removing these nuisances, and making good the above mentioned damages, for they are evidently part of the work of that building, and valuation of the £6,000 above mentioned, which would be of great beauty and security both to the tower and church, and of more service to the public than the laying out all the money on a tower surrounded with encroachments.

7. We humbly move that the ground brought for sites of the churches of Limehouse, Wapping, Spittlefields and Westminster may be walled in with brick, to prevent the harm continually done by the mob to the buildings and works.

8. The porches of the new church in Westminster want covering very much, the rest of the church being all covered in, and the earth brought by the scavengers should be so disposed next the walls of the church, that the rains may not run in the foundations.

9. We desire to secure all the fabricks of such churches as are covered by fixing up the doors, windows, bars and glass, to hinder idle people and boys from getting in, and finding ways to get upon the roofs of such churches as they are finished, where they are doing continual mischief. It is also highly necessary that the said fabricks should be put into the custody of some careful person in the neighbourhood of each of them.

10. We humbly desire the above mentioned works may be performed with all convenient expedition, being of immediate service to preserve that is done, and that the Board will keep some money in their hands to imprest such sums to the workmen, as may enable them to perform the particulars above laid, all which is humbly submitted . . .'

254. [p. 108] 5 May 1720

1. Treasurer reported that he had viewed Sir Ed. Gould's books without finding the receipt of any such sum (minute 2, 28 Apr. 1720). To discourse late Treasurer and others and report to next meeting.

2. Surveyors submitted estimate of the particulars mentioned in their memorial. To discourse the several workmen concerned, and report at next meeting whether they are content to proceed on such encouragement as the Board can at present give.
3. Some of the Commissioners being obliged to attend House of Commons, the Board broke up without considering remaining minutes of last meeting.
Ordered that the messenger add to his summons a request that Commissioners will assist early at the next meeting.

255. [p. 109] 12 May 1720
1. Treasurer reported that he had made inquiries at Mr Auditor Foley's office in the Exchequer: no part of the £460 [for the Queen's statue] had been remitted, but all had been paid into the Exchequer in the final balance of the account, forming part of that given in to the Commissioners on 7 Apr. last.
2. Treasurer to state balance of money in his hands monthly.
3. Appointed committee to consider the Dean of Rochester's petition, to meet this day week, to report to the next meeting (Deans of Canterbury and Ely, Waugh, Waddington, and Ellis; three a quorum).
4. Skeat reported on letting of Bermonsdey and Shadwell sites (minute 6, 28 Apr. 1720); Solicitor to make lease accordingly, at tenant's expense.
5. Grantham agrees to pay for the tree cut down at Surveyors' valuation.
6. Tenant will make good the poling and deduct from his rent price set by Surveyors.
7. Solicitor reported that he had examined Johnson's agreement, and found no foundation for his claim (minute 7, 28 Apr. 1720).
8. Agreed that £166. 13*s*. 5*d*. be paid to Thos Frenchfield, Esq, as prayed by minister and trustees of St George's chapel [Ormond Street], in part of £1,200 to be paid to the trustees to convert chapel into a parish church. Secretary to prepare warrant.
9. Secretary to prepare warrant for Treasurer to pay the workmen concerned five shillings in the pound, in part of account for 1718.
10. Dunn and Townsend promised to finish north and west walls of St Mary Woolnoth without delay; they would go forward in a week's time.
11. Secretary's bill of incidentals to be examined at next meeting.

256. [p. 111] 19 May 1720
1. Committee delivered report on Dean of Rochester's petition concerning his being minister of St Mary le Savoy alias le Strand; to be entered after the Minutes.
2. Warrant signed for payment of £166. 13*s*. 5*d*. to Frenchfield.
3. Solicitor's bill for law charges, 30 Oct. 1718–28 May 1720, £109. 8*s*. 7*d*., referred to Hiccocks and Meller, or either, to examine and settle.
4. Solicitor to prepare assignments to Commissioners of leasehold interests in site of St George's chapel, etc. [Ormond Street], on execution whereof the Commissioners are to pay £1,500 consideration.
5. Advertisement ordered for lime-burners' proposals for lime.
6. [Report of committee on Dean of Rochester's petition] Because of the

partition of St Mary le Strand parish, Acts of 10th Anne do not apply. But Dr Prat was licensed to the cure of souls of the parishioners of St Mary le Savoy alias le Strand in 1697 and has since been regarded as the sole lawful minister.

257. [p. 113] 25 May 1720
[1.] Read proposals for lime from Jas Brown, John Mackereth, and John Brown.
2. Surveyors to prepare form of contract with John Brown, lime-burner, of St Bride's.
3. Signed the book of works of St George's chapel [Ormond Street], being complete.
4. Surveyors to estimate charge of fencing site in Old Street; Skeat to consult Wilson about preventing soil being laid there in future.
5. Hawksmoor reported that ground in Cripplegate [Old Street] purchased of Ironmongers' Company is large enough for erecting a tabernacle without obstructing building a church on another part of it when Board is enabled to do so.

258. [p. 115] 22 June 1720
1. Skeat to give an account of all houses and grounds purchased by this Commission on which no public building is erecting, the uses they are now put to, and what advantage may be made of them until churches are built thereon.
2. All moneys received by Agent for rent to be paid to the Treasurer on account.
3. Secretary to prepare warrant for paying officers' salaries to midsummer.
4. Advertisement ordered for proposals from diggers, bricklayers and masons for building church near Hanover Square, to be received in two weeks' time.
5. Surveyors and Agent to survey two houses belonging to Dr Yeats, and plot of Sir R. Grosvenor's in Hanover Square, and report to next meeting whether either house is fit for a minister's house, and at what price, and whether ground is proper for a churchyard, and at what price, and, if necessary, for a house also.

259. [p. 116] 6 July 1720
1. Agent submitted account of houses and grounds (minute 1, 22 June 1720); to perfect it for next meeting.
2. Signed warrants for officers' salaries (£560) and half-year's rent (£37. 10*s*.)
3. Surveyors and Agent to view Mrs Hastings's ground in Shadwell and remove fence if it stands on her ground.

260. [p. 117] 20 July 1720
1. Signed application to Treasury for £23,000.

261. [p. 118] 28 July 1720
1. Read letter from Treasurer about application to Treasury; another application drawn up and signed.
3. In consideration for gift of site for church near Hanover Square by General Steuart, a pew in the south gallery, 8 ft × 10 ft, to be given to him.

262. [p. 119] 15 Sep. 1720
1. Warrants to be prepared for Solicitor's and Secretary's bills (£103. 5*s*. and £65. 11*s*. 6*d*. respectively), formerly examined and settled.
2. Application of 20 July for £23,000 returned by the Treasury, desiring the Commissioners to sign another application for £28,000, including £5,000 for Greenwich Hospital and Westminster Abbey. Being informed that Treasury have signed warrant for taking in £28,000 in loans on coals, signed such application dated 20 July, the other being cancelled.

263. [p. 121] 27 Oct. 1720
1. Signed two warrants for Solicitor (£103. 0*s*. 3*d*.) and Secretary (£50).
2. Surveyors to prepare for next meeting a design and estimate for church to be built near Hanover Square.
3. Advertisement ordered for proposals from diggers and bricklayers for church near Hanover Square.
4. Watchman to be appointed to take care of covering of Limehouse church.
5. A gateway into the ground purchased of Mr Hastings to be made up with a brick pier and plain gates.
6. Read petition from the workmen. Surveyors and Treasurer to apportion the sums to be paid them by next meeting.

264. [p. 123] 3 Nov. 1720
1. James and the Treasurer apportioned sums to be paid to the workmen. Warrants signed accordingly.
2. Low Wapping site bought of Bastwick Johnson, Esq.
3. Messenger to give Solicitor notice to attend next meeting with all papers relating to Futrel's estate.
4. Solicitor to prosecute Geo. Luck, John Luck and Thos Griffin for laying rubbish on the ground bought from the Ironmongers' Company in Cripplegate parish.
5. James submitted design and estimate for church to be built near Hanover Square; consideration postponed.

265. [p. 125] 10 Nov. 1720
1. Messenger in summons for next meeting to desire the Commissioners to meet at 10 o'clock next Wednesday [16 Nov.] 'upon an Extraordinary occasion'.

266. [p. 126] 16 Nov. 1720
1. General Steuart to be desired to direct Gibbs to attend next meeting with design he has prepared for new church near Hanover Square.

2. Solicitor and Agent to meet Surveyors at Mrs Futrel's ground for ascertaining boundaries and descriptions to be inserted into the conveyance.

267. [p. 127] 23 Nov. 1720
1. Dr Bennet to be desired to attend next meeting.
2. Advertisement for diggers and bricklayers proposals for church near Hanover Square against next meeting.
3. Gibbs submitted his design for a new church; consideration deferred.

268. [p. 128] 7 Dec. 1720
1. Diggers and bricklayers submitted their proposals; referred to Surveyors, to report to next meeting.
2. Read petition of Walwin Parker and James Smith for leave to build a shed on ground bought of the Ironmongers' Company for a minister's house in Cripplegate. Solicitor to contract with them for 20*s*. p.a., on a month's notice.
3. James to contract the expensive parts of his design for new church near Hanover Square so that it do not exceed £10,000.

269. [p. 129] 14 Dec. 1720
1. Approved James's plan for new church near Hanover Square.
2. Deans of Worcester and the Arches to inform General Steuart of Board's decision, and James to accompany them with his plan.

270. [p. 130] 22 Dec. 1720
1. The Deans of Worcester and the Arches reported they had informed General Steuart of Board's resolution.
2. Surveyors to ensure that work at the Strand church is to be finished with expedition; and to give notice for workmen to attend next meeting to agree for works not yet contracted.

271. [p. 131] 5 Jan. 1720/21
1. Resumed consideration of the bill for settling a maintenance on ministers, etc. After making some progress, adjourned to next meeting.

272. [p. 132] 11 Jan. 1720/21
1. Board will accept proposals for new church near Hanover Square; and upon condition that suitable workmen will undertake the work at prices commonly allowed by Board, under its direction, and accept in payment tallies on new churches' loan, will put it in hand forthwith. Churches not yet finished to go on hand in hand with that near Hanover Square.
2. Petition of St Mary le Strand churchwardens to be referred to Bishop of London.
3. Surveyors to submit to next meeting estimates of finishing Strand and Deptford churches and covering Spitalfields church, and securing from weather the others still building. Treasurer to submit account of debt.

273. [p. 134] 14 Jan. 1720/21
1. State of debt of the churches submitted.

2. Both Surveyors to provide at next meeting estimate of sums due for work done but not brought to account by March 1719; and of cost of completion of churches nearly finished as well as of St Mary Woolnoth.
3. Treasurer to submit account of balance in his hands at Michaelmas last, and estimate of net produce of the fund applicable to the Board in year to Michaelmas 1721.
4. Barlow stated that ground offered for cemetery for Hanover Square church now disposed of, but another site available; Skeat to report to next meeting.
5. Hawksmoor submitted estimates of finishing Strand and Deptford churches, covering Spitalfields, and securing the others.

274. [p. 136] 19 Jan. 1720/21
1. Skeat reported on cemetery for Hanover Square church.
Treasurer and Surveyors delivered papers required; the fund of £21,000 p.a. will in the year 1726 inclusive bring in £75,000. Present debts for finishing and securing churches amount to £66,685. 5*s*. 7½*d*.
2. Memorandum: it is a question whether the [fund for the] year 1725 is not entirely applicable for the maintenance of ministers, according to Act of 1 Geo. I.

Board told Dr Green and others from St Martin's in the Fields that they could not procure tallies for the money to be spent on church near Hanover Square, but must refer that to gentlemen who had encouraged the affair.

N.B. Present yearly sum paid to the Commissioners is £21,000, but out of that they doubt whether they must not pay to Westminster Abbey and Greenwich Hospital £10,000 p.a., or a lesser sum pro rata.

275. [p. 138] 23 Jan. 1720/21
1. Particulars from which general estimate arises (2nd article, 19 Jan. 1720/21) to be entered upon the books. [Marginal note: This order has since been recalled.]
2. Skeat to treat with proprietors of ground proposed for cemetery for Hanover Square church.
3. Resolved that the Commissioners will from time to time apply to Treasury for striking tallies for satisfying workmen engaged on Hanover Square church under Board's order. Copy of this minute and the preceding to Dr Green.
4. The joiners and carvers to submit draught of altar-piece, pulpit and desk of Deptford church, with an estimate, and an account how far they have proceeded; they are to go no further until they receive further directions from the Board.

276. [p. 140] 26 Jan. 1720/21
1. James submitted draught of Deptford altar piece, etc., as designed by Archer, which appears very expensive. James to reduce it to as plain and cheap a form as the work already done will allow. Joiners and carvers to proceed according to the directions of the Surveyors.

277. [p. 141] 6 Feb. 1720/21
1. James submitted modified design for the Deptford altar-piece, etc., which was approved; to be put in hand immediately.
2. Scaffolding and fence on north side of the church in Lombard Street to be removed forthwith; workmen to move their materials into the body of the church or the churchyard.
3. Dunn and Townsend to attend the next meeting.
4. Green submitted copy of minute of Commissioners for building St Martin's church, for lending £2,000 to this Board towards forwarding church near Hanover Square.
5. Read letter from Barlow regarding ground proposed by Sir R. Grosvenor for church yard for that church. Agent and Surveyors to treat with owner.
6. Stephen Whitaker to be employed to dig foundation for the church near Hanover Square and carry off earth etc.; to begin immediately. Digging 6*d*. a yard solid; carting, 14*d*. a yard solid; labourer to level the work at 1*s*. 8*d*. per day.
7. Geo Whitton to be employed as bricklayer at church near Hanover Square; contract to be made with him immediately.
8. Surveyors to appoint a carpenter to fence in the ground near Hanover Square, at lowest prices, as soon as possible.
9. Foregoing three resolutions to be imparted to Dr Green.
10. Warrant to be prepared for paying officers' salaries to Christmas last.

278. [p. 143] 19 Feb. 1720/21
1. Commissioners made some progress in consideration of bill for settling a maintenance on the ministers.
2. Advertisement ordered for masons' proposals for church near Hanover Square.
3. Notice to be given in next summons that the yearly election of officers will then be held.

279. [p. 144] 26 Feb. 1720/21
1. A debate arising whether all the same officers should be continued, and with the same salaries, and few Commissioners being present, consideration was adjourned; notice to be given in next summons.

280. [p. 145] 2 Mar. 1720/21
Agreed that the same officers shall be continued for one year from 14 Jan., but at reduced salaries (Treasurer £200, Secretary £150, Surveyors £150, Solicitor £60, Agent £60, Messenger £40).

281. [p. 147] 9 Mar. 1720/21
1. Skeat to offer £300 to Sir R. Grosvenor for ground near Oliver's Mount proposed by him for cemetery for Hanover Square church.
2. Skeat to inquire how the ground in Old Street may be turned to best account.
3. Solicitor to attend next meeting with the writings on St George's chapel.

4. Treasurer to prepare application to Treasury for taking in money at six per cent.
5. Joshua Fletcher to be employed as mason at church near Hanover Square.

282. [p. 149] 20 Mar. 1720/21
1. Skeat reported on cemetery for church near Hanover Square. Agreed that £315 (insisted on by Sir R. Grosvenor and Mr Robt Green) be given, provided a good title can be made. Solicitor to apply to Sir R. Grosvenor for the title.
2. Resolved that if trustees of St George's chapel [Ormond Street] advance £1,153. 6*s*. 7*d*. upon loan now opened at four per cent, it shall be issued for discharge of the debt remaining due to them.
3. Read petition of Thos Hollins; referred to Surveyors.

283. [p. 151] 30 Mar. 1721
1. Solicitor to engross deed to be executed with trustees of St George's chapel.
2. Surveyors to employ Skeat [smith] to prepare four fanes for pinnacles of St Michael Cornhill.
3. Unless Dunn and Townsend attend next meeting and comply with directions about church in Lombard St (minute 2, 6 Feb. 1720/21), they will forthwith be superseded, and subjected to the penalties in the contract.

284. [p. 153] 3 Apr. 1721
1. Dunn and Townsend attending were ordered to finish the cornice of the north side of St Mary Woolnoth within five weeks, and promised to comply.

285. [p. 154] 17 Apr. 1721
1. Agent submitted proposals for parts of the ground in Old Street from Jas Wilson, bricklayer, and John Wilson.
2. Wilson to be allowed the ground upon which a church is intended to be built, to be cleared and given up at three months' notice.
3. James Wilson to attend next meeting.
4. The plumber at Spitalfields church to attend next meeting.
5. Warrant to be prepared for paying £160. 12*s*. 1*d*. to Grove in pursuance of Surveyors' report of 30 Mar. 1720/21 on his account.

286. [p. 156] 27 Apr. 1721
1. John Wilson to attend next meeting.
2. Price of lead having risen since Spitalfields contract was made, 18*d*. per cent to be allowed beyond the contract, provided it be finished by Michaelmas next.
3. Pridie, painter, to execute gilding of vanes of St Michael Cornhill.

287. [p. 157] 3 May 1721
1. John Wilson attending, the Board refused to let him the ground in Old

Street upon which a church is intended to be built unless he consented not to raise it above present level, with which he would not comply.
2. As price of lead is falling, minute 2, 27 Apr. 1721 is set aside. The plumber at Spitalfields church to have such advance above his contract price as agrees with current price of lead when the work is done, provided church be covered before Michaelmas next.
3. Gibbs to be desired to send back model of the church in the Strand.
4. Acts of Parliament about church building to be re-printed (300 copies) with Act of 5 Geo. I for continuing the coal duty, and an abstract of them all at the end. Solicitor to take care of the impression.
5. Appointed committee to prepare bill for maintenance of ministers; to meet at Master of the Temple's house for convenience of having assistance of Mr Ward [counsel]; Deans of Canterbury, Ely, Worcester, Chichester, the Arches and Gloucester; Cannon, Ellis and Philipps, or any other member pleased to come.

288. [p. 159] 26 Oct. 1721
1. Solicitor's bill referred to Meller or Hiccocks to settle and report.
2. James delivered a memorial on the state of the churches; referred to next meeting.

289. [p. 160] 9 Nov. 1721
1. Surveyors to offer Devall 15*s*. per cent for lead covering of Spitalfields church, provided he puts it in hand immediately; if he refuses, they are empowered to employ any other plumber that will undertake it at this rate. As the boards have long been exposed to weather and may be attacked by worm, Surveyors are to cover them with pitch and tar before lead be laid on.
2. The workmen's petition to be considered at next meeting.
3. Commissioners to be summoned for next Monday to consider bill for the maintenance of ministers.

290. [p. 161] 13 Nov. 1721
1. Perused bill for the maintenance of ministers. Solicitor to consider proviso about continuance of payment of tithe on arable land, etc., and prepare a new clause, obtaining Mr Ward's opinion, to submit to next meeting.

291. [p. 162] 16 Nov. 1721
1. Treasurer to pay executrix of Mr Stanley Smith for goods sold and delivered at St George's chapel, and work done, £8. 10*s*.
2. Warrants to be prepared for paying Solicitor's bill, settled by Mr Hiccocks, and the above executrix.
3. Perused bill for maintenance of ministers, and made amendment, to be referred to Mr Ward.

292. [p. 163] 20 Nov. 1721
Two copies of the bill to be written out by Solicitor for next meeting.

293. [p. 164] 23 Nov. 1721
1. Surveyors to submit designs of church in Lombard Street to next meeting for reconsideration.
2. Solicitor submitted two copies of the maintenance bill; Secretary to attend Attorney-General with one, Mr Lowndes with the other.

294. [p. 165] 27 Nov. 1721
1. Secretary to acquaint widow of the late Treasurer that she should submit Leacroft's last quietus and all papers relating to his accounts as soon as possible.
2. Secretary reported that he had delivered copies of the bill to Attorney-General and Mr Lowndes.

295. [p. 166] 14 Dec. 1721
Read petition of Jonas Stephenson about Strand church; referred to Surveyors.

296. [p. 167] 1 Feb. 1721/22
1. Notice to be given in next summons for electing officers and settling their salaries.
2. Nathaniel Blackerby Esq. presented a commission from the King dated 10 Jan. 1721/2, appointing him Treasurer.
3. Surveyors to view parsonage house of St Michael Cornhill, which has suffered damage from building the tower, that reparation may be made.
4. Late Treasurer having advanced £333. 18*s*. 1*d*. to John Gilham, joiner, for work at Deptford and Greenwich churches, John Granger, Esq., to be repaid from first imprest money issued to Commissioners the same sum, advanced by him at their request to enable Leacroft's administrix to pass her accounts with Auditor of the Imprest.
5. The several sums of £200, being a year's salary due to Leacroft at Christmas last, and £75, due then for rent of this house, and £54. 4*s*. 6*d*. paid for fees at Treasury and Exchequer, to be allowed to Mrs Leacroft upon account. Certificate that Blackerby has given security in the Court of Exchequer for due execution of his office as Treasurer to the Commission.

297. [p. 169] 8 Feb. 1721/22
1. Agreed that the same officers and salaries shall be continued for a year from 14 Jan. last.
2. Treasurer to prepare memorial to Treasury for remainder of the £28,000 formerly applied for by memorial dated 20 July 1720; and to wait on bishops for their signatures.
3. Warrant to be prepared for paying Solicitor's bill of £98. 17*s*. 9*d*.
4. Warrant to be prepared for paying officers' salaries to Christmas last.
5. The fifth order of 1 Feb. to be signed by five or more Commissioners.
6. The several officers to have a copy of last print of book of Acts of Parliament relating to this Commission.

298. [p. 171] 8 Mar. 1721/22
1. Treasurer stated that Treasury had ordered the striking of fictitious

tallies for £2,000 only. A new memorial to be drawn by the Treasurer with the assistance of the Secretary, Solicitor and Surveyors, representing the very great difficulty of disposing that sum until the whole amount applied for be granted.
2. Surveyors reported that damage to parsonage house at St Michael's Cornhill may be repaired for about £25. Strong, the mason, to attend the next meeting.

299. [p. 172] 15 Mar. 1721/22
1. Read Treasurer's memorial to Treasury; recommitted to Treasurer to perfect and send to Commissioners to sign.
2. Read petition from St Michael's Cornhill. Surveyors to submit account of money already spent on finishing tower according to the model, and of what remains to be done, with an estimate.

300. [p. 173] 22 Mar. 1721/22
1. Workmen employed on tower of St Michael's Cornhill to deliver their bills forthwith, to be settled by this day fortnight, and Surveyors then to submit report.

301. [p. 174] 5 Apr. 1722
1. Mrs Leacroft submitted 12 books of works done at the churches between 1 Jan. 1717/18 and 25 Mar. 1719/20.
2. Treasurer reported that Treasury had advanced him a further £1,563. 7*s*. 6*d*. in money and tallies. Surveyors to measure the work done at the new churches and make up the accounts from 1719 to 25 Mar. 1721/2 by this day fortnight.
3. Surveyors to lay before next meeting an estimate of necessary expenses of finishing Strand and Deptford churches.
4. Warrant to be prepared for paying £1,127. 6*s*. 7*d*. to trustees of St George's chapel, residue of purchase money, after £26 deducted, expended by Hawksmoor and Skeat. Another warrant to be prepared for paying Hawksmoor and Skeat £26 for work done.
5. Groves's memorial referred to Surveyors for report.

302. [p. 175] 12 Apr. 1722
1. Signed warrants for £1,127. 6*s*. 7*d*. and £26.

303. [p. 176] 19 Apr. 1722
1. Surveyors submitted estimate of expenses for finishing Strand and Deptford churches.
2. Surveyors to agree on lowest possible terms with Townsend, mason, for paving in Strand church, so that it be finished out of hand.
3. Josh. Fletcher, mason at church near Hanover Square, petitioned for an allowance for being obliged for want of room on site to lay his stone and work in Hanover Square at a distance from the work. To deliver his estimate of the charge to next meeting.

304. [p. 177] 26 Apr. 1722
Adjourned.

305. [p. 177a] 8 June 1722
1. Warrants to be prepared for paying £6,850 due to artificers up to 25 Mar. 1719, and £2,000 for work at church near Hanover Square.

306. [p. 178] 15 June 1722
1. Read petition from some inhabitants of Wapping. They were told their church would be finished with all convenient speed.
2. A review by the Surveyors of account due to the contractors showing that £849. 19*s*. 11*d*. ought to be added to the £6,850. 0*s*. 10*d*. [*sic*], above-stated, a warrant was signed for £7,699. 19*s*. 11*d*. instead.
3. Warrant to be prepared for paying £54 to Mr Basket for printing the Acts of Parliament.

307. [p. 179] 11 July 1722
1. Warrants signed for paying John Basket £54, the officers' salaries to Midsummer last, £405, and a half-year's house-rent to Mrs Leacroft, £37. 10*s*.
2. Mrs Leacroft was called in and desired to give a positive answer by next meeting whether she will surrender the lease of this house taken by Leacroft for the use of this Board.
3. Signed memorial to Treasury for £10,000 in money and tallies.

308. [p. 180] 25 July 1722
1. Mrs Leacroft after much debate declared that having a right to this house by virtue of the lease, as her late husband's administrix, she could not leave it without great inconvenience, but that if the Commissioners would think fit to leave it, she must submit.
2. Signed memorial to Treasury for issue of £1,301. 18*s*. 8*d*., the balance of Leacroft's account.

309. [p. 181] 8 Aug. 1722
1. Whereas Mrs Leacroft refuses to leave this house and deliver up the lease, Agent to look out for a convenient room for the Commissioners' meetings in Lincoln's Inn or thereabouts.
2. Agent to report what sites purchased and not yet made use of.
3. Examined, allowed and signed the books of works for 1719.

310. [p. 182] 24 Oct. 1722
1. Allowed and signed the books of works for 1720.
2. Signed warrant for payment of £6,028. 13*s*. 7*d*.
3. Read petition from inhabitants of St Clement Danes and St Mary le Strand; referred to another meeting.
4. Read petition from Sam. Preedy, painter, for painting the stone work over altar in Strand church; work to be done on the foot of former contract.
5. Warrant to be prepared for paying John Gilham £333. 18*s*. 1*d*.

311. [p. 183] 1 Nov. 1722
1. Having considered petition from St Clement Danes and St Mary le

Strand about a watch house, and Sir J. Philipps having been desired to speak to Jennings and Hoare, he reported that they could recollect no promise ever made by the Board about building a watch house.
2. Secretary to desire Farrer to make further inquiry of Annesley; and Gibbs to attend next meeting.
3. Signed warrant for paying £333. 18*s*. 1*d*. to Gilham.
4. Surveyors to report to next meeting on delays and obstruction of the building of St Mary Woolnoth and Hanover Square churches.
5. Next meeting to consider bill for maintenance of ministers; notice to be given on the summons.
6. Read petition from John Foltrop, Jas Groves and Ezekiel Cook. Treasurer to stop payments to John Grove till further notice.
7. Next meeting to consider Marshall's request that Commissioners apply to Bishop of London to consecrate St George's chapel according to precedent of application for consecrating church yard.

312. [p. 185] 8 Nov. 1722
1. Signed application to Bishop of London to consecrate St George's chapel; copy to be entered into the books.
2. Dean of Canterbury to have leave to place a stable and coach house on ground appointed for a church yard at Deptford till Commissioners want it for use of minister.
3. Considered the bill for maintenance of ministers.
4. Surveyors submitted memorial regarding St Mary Woolnoth and Hanover Square churches.
5. Books and state of accounts to be considered at next meeting.
6. Workmen concerned in churches of St Mary Woolnoth and near Hanover Square to attend next meeting.
7. Blank warrant to be prepared for paying moneys due to workmen.
8. Gibbs reported that he knew nothing about the watch house near church in the Strand.
9. Surveyors to agree with Simmons for making and carving a reading desk and for joiner's and carver's work about altar of Strand church.

313. [p. 187] 15 Nov. 1722
1. Dean of Arches to be desired to report at next meeting on two houses in Duke Street.
2. Solicitor or his clerk to attend Dr Henchman, Chancellor of London, with purchase deeds of St George's chapel in order to prepare instruments for consecrating church.

314. [p. 188] 23 Nov. 1722
1. Examined books for 1721.
2. Dean of Gloucester to be desired to examine Secretary's bill of incidents.
3. Read letter from Simmons, joiner at Strand church; Simmons called in; affair referred to next meeting.

315. [p. 189] 7 Dec. 1722
1. Approved and signed books of works for 1722 for Bloomsbury,

Deptford, Hanover Square and Spitalfields churches, St George's chapel and outworks.
2. Blank warrants to be prepared for payments to the workmen.
3. Read petition delivered by Simon Michell Esq. about Aylesbury chapel, Clerkenwell; Surveyors to report thereon to next meeting.

316. [p. 190] 20 Dec. 1722
Read Fletcher's petition; he was called in and heard.
1. Signed warrant for paying moneys due to workmen for 1721.
2. Warrant to be prepared for impresting £394. 3*s*. 6*d*. to John Simmons, joiner.
3. Read workmen's petition about receiving interest on their tallies.
4. Ground bought of Hastings in St Paul Shadwell to be let to Eusebius Pattenden at £7 p.a., he paying all rates and taxes, for seven years from Christmas next, at a half-year's notice. Solicitor to prepare a lease as usual.

317. [p. 191] 3 Jan. 1722/23
1. Signed books of Limehouse and Wapping churches and St Michael Cornhill, examined on 7 Dec. 1722.
2. Simmons' warrant signed.

318. [p. 192] 24 Jan. 1722/23
1. Solicitor to prepare abstract of intended bill for maintenance of the ministers.
2. Upon report from the Surveyors that Deptford and Strand churches are in a manner finished, those two are forthwith to be finished; Surveyors to give orders to the workmen to proceed thereon, and also on St Mary Woolnoth and Hanover Square churches.
3. On petition and memorials from minister and inhabitants of Spitalfields, those gentlemen were assured that Commissioners will order finishing their church as soon as it can be done.
James to submit an estimate for finishing that church, and particularly what will suffice if finishing the steeple be deferred.

319. [p. 194] 31 Jan. 1722/23
1. Solicitor submitted abstract of bill for maintenance of the ministers.
2. Deans of Canterbury, Worcester and Chichester, or any two, to wait on chancellor of the Exchequer with a copy of the bill and abstract, and pray his favour. Solicitor to prepare a fair copy and six copies of abstract.
3. Notice to be given in next summons for electing officers and settling their salaries.
4. James submitted estimates for finishing Hanover Square, Deptford, St Mary Woolnoth and Strand churches.
5. Memorial to Treasury for [blank] to be prepared.

320. [p. 195] 7 Feb. 1722/23
1. Agreed that same officers and salaries be continued for a year from 14 Jan.

2. Signed memorial to Treasury for £20,000.
3. The gentlemen desired to wait on the chancellor of the Exchequer with the bill, to acquaint him at the same time how moneys applied for are to be disposed of.
4. Talman's account for Queen's statue to be inquired after and submitted at next meeting.

321. [p. 196] 14 Feb. 1722/23
1. Considered bill for maintenance of the ministers; some amendments made. Solicitor to prepare fair copy and several copies of abstracts.

322. [p. 196a] 19 Feb. 1722/23
1. Fair copy of bill with amendments read, and further amendments made.
2. Deans of Canterbury and Chichester reported they had waited on the chancellor of the Exchequer. He had perused the abstract, and promised his assistance. They had acquainted him with Commissioners' intent to lay out money now applied for in finishing Deptford, Strand, St Mary Woolnoth and Hanover Square churches, whereon he promised that such loan shall be granted.
3. Deans of Canterbury, Chichester and Gloucester, or any two, to consult with Farrer about proper persons to bring in the bill, and take his advice whether abstracts should be printed for MPs.

323. [p. 197] 22 Feb. 1722/23
1. Dean of Gloucester reported that he and Deans of Canterbury and Chichester had consulted Farrer, who thought there was no necessity to deliver printed abstracts to MPs.
2. Solicitor to attend Solicitor-General forthwith with fair copy and abstracts, and wait on the chancellor of the Exchequer with another copy as soon as it can be finished.
3. Read memorial of inhabitants of St Mary le Strand; referred to next meeting.

324. [p. 197a] 7 Mar. 1722/23
1. Advertisement ordered for carpenters and plasterers to submit proposals for church near Hanover Square.
2. Surveyors to direct iron work of fence of Strand church to be painted forthwith.
3. Inhabitants of St Mary le Strand (Nicholson, Sparkes and others) heard on their memorial; further consideration adjourned.

325. [p. 198] 21 Mar 1722/23
1. John Meard to be employed as carpenter at church near Hanover Square, his proposal being the lowest.
2. Isaac Mansfield to be employed as plasterer there, his proposal being the lowest.
3. Preedy to paint rails and iron work around Strand church if he agrees to the Surveyors' terms, at not more than 10*d*. per yard.

4. Skeat reported receiving letter from Blackmore How Wardell for renting ground in Upper Wapping. Church yard site to be let to them for £4 p.a. for three years from Lady Day next, at six months' notice.
5. Read petition of workmen employed during 1718–20 who were paid in tallies and orders at four per cent, praying for interest between date of the order and the time they were issued.
6. Treasurer to consult with Lowndes whether it would be proper for Board to direct interest to be paid to the workmen, or whether he must charge himself in his accounts therewith; and if so, then how interest is to be paid.

326. [p. 200] 28 Mar. 1723
1. Agent to prepare rental of pieces of ground let by Commissioners, to be entered into the minute book.
2. Designs of church in Lombard Street to be submitted at next meeting.
3. Agent to report on a proper site for a church, etc. in St Botolph Aldgate.
4. Read petition from Tufnell's executors about stone bought for church in St Olave Southwark; no objection to their taking back the stone.

327. [p. 201] 9 May 1723
1. Agent reported that he was inquiring after two sites in St Botolph's Aldgate.
2. Warrant signed for £315, counsel having approved Sir R. Grosvenor's title for ground for church yard for Hanover Square.
3. Petition of Geo. White, complaining of damage to coach house and stable near new church in Bloomsbury. Surveyors to report.
4. Objections reported to be made against the bill for a maintenance for the ministers to be considered at the next meeting.
5. Advertisement ordered for plumbers' and joiners' proposals for churches in Hanover Square and Lombard Street.

328. [p. 203] 16 May 1723
1. James reported on White's petition. Surveyors immediately to remove fence into the range of the fronts of the houses, to open a passage into White's stable.
2. Considered objections against the bill; referred to next meeting.

329. [p. 204] 24 May 1723
1. Philipps, Hiccocks, and Melmoth to view Aylesbury chapel, Clerkenwell, attended by Surveyors, and report whether it is capable of conversion to a parish church.
2. Fletcher, mason at church near Hanover Square, to attend next meeting.
3. On petition from inhabitants of St Margaret's Westminster for finishing church near the Horse Ferry, the gentlemen were called in. Resolved, that the church shall be forwarded as soon as consistent with engagements elsewhere.
4. Treasurer reported a [Treasury] minute: '8th April 1723. Deliver the

Talleys and Orders to the Workmen with the Interest due thereupon.'
5. Surveyors presented abstract [given] of plumbers' proposals from Geo. Devall, H. Savage, J. Fincher & Js Slater, D. Arnot, Geo. Osmond, and Robt Evans, and reported that Fincher & Slater are the best plumbers, and David Arnott the most reasonable. Fincher & Slater to be employed at Hanover Square church, and Arnot at St Mary Woolnoth. Surveyors to report on joiners' proposals at next meeting.

330. [p. 207] 30 May 1723
1. Philipps and Hiccocks reported that Aylesbury chapel will conveniently hold about 1,000 (700 in pews and 300 in aisles). Approach avenues are very good. Surveyors delivered report and plans.
2. Surveyors reported on joiners' proposals. Appleby to do the work at Lombard Street and Meard that at Hanover Square church, these being cheapest.
3. Fletcher attended. Being acquainted that Board thought him very dilatory, he alleged want of stone because of contrary winds. But now he was so well supplied that he could make it ready for roof in about two months.
4. Read Michell's proposal for Aylesbury chapel; referred to another meeting.

331. [p. 209] 6 June 1723
1. Michell's proposals deferred to next meeting, James being out of town.
2. Surveyors and Secretary to submit petition of St Mary le Strand and plan of parish at next meeting.

332. [p. 210] 13 June 1723
1. Considered Surveyors' report on chapel in St John's Square, Clerkenwell, and two houses and ground at east of chapel; and heard Michell. Resolved to pay him £3,000 for chapel, houses and ground, including two long vaults under chapel and a right of passage all over the ground in west front of chapel, Michell making a good title, free from incumbrances; £50 to be abated in lieu of good title to and conveyance of vault in south-east corner of chapel. Solicitor to settle title and conveyances with counsel.
2. St Clement Danes and St Martin in the Fields to be acquainted that inhabitants of St Mary le Strand are petitioning for parts of those parishes to be added to theirs; to be considered at next meeting.
3. Surveyors submitted a model of the roof of Bloomsbury church which is in form of a cupola instead of a flat roof as at first intended. The said roof to be erected with a cupola in form of said model.

333. [p. 212] 20 June 1723
No person attending on behalf of parishioners of St Mary le Strand, matter referred to next meeting.

334. [p. 213] 5 July 1723
1. No representatives of St Clement Danes and St Martin in the Fields

appearing, to offer reasons why parts of their parishes should not be annexed to St Mary le Strand, resolved that Board will proceed to a determination at next meeting; notice to be given to ministers and churchwardens.
2. Signed warrant for payment of £315 to Sir R. Grosvenor, the Solicitor objecting to the form of the previous one.
3. Allowed Secretary's bill of incidents.

335. [p. 215] 12 July 1723
1. Received objections of parishioners of St Martin in the Fields to part of their parish being annexed to St Mary le Strand; and those of St Clement Danes desired another fortnight: allowed.
2. Solicitor to attend this day fortnight.

336. [p. 216] 26 July 1723
1. Solicitor reported that Ward, Commissioners' counsel, had approved Michell's title to chapel in St John Street [Aylesbury Chapel].
2. Churchwardens of Wapping petitioned for hastening the finishing of their church. Surveyors to submit with all convenient speed estimates for finishing the churches in Spitalfields, Westminster, Limehouse, Wapping and Bloomsbury.
3. Secretary to prepare warrants for paying the officers a year's salary to Midsummer last, a year's house rent to Mrs Leacroft, and a blank for impresting money to the Secretary to pay his incidental charges.
4. On considering petition of St Mary le Strand and hearing inhabitants of St Martin in the Fields and St Clement Danes, resolved that there be added to St Mary le Strand about 30 houses on south side of Exeter Street and about the same on north side of Whiteheart Yard, towards the east end, out of St Martin's; and out of St Clement Danes about 45 houses bounded on west by Burleigh Street and on south by the Strand, including Exeter 'Change.

337. [p. 218] 9 Aug. 1723
1. Secretary delivered a memorial setting forth the sums necessary to finish the churches at Spitalfields, Westminster, Limehouse, Wapping and Bloomsbury.
2. Signed warrants for salaries and an imprest of £50.
3. Mr Hammond delivered a representation on the part of Lord Northampton, and other parishioners of Clerkenwell, with objections to the agreement with Michell. Michell to have a copy of the representation, to remark on it by tomorrow night; the Secretary to deliver the same to Hammond for a reply to be laid before next meeting.
4. Lord Carpenter and some of St Martin's parish appeared, claiming that there was an error in the plan in that it did not show that Little Catherine Street and some adjoining courts are part of St Martin's. The parish to draw an exact plan as far as it borders on St Mary le Strand, and deliver a duplicate to the Secretary for the parishioners of St Mary le Strand to respond before the Board on the 16th.

338. [p. 220] 16 Aug. 1723
1. Signed memorial to Treasury for opening a loan of £25,000.
2. Some further progress made regarding Aylesbury chapel and the division [*sic*] of St Mary le Strand; further consideration adjourned.

339. [p. 221] 23 Aug. 1723
1. Treasurer having desired Mr Treker to deliver memorial for a loan to Treasury, Secretary to deliver memorial to Treker at Treasury Chamber.
2. Further considered: parish of St Mary le Strand. Finding that Little Catherine Street and some adjoining courts are in St Martin and that two houses belonging to St Paul Covent Garden are separated from the parish by a broad street and they adjoin those parts intended to be added to St Mary le Strand, resolved that the 30 houses on the north side of White Hart Yard shall not be taken into St Mary le Strand, but that the addition be: out of St Martin's, the line of about 30 houses on the south side of Exeter Street, and the houses in Little Catherine Street and adjoining courts, and houses according to a survey thereof taken by James; and out of St Clement Danes, the houses bounded on west by Burleigh Street and on south by the Strand, including Exeter 'Change, in all about 45; and out of St Paul Covent Garden, the two houses marked 'c' in the said plan. Surveyors to make plan of the new parish.
3. Having fully considered question of Aylesbury chapel, and the objections, resolved that it be converted to a parish church. Agreement with Michell to be completed, and a warrant prepared for the purchase money out of next moneys coming in not already appropriated, with four per cent interest after nine months from now if the money be not sooner paid.

340. [p. 223] 13 Sep. 1723
1. Surveyors to submit account at next meeting of works most necessary to be put in hand immediately to fit churches for divine service (minute 2, 26 July last).
2. Solicitor to attend consecration of chapel in Ormond Street and present endowment to the bishop in the Commissioners' name.
3. Divine service to be performed in chapel purchased of Mr Michell in the same manner as at present, and Michell to take management thereof till further order.
Surveyors to report on a proper district for a parish to be allotted to the chapel, informing authorities of St James Clerkenwell.
4. Agent to inquire for parsonage house or site in St Mary le Strand.
5. Read petitions from inhabitants of Hanover Square complaining of Fletcher's dilatoriness in finishing church; and those of Limehouse complaining of Wingfield and Mahew, joiners, for not performing their contracts; referred to Surveyors.
6. Read petition of Stephen Hall for a consideration for looking after Spitalfields church; referred to Surveyors.

341. [p. 225] 27 Sep. 1723
1. Agent reported he had found neither house nor site in St Mary le Strand; to make further inquiry.

2. Solicitor reported he had yesterday presented the endowment for St George's chapel [Ormond Street] to the bishop.
3. James submitted plan of parish of St Mary le Strand as now established.
4. James submitted account of works necessary at churches mentioned in minute 2 of 26 July last.
5. Surveyors to direct the workmen at the several churches to go on without loss of time; contracts to be made with others, for works not already contracted for, as soon as may be.

342. [p. 226] 11 Oct. 1723
1. Read petition from East Greenwich for building a steeple and doing other works. They were told that the £25,000 to be raised by loan was not for building steeples but only to prepare for worship five of the churches already begun, but that Board was willing to receive representations about things they thought still wanting.
2. Read petition from St Mary le Strand. A font to be built in the church, and placing of some seats with regard to the situation of pulpit referred to Surveyors to report.
The Commissioners adhere to division of the parish already made.
3. Treasurer and Solicitor to prepare list of parish officers for St George the Martyr [Ormond Street], and refer it to Melmoth and Farrer.

343. [p. 227] 17 Oct. 1723
1. Solicitor submitted list of officers for St George the Martyr, formed with the assistance of Philipps and Farrer. William Chambers, Esq, of Ormond Street and Wm Proby, Esq, of Devonshire Street to be churchwardens; Valentine Hilder, Esq, of Glowster Street, captain of militia, and Rich. Brown-John of Ormond Street, coffee man, overseers; John Cox of Devonshire Street, corn chandler, and John Hurst of Eagle Street, undertaker, sidesmen; Rich. Barret of Glowster Street, grocer, and Thos Kirk of Devonshire Street, chandler, constables; John Saunders of Orange Street, silversmith, and Robt Pepper of Devonshire Street, pastrycook, headboroughs; Robt Beerford of Eagle Street, builder, and Hercules Brailsford of Orange Street, plumber, surveyors; Ed. Bates of Orange Street and Rich. Haberly of Devonshire Street, scavengers.
2. Advertisements ordered for joiner's works at Westminster and Limehouse, plumber's at Bloomsbury and painter's at Spitalfields churches.
3. Treasurer and Solicitor to prepare list of vestrymen for St George the Martyr and refer it to Philipps, Melmoth and Farrer.

344. [p. 229] 25 Oct. 1723
1. Read letter from Dean of Canterbury. Surveyors to direct workmen to cover in Deptford parsonage with all convenient speed, and parish to specify further works necessary for making church ready for worship.
2. On petition from East Greenwich: works specified on 1 May 1718, not yet done, amounting to £370, to be forthwith put in hand, and some joiner's work also.

3. Read petition from Stratford Bow. James forthwith to prepare plan for a minister's house not exceeding £800.
4. Read letter from John Wingfield, joiner, concerning contracts for Limehouse church. James to acquaint him that he must give security for performing his contract, and give in prices for works not contained in contract.
5. Authorities of St James's Clerkenwell to be notified that the Board will at its next meeting settle a district to be allotted to St John's chapel.
6. Wm Langley to be employed for joiner's work at Westminster, his price being lowest; Solicitor to prepare contract.

345. [p. 231] 1 Nov. 1723
1. James reported that Grove, carpenter at Deptford, being lately dead and his executors not being willing to finish the works, he ordered Meard to finish carpenter's works at church and parsonage.
2. Holding to be appointed partner with Wingfield for joiner's work at Limehouse, his former partner Mahew having left the kingdom.
3. Consideration of district for St John's chapel Clerkenwell deferred, Mr Hammond on the part of the parishioners of St James's requiring more time.

346. [p. 232] 8 Nov. 1723
1. Sir J. Philipps, Melmoth concurring (Farrer being out of town), delivered list of 50 persons proper to be of the vestry of St George the Martyr.
2. Vestry to consist of 30, with minister and churchwardens for the time being.
3. Every Commissioner present to have a copy of the list by Monday night, and bring paper rolled up, written with 30 names for the vestry.
4. Sam. Worrall to finish carpenter's work for Spitalfields church, *vice* Grove deceased, on basis of Grove's contract.
6. [*sic*] Agent submitted plan for site for parsonage house and church yard for church in the Strand, proposed by Mr Moses West for £1,000. James and Skeat to report.
7. Preedy to do painter's work at Spitalfields church.
8. Fincher complaining that he cannot perform his contract for plumber's work at church near Hanover Square because of the rise in price of lead, the Board allow increase or reduction in the contract price consistent with current price of lead at the time the work is done.
9. Osmond, plumber, to be employed to cover in Bloomsbury church, the Board agreeing to make increase or reduction in his price consistent with current price of lead when the work is done.

347. [p. 234] 15 Nov. 1723
1. The present churchwardens to be two of the 30 to compose standing vestry of St George the Martyr.
2. Elected 28 other vestrymen; approved by Bishop of London. Ordered that the said gentlemen be the vestry; Sir Robt Raymond (attorney-general), Sir P. Yorke (solicitor-general), Chas Downing, John Whetham, Wm Kinnaston, Jas Lightbone, Thos Huxley, Esquires, Capt

John Long, all of Red Lion Square; Sir Harry Bateman, Sir Ed. Gould, Robt Thornhill and Walt. Plommer, Esquires, of Queen's Square; William Chambers, Thos Andrew, Thos Trenchfield, gent., Rich. Benion, baker, of Ormond Street; Wm Proby, Wm Higginson and Robt Pauncefoot, Esquires, of Devonshire Street; Andrew Broughton, Esq, Rich. Barets, Esq, grocer of Glocester Street, Hy Martin, Esq, of East Street, Thos Thayer, Esq, Graves Martin, Esq, of New Street, Thos Penny, apothecary of Red Lion Street, John Trower, baker of Lee Street, Ralph Prior, oilman, Ed. Bates, tallow chandler of Theobalds Row.

3. Solicitor to prepare instrument of appointment, to which Commissioners are to set their hands and seals, for next meeting.

4. James submitted memorial about division of St James Clerkenwell. Copy to be given to Michell, who is to bring his remarks by next meeting.

5. Treasurer to advance by imprest £15 to Hall for looking after Spitalfields church and repairing fences.

6. James submitted account of works necessary in and about Deptford church; several were agreed to and others rejected as noted in margin of the account.

7. Mrs Leacroft presented bill of fees for passing the accounts of her late husband; referred to next meeting. Secretary to consult the books and see what Board's practice has been.

348. [p. 236] 22 Nov. 1723

1. Signed warrant for paying £15 to Hall.

2. Michell brought in remarks on memorial delivered by James touching division of Clerkenwell.

3. Mrs Leacroft's final bill referred to Hiccocks and Melmoth.

4. Read petition from John Foltrop, Ezekiel Cook and Jas King praying that £129. 13*s*. 5*d*. due to John Grove, carpenter at Millbank church, may may be paid upon their producing a letter of attorney. Resolved that the money cannot be paid regularly and with safety.

5. Having considered manner of pewing the churches now in hand, unanimously resolved that in all churches now building or hereafter to be built the pews shall be single.

6. Read petition from Rev Mr Trebeck for providing a parsonage house for church near Hanover Square. Agent to inquire for house or site.

7. Solicitor submitted draft instrument for appointing vestry of St George the Martyr; approved, and to be engrossed to be signed at the next meeting.

8. Hammond appeared on behalf of inhabitants of St James Clerkenwell and desired a week to make his remarks on Michell's paper, and that he might have a copy of it; granted.

9. The work at Strand church mentioned in James's memorial to be finished forthwith.

10. Warrant to be prepared for paying workmen up to Lady Day 1723.

349. [p. 238] 28 Nov. 1723

1. Agent mentioned two houses proper for minister's house for church near Hanover Square.

2. Signed instrument appointing vestry of St George the Martyr.
3. Hiccocks and Melmoth reported they had examined Mrs Leacroft's final bill for £80. 13*s*., which was allowed.
4. Hammond delivered his remarks on Michell's paper. All the papers referred to Dr Waddington, Ellis and Melmoth to report on division of the parish at next meeting. James and Solicitor to attend.
5. James reported that font for Strand church was ready. Ordered all despatch in clearing church and setting up font. When this done, Bishop of London to be desired to consecrate the church.
6. Warrant to be prepared for paying £80. 13*s*. to Mrs Leacroft.

350. [p. 240] 6 Dec. 1723
1. Read report of Waddington, Ellis and Melmoth with some other papers about the intended district in Clerkenwell. Resolved that north boundary of new parish be made by a line passing from the west end of Mutton Lane over Clerkenwell Green through Aylesbury Street to St John's Street, thence returning south through the middle of St John's Street and passing through Sutton Street alias Swan Alley into Goswell Street and thence the limits as made by the ancient bounds of the parish on side next the Charterhouse ground and continued to south-west corner next Cow Cross. Solicitor, with James's assistance to prepare deed accordingly.
2. Signed warrant for paying £80. 13*s*. to Mrs Leacroft.
3. Read petition of executors of Ed. Tufnell and Joshua Fletcher who undertook to furnish stone for building church in St Olave's Southwark; referred to Surveyors.
4. Laying out of districts for churches now building and such chapels as may be converted into parish churches to be considered at next meeting, and what chapels are fit to be so converted.
5. Surveyors and Agent to view two houses in Grosvenor Street proposed for a minister's house for church near Hanover Square.
6. John Grove having assigned his contract for Westminster church to John Lock, Lock to proceed with remaining works on foot of Grove's contract.

351. [p. 242] 11 Dec. 1723
1. Executed deed dividing parish of St James Clerkenwell.
2. John Meard, carpenter, to carry on carpenter's work of Limehouse and Wapping churches on foot of [Jas] Grove's contract.
3. Simmons to attend next meeting to settle accounts for 1723.
4. Surveyors to give directions for a font for St John Clerkenwell; when ready, to report to Bishop of London so that he may consecrate. Solicitor to attend consecration of Clerkenwell and Strand churches to present the deeds in the Commissioners' name.
5. Solicitor and Surveyors to consider proper districts to be laid out for churches now building, with assistance of such inhabitants as they judge convenient, and then to draw a plan of each district to lay before the Board.
6. Dean and Chapter of Westminster to be asked whether they have any

objection to converting chapel now called the new chapel in Westminster into a parish church.

7. Trustees of chapel in King Street Golden Square to be applied to, whether they have any objection to its being converted into a parish church.

8. Secretary to make separate copies of the foregoing minutes and wait on Bishop of Rochester (Dean of Westminster) and Dr Clarke, Rector of St James's, with them.

352. [p. 244] 19 Dec. 1723

1. Nicholson and other inhabitants of Strand parish delivered memorandum of works wanting in the church; several ordered to be done.

2. Simmons attended to settle accounts for 1722 [*sic*]; his bill allowed.

3. Examined and signed books of works for 1722.

4. Read petition from Arnot, plumber for church in Lombard Street, praying an allowance because of the increase in the price of lead. Allowed addition or abatement consistent with price of lead when work is done.

353. [p. 245] 10 Jan. 1723/24

1. Solicitor to prepare draft of deed in pursuance of order of vestry of St Giles Cripplegate dated 15 Oct. 1723.

2. Waddington and Peck, assisted by Treasurer, Solicitor and Agent to consider of persons proper to be officers and vestry of new parish of St John Clerkenwell, by next meeting.

3. Trustees of King Street chapel delivered a presentation why their chapel should not be converted into a parish church.

4. Jenner proposed a house in Grosvenor Street for £1,300 for minister of church near Hanover Square; agreed, if it can be made freehold at that price.

5. Bill for settling a maintenance on the ministers of the new churches to be considered at the next meeting, and notice to be given in summons.

6. Surveyors to report on condition of houses and ground at east end of chapel lately purchased of Michell [Aylesbury Chapel].

354. [p. 246] 17 Jan. 1723/24

1. Dr Bennet proposed that Cripplegate parish should obtain Chancery decree to make a good title to ground proposed by them to be added to site for new church intended to be bought of Mr[s] Fewtrell. Further consideration deferred until Dr Bennet obtains such decree.

2. Vestry of St John Clerkenwell to consist of 20 persons and minister and churchwardens for the time being; every Commissioner present to have by Monday night a copy of the list delivered by Waddington and Peck, and bring in writing on a paper rolled up names of 20 such persons to compose the vestry.

3. Considered the bill for maintenance of the ministers and made some progress therein.

4. Petition of Foltrop, Cook and King referred to next meeting; Treasurer to attend.

355. [p. 247] 23 Jan. 1723/24
1. Reconsidered minute 2 of last meeting: Waddington and Peck with assistance of Treasurer, Solicitor and Agent to bring in larger list of persons proper to be the vestry.
2. Following to be appointed officers for St John Clerkenwell: John Ekins and Simon Michell, esquires, churchwardens; Wm Bury, esq., and Aaron Gibbs, gent., sidesmen; Wm Gambell and Geo. Greaves, carpenter, overseers of the poor; Edward Hutchins, gent. and Wm Wiggins of Turnmill St, tallow chandler, surveyors of highways; Thos Bradley, cheesemonger, and Sam. Jeacock, baker, scavengers; Joseph Jackson, bricklayer, and Hy Jeffreys of Bartle's [Bartlet's] St, cutler, constables; John Banks, barber, and Thos Wood, tobacco pipe maker of Turnmill St, headboroughs.
3. Petition from Dr Marshall, Nich. Jeffreys and Edm. Fenwick, esquires, that they have lately erected a chapel near Red Lion Street, and proposing to convey their interest to the Commissioners that it may be converted into a parish church. Ordered that application be made to obtain a clause in an act of parliament to enable the Commissioners to treat with proprietors of chapels erected after the ninth of Anne, as well as for those already then built. Solicitor to prepare such a clause.
4. Solicitor to report on sufficiency of letter of attorney of John Grove and the bond of indemnification offered to Board by John Foltrop and others against double payment of £129. 13*s*. 5*d*. ordered to be paid to John Grove by warrant dated 24 Oct. 1722.
5. Officers appointed for St Mary le Strand: Jas Gascoigne and Robt Poney churchwardens; Jas Cornish and Peter Annet, overseers; John Matthews and Thos Towell, scavengers.

356. [p. 249] 25 Jan. 1723/24
1. Considered bill for maintenance of the ministers, and made some progress therein. Final consideration to be referred to next meeting, and no other business to intervene.

357. [p. 250] 31 Jan. 1723/24
1. Waddington delivered larger list of persons proper for vestry of St John Clerkenwell. Commissioners to have a copy, and each to bring written list of 20 names rolled up.
2. Read petition from Company of Parish Clerks setting forth that they are not enabled by their charter to receive weekly bills from any of the new churches. Solicitor to prepare clause for endowment bill pursuant to prayer of petition.
3. Warrants to be prepared for paying half year's salary to officers and half year's rent to Mrs Leacroft.
4. Read report from Solicitor of Grove's letter of attorney and Foltrop's bond; Treasurer to pay Foltrop and others sum of £129. 13*s*. 5*d*.
5. Considered bill for maintenance of the ministers and made several amendments therein.

358. [p. 251] 7 Feb. 1723/24
1. Lists of persons to compose vestry for St John Clerkenwell being

brought in, it appeared the majority fell on: Thos. Pinder, Matt. Howit, Robt Tothill, Thos Isted, Wm Brooke, John Ekins, Simon Michell, Edward Lovibond, Wm Bury, Chas Floyer, John Forster, Rich. Lechmere, esquires; Robt Dymond, Rich. Templar, gent.; Wm Croaker, mercer, Nich. Goodwin, brewer, Wm Downing, printer, Wm Gamble, silversmith, Abr. [illegible] salesman, Geo. Greaves, carpenter.

Bishop of London consenting, ordered that the list be the vestry. Solicitor to prepare instrument.

2. Solicitor brought clauses to enable Commissioners to build with brick, and to enable Company of Parish Clerks to receive accounts of christenings and burials from clerks of the new churches; read, and directed to be added to the bill. The bill as now settled to be offered to parliament.

3. Bishop of London to be desired to advise with Chancellor of the Exchequer about the most proper method of bringing the bill into the House of Commons.

4. Copies of bill to be given to Chancellor of the Exchequer, Speaker, person introducing it, and Mr Scrope, Secretary of the Treasury. Also a brief of the bill and a copy of a paper for filling up the blanks.

5. Commissioners at next meeting to proceed to annual election of officers; notice to be given in summons.

6. Warrants signed for payment of officers' salaries to Christmas last, and one year's rent.

359. [p. 253] 14 Feb. 1723/24

1. Bishop of London reported that he had applied to Chancellor of the Exchequer and others about most proper method to bring in the bill, and had received very favourable answers.

2. Solicitor to prepare two dozen briefs of bill for next meeting, and to make out copies of bill for attorney-general and solicitor-general.

3. Agreed that the same officers be continued for a year at same salaries.

4. Agreed that a gratuity of 50 guineas be given James for his past services and more than ordinary attendances upon the works and this Board.

5. Philipps, Waddington, Deans of the Arches and Chichester, Hiccocks and Melmoth to be desired to attend and solicit bill for maintenance of ministers while it is depending in the Commons.

6. Agreed to a proposal of Sir R. Grosvenor's for sale of ground rent of a house in Grosvenor Street proposed for minister's house: Board to give 30 years purchase and bear all legal charges. Resolved to purchase the said house of John Jenner for £1,300.

7. Executed instrument for settling vestry of St John Clerkenwell.

8. Secretary to remind Board at next meeting to consider one year's interest due to Sir R. Grosvenor for purchase money of ground near Oliver's Mount bought for churchyard for church near Hanover Square.

360. [p. 255] 20 Feb. 1723/24

1. One year's interest on the purchase money to be paid to Sir R. Grosvenor if he insists on it.

2. Empowered the six members appointed to attend the bill in parlia-

ment to employ a solicitor to follow bill through both Houses and give them notice when it is necessary for them to attend, etc.

361. [p. 256] 27 Feb. 1723/24
1. Read report about minister's house and church yard for St John Clerkenwell; referred to another meeting.
2. James delivered three papers about Millbank church: account of total expended, account of extraordinary expenses because of the tenderness of the foundation, and account of money necessary to finish church.
3. Treasurer to imprest £200 to Jenner, part of £1,300 for his house.
4. Treasurer to bring in account of monies already received at Exchequer for the Commission.
5. Agent to procure best information available about perquisites likely to arise from districts assigned for new churches.

362. [p. 257] 3 Mar. 1723/24
1. James to estimate for making a parsonage house for St John Clerkenwell on the foundation of two old houses bought from Michell; and Agent to inquire after a suitable house. Other affairs about new parish referred to another time.
2. Petition from inhabitants of St Mary le Strand for appointment of a vestry to be considered at next meeting.
3. Ordered advertisement for joiners to bring in proposals for Spitalfields church.
4. Petition from Dunn about payment for his work at St Mary Woolnoth; referred to Surveyors to report at next meeting.
5. Agent to inquire about £1,100 paid to trustees of Ormond Street chapel and how the sum has been applied; Solicitor to attend next meeting with the deeds.
6. Bishop of London acquainted Board of great readiness shown by Mr Poultney [Pulteney] and Mr Onslow to promote the bill. On discoursing with several MPs they found it advisable in order to facilitate the bill's passing that estimate be made of perquisites and other profits arising from districts annexed to new churches, to be laid before the House.
7. Resolved that Bishop of London be desired to return Board's thanks to Pulteney and Onslow.
8. Resolved that this Board judges it impossible to make the inquiries expected from them so as to be ready to present them to House of Commons with a view to passing the bill this session. Board will immediately commence inquiries so as to lay information before House at opening of next session.

363. [p. 259] 13 Mar. 1723/24
1. James brought in a plan for a minister's house for Stratford Bow, estimated at £800.
2. Surveyors to bring estimates by next meeting for building parsonage house for St John Clerkenwell; other matters concerning that parish referred to a fuller Board.

3. Dean of the Arches, Ellis, Treasurer, Solicitor and Agent to consider list of proper persons for vestrymen for St Mary le Strand.
4. James to attend next meeting, when joiners' prices for Spitalfields church to be considered.
5. Solicitor to attend next meeting with purchase deeds of Ormond Street chapel.
6. Secretary to write out minutes about said chapel and lay them before next meeting with the papers belonging thereto.
7. Board will at next meeting consider table of burial fees for St George the Martyr.
8. Bishop of London reported that he had thanked Pulteney and Onslow.

364. [p. 261] 20 Mar. 1723/24
1. Dean of the Arches and Ellis assisted by Treasurer, Solicitor and Agent brought in list of proper persons for vestry for St Mary le Strand.
2. Resolved that vestry consist of 14 persons and minister and church wardens; every Commissioner present to have copy of list of names by Monday night, and bring 14 names in writing in a paper rolled up.
3. Michell to submit proposal for house formerly proposed by him for parsonage for St John Clerkenwell; other matters about parish deferred.
4. Joiners' proposals for Spitalfields church referred to Surveyors to report who is lowest.
5. Table of burial fees for St George the Martyr to be considered at next meeting.
6. Treasurer to advance £700 to Dunn for work at St Mary Woolnoth; and to labourers for taking care of lead at the churches in Bloomsbury and near Hanover Square such sums as Surveyors advise to be proper.
7. Solicitor to have fresh directions to prosecute any who lay dirt or rubbish on site purchased in Old Street.
8. Advertisement ordered for painters' and glaziers' proposals for Bloomsbury and Hanover Square churches.
9. Renewed minute of 11 December last about districts for new parishes; the officers appointed to go on without loss of time.

365. [p. 263] 27 Mar. 1724
1. Gabriel Appleby to be employed as joiner at Spitalfields church, as the lowest proposal.
2. Consideration of burial fees for St George the Martyr deferred until report made about money transferred for purchase of seats.
3. £650 to be paid Michell for house proposed by him for a parsonage for St John Clerkenwell, he making a good title and laying out £50 on the house as Surveyors appoint.
4. Scriven to be employed as glazier at Bloomsbury and Hanover Square churches, as lowest proposal.
5. Petition of William Prat about his claim to Aylesbury chapel [Clerkenwell] referred to Solicitor.
6. Michell's title deeds to be referred to counsel.

7. Geo. Clayfield to be employed as painter at Hanover Square and Bloomsbury churches.
8. Advertisements ordered for bricklayers' and carpenters' proposals for minister's house, Stratford bow.
9. Read petition from Osmond, plumber; £500 to be imprested to him for carrying on works in his churches; and upon Fincher's petition, £400 to him likewise for Hanover Square church.
10. The following were elected as vestrymen for St Mary le Strand: Wm Foley, Esq., Robt Nicholson, pewterer, Robt Sparks, brazier, Wm Wilson, draper, Fcs Sawle, draper, Robt Shelly, draper, John Walsh, instrument-maker, Robt Powney, stationer, Thos Phill, upholder, John Verdon, shoemaker, Patricius Underwood, stuffman, Jacob Tonson, bookseller, Adam Hog, tailor, Chas Danvers, draper. Bishop of London consenting, ordered that minister and churchwardens for the time being, and the 14 named, be the vestry.
11. Solicitor to prepare instrument for appointing the vestry.

366. [p. 265] 10 Apr. 1724
1. On account of Solicitor's absence, Michell's title referred to next meeting; Solicitor to have notice to attend.
2. Referred to next meeting a proposal of Mr Pomeroy and Mr Newman concerning a passage from Ratcliffe Highway to new church at Wapping; Surveyors to have notice to attend.
3. Warrant to be prepared for paying a quarter's rent to Mrs Leacroft.
4. Hester to be employed for brickwork at parsonage house, Stratford Bow, and Meard for carpenter's work.
5. Manner of contracting with the workmen employed to be considered at next meeting.
6. Solicitor to submit contract with Wilson for the ground in Old Street.
7. Surveyors to be reminded at next meeting to make due progress in laying out districts for the new churches.
8. Read petition from vestry of St John Clerkenwell for £150 for supplying defects. Agreed that £150 be given, the Commissioners' resolution that they will have no concern with any additions or improvements in new churches after consecration not being understood by petitioners at time of consecration.

367. [p. 267] 24 Apr. 1724
1. Warrant to be prepared for paying Michell £650 for house for the minister, St John Clerkenwell, he giving a note to the Treasurer for £50 to be laid out on the house as Surveyors shall direct.
2. Rejected Pomeroy and Newman's proposal.
3. Surveyors to report on Mary Goodchild's petition about price of groining at Spitalfields church.
4. Vestry of St John Clerkenwell to be informed that Surveyors are directed to inspect application of £150 for covering ceiling floor of church with boards, enlarging vestry room and making new altar piece and rail at communion table.

368. [p. 268] 1 May 1724
1. Mrs Goodchild to be allowed 6*d*. per foot for groining, that being the general price.
2. On petition of Isaac Mansfield, plasterer, Treasurer to pay him £500 by imprest for work done in Spitalfields, Hanover Square and Westminster churches.
3. Warrants to be prepared for pay £1,100 to Jenner for his interest in house in Grosvenor Street, and £135 to Sir R. Grosvenor and others for ground rent.
4. Marshall reported from trustees of St George's chapel, Ormond Street, that they are ready to give satisfaction to Board for money paid them for purchasing pews, but they desire written statement of what Board requires.
5. Deans of Chichester and the Arches to draw up what they conceive proper to be delivered to the trustees and lay it before next meeting.
6. Solicitor's bill of fees being delivered to Melmoth and Hiccocks, ordered warrant to be prepared for £143. 10*s*. 9*d*.
7. Signed Michell's warrant for £650.

369. [p. 270] 15 May 1724
1. Bennet submitted paper on difficulty of conveying some ground belonging to St Giles Cripplegate adjoining Mrs Fewtrell's ground; referred to Solicitor to take advice.
2. Dean of Chichester being out of town and Dean of the Arches being obliged to attend elsewhere, the deans to bring answer to Ormond Street chapel trustees to next meeting.
3. Marshall to obtain copy of burial fees of St Andrew Holborn for next meeting.
4. Read petition from Commissioners appointed to inspect decoration of church near Hanover Square signifying that they intend an organ for the church and desire Commissioners to build a loft for it. Resolved that Board conceive themselves not at liberty to proceed further than providing convenient seats for parishioners.
5. A plain brick wall five ft high to be built to enclose ground purchased of Sir R. Grosvenor for a burial place for church near Hanover Square.
6. Signed warrants for paying £135 to Sir R. Grosvenor, £143. 10*s*. 9*d*. to Solicitor, and £1,300 to John Jenner.
7. Bennet reported that, having acquainted vestry of St Giles Cripplegate that he had delivered to Commissioners the vestry's agreement to convey to them Bear and Ragged Staff Yard provided they would allow parishioners to bury in the ground in Old Street, and that Commissioners had answered that they were willing, as soon as conveyance was made, to divide the parish and give parishioners of Old Street church district free leave to bury there, vestry unanimously acquiesced.

370. [p. 272] 18 June 1724
1. Trustees of St George the Martyr in whose hands £1,153. 6*s*. 7*d*. was left for purchasing pews desiring to know in writing what Board requires of them,

2. Agreed that trustees do lay before Board at next meeting an account of how the money has been applied; whether any pews have been bought, and of whom and for what; in whom such pews are now vested, and in whose hands the remainder of the money now is; whether any has been placed out at interest, and on what security.
3. Copy to be given to Dr Marshall for the trustees.
4. Sjt Baines reported that Duke of Montagu ready to come to agreement for the more effectual division of St George the Martyr from St Andrew Holborn; will agree to any division of rights and dues between the rectors which the Board think proper, provided the patronage of St George the Martyr be vested in him and his heirs.
5. Agreed that the Board is satisfied that the duke is patron of St Andrew Holborn, and will treat with him as such.
6. Agreed that the patronage of St George the Martyr be vested in the Duke of Montagu and his heirs in the same manner as the patronage of St Andrew Holborn is now vested; and that all rights, etc, arising from the district allotted for St George the Martyr be forever vested in the rector of the parish by such settlements as counsel shall direct.
7. Solicitor to prepare draft of such a settlement.

371. [p. 274] 29 June 1724
1. Bishop of London reported that Marshall had informed him that the money for purchasing pews in St George the Martyr was in the hands of Mr Chambers who is at Bath; at his return a satisfactory account would be given.
2. Mrs Goodchild declines finishing bricklayer's work at Limehouse church. Lucas, recommended by Hawksmoor, to be employed to finish it on terms of the late Goodchild's contract.
3. Hawksmoor to deliver his draft of division of parish of Deptford with a district for the new church to the parish authorities, to report their opinion.
4. Bills of Busby for watching Bloomsbury church and Newsham for watching that near Hanover Square referred to Surveyors.
5. Solicitor presented draft for the further division of St George the Martyr which was read, and ordered to be engrossed.

372. [p. 276] 13 July 1724
1. Hawksmoor submitted drafts for division of parishes of St Margaret Westminster and St Giles in the Fields.
2. Hawksmoor to deliver same to parish authorities for their consideration.
3. Warrant to be prepared for paying £315, one year's interest, to Sir R. Grosvenor.
4. Treasurer to pay John Busby and Sam. Newsham, watchmen of Bloomsbury and Hanover Square churches, £10. 16*s*. each for watching for 24 four weeks to 4 July.
5. James to acquaint Rector of Stepney and churchwardens of the hamlets of Ratcliff, Bethnal Green, Mile End Old and New Town with division intended for new parishes of Spitalfields, Wapping–Stepney and Limehouse, for their consideration.

6. Treasurer to pay following sums by imprest: to Whitton, bricklayer (Hanover Square) £300; Mansfield, plasterer (Hanover Square) £300; Holden, joiner (Limehouse) £250; Wilkins, plasterer (Wapping) £200.
7. Solicitor to lay before Ward [counsel] proviso he had drawn up concerning agreement with Duke of Montagu for dividing parish of St Andrew Holborn, with two queries, and take his opinion.

373. [p. 278] 27 July 1724
1. Signed warrant for paying £315 to Sir R. Grosvenor.
2. Hawksmoor reported by letter delivering plans of parishes of St Margaret Westminster and St Giles in the Fields, but Bishops of Rochester and Bangor being out of town he thought the parishes could not make their report till their lordships' return. Dean of Canterbury and inhabitants of Deptford had agreed to plan proposed.
3. Marshall snr reported that Mr Harvey of Comb and his son were willing to join Duke of Montagu in a proper instrument for dividing St Andrew Holborn; Solicitor to prepare draft agreement pursuant to Ward's opinion of 15 July.
4. The two Rectors of Stepney attending were called in and heard concerning districts for the new parishes. Ordered that entire hamlet of Spitalfields be parish of the new church.
5. The inhabitants of Mile End Old Town appeared to show cause that the hamlet ought to be left undivided and part of district of the mother church.
6. Some of principal inhabitants of Ratcliff and Limehouse submitted written states of these hamlets.
7. Notice to be given to minister and principal inhabitants of Poplar to show why it should not be added to Limehouse.
8. Referred to Surveyors petitions of Strong and Fletcher for imprest money to enable them to carry on works, as also Edward Leny's complaint of damage to his house by building of Bloomsbury church.

374. [p. 280] 31 Aug. 1724
1. Referred to Surveyors petitions of Goodchild, Mrs Goodchild, Dunn, Walshaw, Whitaker and Sarah Plumpton.
2. Advertisements ordered for joiners' and plasterers' proposals for Bloomsbury church, for glaziers' for Spitalfields, and plasterers' and glaziers' for Lombard Street churches.
3. On a representation from East India Company, resolved that Commissioners have no objection to their proposed application to parliament, and that meantime they are ready to come to conditional agreement for converting Poplar chapel into a parish church; Commissioners also willing to suspend settling what shall be added to Limehouse parish for a month to enable Company to make their proposal, further deferment being inconvenient to Board.
4. Treasurer presented a memorial that an overpayment had been made to Frenchfield for St George's chapel; copy to be delivered to Frenchfield and he desired to attend next meeting; Solicitor also to attend with purchase deed.

5. Signed warrants for paying £5,250 to workmen, and £21.12*s*. to watchmen for Bloomsbury and Hanover Square churches.
6. Read and confirmed table of burial fees for St Mary le Strand: for the pavement about the church enclosed with iron palisadoes: to rector, £1. 10*s*.; churchwardens, £2; clerk, 5*s*.; sexton, 3*s*.; gravemaker, 2*s*. 6*d*.; bell, 3*s*.; bearers, 6*s*. Signed by minister, churchwardens and seven vestrymen.

375. [p. 283] 14 Sep 1724
1. James reported opinion of memorials and petitions referred to him. Following payments ordered by way of imprest: Strong, mason, £1,500; Dunn, mason, £500; Fletcher, mason, £1,500; Meard, carpenter, £800; Whitaker, digger, £50; John Walshaw, joiner, £300; Joseph Goodchild, glazier, £50; Sarah Plumpton, exec. of Lot Plumpton, £20; Mary Goodchild, bricklayer, £250; Lucas, bricklayer, £150; Turner, painter, £40. Warrant to be prepared for next meeting.
2. Mrs Skeat to carry on smith's work in partnership with Cleave on foot of contract made with Cleave and Skeat, her late husband.
3. Hawksmoor to produce plan of district of new parish of Deptford, to which he reported on 27 July last that Dean of Canterbury and vestry had agreed, and that it be delivered to Solicitor to be enrolled.
4. Board were informed of death of Skeat, their Agent. Although necessary to appoint a successor, the labour being considerably less than formerly, resolved not to allow more than £40 p.a. salary. Resolved that John Prichard be Agent at £40 p.a.
5. Frenchfield having delivered his answer about payment for St George's chapel, which cleared up the matter to Treasurer's satisfaction, ordered Treasurer to lay answer before Auditor of the Imprest, and if further difficulty arises, to lay it before Board.
6. Read petition from governors of Free School of Charity of Queen Elizabeth in St Olave's Southwark about walls of the ground being out of repair; Agent to report to next meeting.
7. Several proposals being submitted, ordered that Joseph Goodchild perform glazier's work at Spitalfields and Lombard Street churches; Mansfield, plasterer's at Bloomsbury; Wilkins that at Lombard Street.
8. Treasurer reported that Auditor complained there were several miscalculations in books of works of the new churches from 1717 to 1722 to his prejudice. Ordered for the future that all books of the new churches be delivered to Treasurer to be examined by him three weeks before warrant for paying workmen be signed.

376. [p. 286] 28 Sep. 1724
1. John Reynolds to do painter's work at minister's house erecting at Bow.
2. Thos Philipps to do joiner's work at Bloomsbury church.
3. Signed warrant for impresting money to workmen totalling £5,160.
4. Agent reported concerning Artillery Ground in St Olave's parish. Resolved that Board not having occasion for the ground do not think it convenient to incur charge of dividing it with a new wall at present; but have directed breaches in the other wall to be made up.

5. Advertisement ordered for ironmongers' proposals for furnishing new churches at Westminster, Great George Street [Hanover Square], Bloomsbury, Lombard Street, Spitalfields, Wapping, and Limehouse with pew locks and hinges according to patterns at the office, and square irons to strengthen pews.

377. [p. 288] 12 Oct. 1724
1. Read memorial from commissioners for decoration of church erecting near Hanover Square, complaining of Fletcher's dilatoriness in carrying on mason's work. Fletcher, called in to answer, received Board's reprimand, and promised to proceed with all despatch.
2. On the complaint of some inhabitants of St Mary Woolnoth of the masons' dilatoriness, masons ordered to attend next meeting.
3. Read petition from inhabitants of Bethnal Green; resolved that Board will receive a proposal from the proprietor for a site for a church etc.
4. Solicitor to attend next meeting about bill for providing an endowment for ministers of new churches.
5. Peck delivered account of burial fees of hamlets of Spitalfields, Wapping Stepney, and Limehouse for one year; which Secretary is to keep till called for.
6. Bishop of Rochester reported that Dean and Chapter of Westminster are willing that new chapel in the Broadway be converted into a parish church. Solicitor to consider proper method of proceeding.
7. Warrant to be prepared for impresting £350 to Gilham for joiner's work at Greenwich and Deptford churches.
8. James delivered boundary for new parish at Limehouse; which Secretary is to keep.
9. Solicitor's bill referred to Hiccocks and Melmoth for examination and settlement.
10. Surveyors to report at next meeting on smiths' proposals for locks, etc.

378. [p. 290] 26 Oct. 1724
1. Melmoth having examined Secretary's bill, warrant to be prepared.
2. Secretary to new model bill for providing a maintenance for ministers by next meeting.
3. Signed warrant for paying £350 to Gilham.
4. Goff to be employed for making locks and hinges and squares and keys for churches of Hanover Square, Westminster and Bloomsbury, and Robins for St Mary Woolnoth and Spitalfields; Cleave for Limehouse and Wapping.
5. On petition by Langley, joiner at Westminster church, ordered £300 to be imprested and warrant prepared.
6. Hawksmoor submitted district taken out of Deptford; Solicitor to take care that the district be enrolled. [Boundary details given at length.]
7. Solicitor to take care that district to be Limehouse parish be enrolled. [Details of boundaries given.]

379. [p. 293] 6 Nov. 1724
1. Bishop of Rochester reported that Dean and Chapter of Westminster

desire longer to consider question of converting Broadway chapel to a parish church.
2. Solicitors brought new modelled bill for maintenance of ministers, and Commissioners made some amendments.
3. Read letter from Hester, bricklayer for minister's house at Bow; ordered £150 to be imprested to him and a warrant to be prepared.
4. Ellis desired to settle Secretary's bill of incidents.
5. Secretary to prepare conveyance from Mrs Fewtrell for site for a new church in parish of Cripplegate, and a conveyance from vicar and churchwardens to Commissioners.

380. [p. 294] 13 Nov. 1724
1. New modelled bill for maintenance read and after some amendments approved by Commissioners. Solicitor to wait on Onslow with the bill for his perusal.
2. Ellis having examined Secretary's bill, it was allowed; warrant to be prepared for £50.
3. Read White's proposal for a site for a church at Bethnal Green; Surveyors to view and report.
4. Agent to wait on Deacon to deliver amount of annual produce of tax on coals for three years last.
5. James to put Hawksmoor in mind of bringing in plans of new districts of Bloomsbury and Millbank.
6. Warrant to be prepared for paying £250 to Lock, carpenter at Millbank church.
7. Treasurer to advance £8 to Busby, watchman at Bloomsbury church.

381. [p. 295] 19 Nov. 1724
1. Agent submitted amount of produce of tax on coals:

for the year ending Christmas	1721	£69,561. 18*s*. 8*d*.
	1722	£67,656. 16*s*.
	1723	£66,595. 7*s*.

2. Hawksmoor submitted plans of districts for Bloomsbury and Millbank.
3. District as submitted by Hawksmoor for Bloomsbury to be district of new parish.
4. Solicitor reported that he had waited on Onslow with endowment bill, who had perused it and thought a clause should be added forbidding any two new churches to be held by one minister. Solicitor to prepare such a clause.
5. Imprest warrant to be prepared for paying £350 to Worrall, carpenter at Spitalfields church.
6. Signed warrants for paying £250 to Lock and £50 to the Secretary.

382. [p. 296] 27 Nov. 1724
1. Resumed consideration of endowment bill and what should be proposed for endowment of each, and what proportion should be appropriated to each out of the £60,000, more or less, appropriated by parliament towards maintaining the ministers.

2. Signed warrant for paying Worrall £350.
3. James submitted plan of and report on site proposed by White for church at Bethnal Green. Agreed to purchase two and a half acres at £4 p.a. at 20 years purchase; White to enjoy rents and profits till foundation of intended church laid.
4. Treasurer to pay Hall £20 for watching Spitalfields church.

383. [p. 297] 30 Nov. 1724
1. Made some further progress in endowment bill with assistance of Pulteney and Onslow who were present.

384. [p. 298] 4 Dec. 1724
1. Made further amendments in endowment bill with assistance of Pulteney and Onslow. Solicitor to prepare several copies.
2. Hawksmoor submitted new districts of Bloomsbury and Millbank to convert them into parishes. Solicitor to take care that these districts be enrolled; and also to prepare draft representation and petition to the King to recommend bill to parliament.
3. Signed warrant for paying Hall £20.
4. Warrant to be prepared for paying David Arnot £250 for plumber's work at Lombard Street church.

385. [p. 299] 11 Dec. 1724
1. Signed warrant for paying Arnot £250.
2. Read draft representation and petition to King to recommend endowment bill to parliament. Solicitor to wait on Dean of the Arches to settle it by next meeting.
3. Solicitor reported that he had delivered copies of the bill to Speaker, Master of the Rolls, Pulteney, Attorney-General and Solicitor-General and Onslow. Ordered to deliver copies to Mr Walpole and Scrope, and prepare abstracts by next meeting.

386. [p. 300] 18 Dec. 1724
1. Dean of the Arches delivered draft representation etc. to King, which was approved. Secretary to prepare fair copy and wait on Commissioners present today for their signatures. Bishops of London, St Asaph, Rochester, Carlisle or any two or more of them be desired to wait on Lord Townshend with representation.
2. Read petitions from Osmond, plumber, Robins, smith, Cleave and Mrs Skeat for imprest money.
3. Letter to be sent to Marshall that Board expect a satisfactory account of money for purchasing pews in St George's church in Chambers's hands, pursuant to his promise of 29 June last.
4. Warrants to be prepared for impresting £300 to Osmond, £120 to Robins, £1,000 to Cleave and Mrs Skeat.

387. [p. 301] 8 Jan. 1724/25
1. Marshall delivered account of pew purchase money for St George the Martyr, which was referred to Dean of Chichester.

2. On petition from Trebeck for a bell for church near Hanover Square, ordered bell to be prepared of not more than 400 lbs weight; Surveyor to give dimensions.
3. Bishop of London reported that he and Bishop of St Asaph had waited on Lord Townshend with the representation etc, and he had promised to further it and lay it before King.
4. Signed warrants for paying Osmond £300, Robins £120, John Cleave £500, and Mrs Skeat, widow of John Skeat, £500.

388. [p. 302] 11 Jan. 1724/25
1. Made further progress in endowment bill.

389. [p. 303] 18 Jan. 1724/25
1. Read petition of parish clerks of St Martin in the Fields, St James, and St Ann, Westminster about their dues and privileges. Solicitor for their relief to prepare clause in endowment bill.
2. Lord Carpenter, Gen. Steuart and others from Hanover Square complained of Fletcher's dilatoriness in finishing masonry, bringing with them a letter from Fletcher that he is willing to quit the work if Board please.
3. James to measure work already prepared, and employ another mason to finish it with all possible speed on basis of Fletcher's contract.

390. [p. 304] 19 Jan. 1724/25
1. Signed warrants for paying half year's salary to officers and half year's house rent.
2. Vestry room for Hanover Square church to be prepared on S.E. corner according to the plan.
3. Mansfield petitioned for imprest for plasterer's work; warrant for £400 to be prepared.

391. [p. 305] 26 Jan. 1724/25
1. Solicitor read endowment bill with amendments made at last meeting, which were agreed to.
2. Read petition from minister and churchwardens of St Mary le Strand; consideration deferred.
3. Signed warrant for paying Mansfield £400.
4. Solicitor to prepare a schedule for filling up blanks in endowment bill and to prepare abstracts.
5. Fletcher to be discharged from mason's work in Hanover Square church, and Strong and Cass to be employed instead.

392. [p. 306] 2 Feb. 1724/25
1. Solicitor submitted abstract of endowment bill. Debates arising on the reading, resolved that Board resume consideration at next meeting, and filling up blanks be considered at the same time.

393. [p. 307] 4 Feb. 1724/25
1. Resumed consideration of endowment bill and finished it to bring it into House of Commons. Solicitor to prepare paper for filling up blanks.

394. [p. 308] 9 Feb. 1724/25
1. Dean of Chichester reported on money in Chambers' hands; to be considered at next meeting.
2. Considered clause about perpetual patronage of St John's church, Clerkenwell; clause to be omitted, Secretary to inform Solicitor, and he to acquaint Pulteney and Onslow and alter the copies accordingly.

395. [p. 309] 11 Feb. 1724/25
1. Dean of Chichester being absent, money in Chambers' hands to be considered at next meeting.
2. Sir Geo. Stonehouse, Bt, appointed to solicit bill of endowment in parliament and Philipps desired to acquaint him therewith.

396. [p. 310] 15 Feb. 1724/25
1. Bishop of London reported that bill will speedily be brought into parliament. Proposed endowments to be entered in the books:
Large parishes and rich: Hanover Square, Bloomsbury and Ormond St,

by a £ rate yearly for each church	£350
whereof a curate £80, the residue to the rector. And no part of the parliamentary fund need be applied thereto.	

2. Large parishes and small rents and many poor:
Westminster, Spitalfields and Wapping,

by a £ rate yearly for each church	£270
by the parliamentary fund	80
	£350
whereof the curate £80, the residue to the rector.	

3. Limehouse, not so large but burdened with poor,

by a £ rate	£200
by the parliamentary fund	100
	£300
whereof to the curate £60, the rest to the rector.	

4. Bow, Strand, St John's, Deptford. Small parishes.

by a £ rate each	£130
by the parliamentary fund	120
	£250
To the curate £50, the rest to the rector.	

397. [p. 312] 22 Feb. 1724/25
1. Smiths' proposals for locks and hinges to church doors to be referred to James.
2. Agent to give Solicitor copies of vestry fees and number of houses, their value and what they pay to land tax and poor in the eleven new parishes.

398. [p. 313] 26 Feb. 1724/25
1. Hinges already made for church doors by Goff, Robins and Cleave to

be delivered to Surveyors' custody and brought to account in the books of the present years. The workmen in general to proceed with no works for the future without direct order of this Board signified to them by Surveyors.
2. Locks for church doors to be provided by persons appointed by a former order to provide locks for pews.

399. [p. 314] 2 Mar. 1724/25
1. Considered some clauses in endowment bill now depending in Parliament.

400. [p. 315] 6 Mar. 1724/25
1. Further consideration of some clauses in endowment bill.

401. [p. 316] 20 Mar. 1724/25
1. James reported Hanover Square church ready for consecration. Adjourned to this day se'night.

402. [p. 317] 20 [*sic; recte* 27] Mar. 1725
1. Jas Heath Esq presented proposal of a house in Church Lane, Limehouse, for the minister; James to view and report.
2. Dean of the Arches and Ellis, assisted by Treasurer, Solicitor and Agent, to consider list of proper persons to be parish officers for St George Hanover Square, and another list for vestrymen.
Commissioners will proceed on yearly election of officers and determination of salaries at next meeting.

403. [p. 318] 31 Mar. 1725
1. Dean of the Arches and Ellis presented list of proper persons for officers and another of about 70 for vestrymen for Hanover Square.
Agreed that Lord Carpenter and Gen. Steuart be the first churchwardens; Benj. Timbrel of Swallow St and Matt. Tomlinson of Portugal St, sidesmen; Thos Edwards of Maddox St, carpenter, Wm Sherwood in Oxford St, distiller, John Dickinson of St James St, saddler, and John Prescot of Piccadilly, baker, overseers of the poor; John Boyce of Maddox St, butcher, —Web, farrier of High Park Corner, constables; Robt Owen of Maddox St, grocer, Hy Micklebury of New Bond St, baker, Thos Gough of High Park Corner, smith, —Kellum, breeches maker, scavengers; —Scot at Queen's Head, Chelsea Bridge, headborough; John Heylyn, Roger Williams of Dover St, and Matt. Tomlinson of Portugal St, surveyors of highways. Secretary to deliver copy of resolution to Lord Carpenter and Gen. Steuart.
2. Vestry of St George Hanover Square to consist of 50, besides minister and churchwardens.
3. Each Commissioner present to have a copy of the list, and bring a paper rolled up containing 50 names.
4. All papers about Ormond chapel to be laid before Board at next meeting, and Treasurer to make demand in Board's name for money paid the trustees for purchasing pews.

5. Secretary to pay Sarah Plumpton, dau. and adminx of Lot Plumpton, watchman at Limehouse and Ratcliff churches, £10; Newsham, £6; Griffith Lloyd £4 for watching the respective churches under their care.
6. Read petition from Astell about money advanced for building Limehouse church. Thos Holden to attend next meeting to answer allegations.
7. Deans of Canterbury, Chichester and the Arches and Dr Gooch, Archdeacon of Essex, to be desired to prepare draft representation to parliament concerning bill of endowment now depending.
8. Annual election of officers, etc., adjourned to next meeting.

404. [p. 321] 3 Apr. 1725
1. Every Commissioner present at liberty to name any person he thinks proper to be of the vestry of Hanover Square though not named in the list presented at last meeting.
2. Surveyor to view minister's house near St George the Martyr and building adjoining wherein is the vestry room, and report to next meeting.
3. Read order from House of Commons directing the Board to lay an account of its proceedings concerning the endowment of the churches: entered in minute book.
4. Deans of Canterbury, Chichester and the Arches, and Dr Gooch brought draft representation about endowment bill pursuant to order of the House of Commons; referred back to make some addition and to finish it.
5. Treasurer and Surveyor to submit account of what proportion of the £360,000 has been expended since Lady Day 1719.

405. [p. 323] 6 Apr. 1725
1. All business adjourned to next meeting except account of Board's proceedings in the endowment of the fifty new churches.
Dean of Chichester, one of the committee, read it to the Board in order to be laid before the Commons. Report to be lodged with Bishop of London for his perusal and use.
2. All minutes on St John Clerkenwell to be printed and attested by Secretary.
3. James and Hawksmoor to attend Committee of House of Commons on Thurs. next with all papers about division of St James Clerkenwell, taking care they have with them a plan of the new parish of St John.
4. All estimates and accounts of perquisites of the several parishes to be delivered to Dean of Canterbury to be by him put into a method for the Board's use.

406. [p. 324] 9 Apr. 1725
1. The bringing in list of vestry of Hanover Square adjourned to Fri. next.
2. Considered draft of account of Commissioners' proceedings on endowment of the fifty new churches; some amendments proposed and referred to committee to make in it against next meeting.
3. Solicitor's bill of disbursements referred to Melmoth, Meller and Hiccocks.

4. Considered report from Deans of Chichester and the Arches on money allotted for purchasing pews in St George the Martyr. Money has, by mistake, been lodged in the hands of trustees of the proprietors of the pews. Uses of the sum are improperly limited in deed between Commissioners and trustees. Commissioners should demand return of the money, and if necessary take proper methods to recover it.

407. [p. 326] 12 Apr. 1725
1. Resumed consideration of report on endowment proceedings, and finished it; to be writ out fair by Wed. [14 Apr.], to be signed by Commissioners.

408. [p. 327] 17 Apr. 1725
1. Secretary reported he had delivered Commissioners' report on their proceedings at bar of House of Commons.
2. Treasurer reported that he had demanded pew purchase money of the Ormond chapel trustees.
3. Meller and Ellis to prepare a scheme to endow parishes willing to submit to a pound rate; Agent to attend them with all necessary papers.
4. Meller reported that Solicitor's bill was reasonable, but contained two blanks which he and Melmoth thought not proper for them to fill; to be considered at next meeting.
5. Table of burial fees for St George the Martyr to be considered at next meeting.
6. Read petition from Ezekiel Cook. Surveyors to adjust measurement of church at the Horse Ferry [Millbank].
7. All members of either House of Parliament now dwelling in parish of St George Hanover Square to be members of vestry. As it appears on inquiry since order of 31 March last that such inhabitants are very numerous and live in the country during summer, other residents must be joined with them to carry on business of church and parish.
8. Vestry of St George Hanover Square to consist of 100 persons, besides minister and churchwardens.
9. Every Commissioner to bring his nominations next Fri. [23 Apr.].

409. [p. 329] 21 Apr. 1725
1. Solicitor to prepare bill in Chancery against trustees of St George the Martyr to recover money paid them to buy up pews.
2. Meller and Ellis presented scheme to endow parishes willing to submit to a pound rate; thanked by Board and desired to perfect it as soon as they can.
3. Petition of St John Clerkenwell adjourned to next meeting.

410. [p. 330] 23 Apr. 1725
1. Treasurer to pay £150 to churchwardens of St John Clerkenwell, pursuant to order of 10 April last, upon their producing bills certified by warrant to be prepared.
3. [*sic*] Solicitor's bill allowed, and an extra 20 guineas for his extraordinary attendance on bill of endowment.

4. Holden attending admitted that Astell advanced him £1,400 for carrying on joiner's work at Limehouse church, and he had assigned his contract to Astell. £550 to be imprested to Astell, and further sums paid him as due upon his performing the work and leaving Holden's assignment in the office.
5. Hawksmoor and Agent having viewed land for a burying ground for St Mary le Strand brought in a plan; deferred to next meeting.
6. Agreed to a list of vestrymen for St George Hanover Square [names not given].

411. [p. 332] 30 Apr. 1725
1. Minister and churchwardens for St Mary le Strand to attend next meeting with plan drawn by James for disposing grounds of church yard for burials.
2. Resolved that same officers elected on 14 Feb. 1723/24, except Agent, since deceased, be continued to first meeting after New Year's Day next.
3. Election of officers to be made annually, the first meeting after New Year's Day.
4. In consideration of the officers' extraordinary trouble during year ending 14 Jan. last, following gratuities be allowed above their salaries: Secretary, £50; each Surveyor, £50; Agent, £20.

412. [p. 333] 7 May 1725
1. James reported that on view of the minister's house, St George the Martyr, and that adjoining, the vestry room is on middle floor of adjoining house, the rooms above and below being let for charity school children, rent of which in counsel's opinion is minister's right.
2. Marshall to be desired to attend Friday next [14 May], with counsel's opinion and deed of purchase.
3. Petitions of Meard, Mansfield, Dunn and Worrall for money referred to Surveyors to report at next meeting.

413. [p. 334] 14 May 1725
1. Marshall attended, with Ward's opinion; consideration deferred.
2. Consideration of burial fees for St George the Martyr deferred.

414. [p. 335] 31 May 1725
[1.] List of persons to compose vestry of St George Hanover Square being brought, the following were named:*
Dukes of Devonshire, Kingston, Grafton, Bolton, Montrose, Roxborough and Manchester; Earls of Leicester, Westmorland, Peterborough, Litchfield, Albemarle, Coventry, Grantham, Powlett, Orkney, Oxford, Ferrers, Sussex, Cadogan and Pomfret; Viscounts Tadcaster and St John; Lords Piercy, Hundson, Delawar, Compton, Carteret, Guilford, Waldegrave, Walpole, Hartington, Burford, Archibald Hamilton, How, Harvey, Carpenter, and Castlemain.
Esquires: Edward Ash, Martin Bladen, Walter Carey, Thos Cartwright, Wm Chetwind, Walt. Chetwind, Godf. Clark, John Conduit, Hy Furness, John Hedges, Robt Sawyer Herbert, Thos Lewis, Thos Pagett, Wm

Pulteney, Sam. Shepherd, Jas Tyrrel, Bowater Vernon, Horatio Walpole, Robt Ruddal Westphaling, Dixy Winsor, Sam. Mollineux, Wm Thomson, John Lance; Sir: John Hind Cotton, Wm Lowther, Edw. Earlne, Robt Furness, Wm Gage, John Guise, Thos Hanmer, Rich. How, Arthur Kay, Wilf. Lawson, Sam. Lennard, Paul Methuen, John Norris, Adolphus Oughton, Wm Strickland, Robt Sutton, Robt Walpole, Wm Wyndham, Jas Clark.
JPs: Sir Thos Clargies, Sir Clem. Cotrell, Col. Dan. Houghton, Wm Burdon, Thos Scot, Nich. Bland, Anthony Corbiere.
Generals Peper and Steuart; Colonels Carpenter, Kerr, John Fane and Jas Allen; Major Wm Ducket.
Messrs: John Heylin, Thos Philipps, Thos Barlow, Benj. Timbrel.
2. Bishop of London consented to the list.
3. Solicitor to prepare instrument of appointment for the Commissioners' signature.
4. Signed warrant for payments to workmen in 1723.

*The entry stops at the colon, and is repeated on p. 336.

415. [p. 339] 4 June 1725
1. Approved and confirmed table of burial fees for St George the Martyr:

	Every corpse interred above 10 years old			below 10 years		
Ground:	Upper	Middle	Lower	Upper	Middle	Lower
To rector	6*s*. 8*d*.	5*s*.	2*s*. 6*d*.	4*s*. 6*d*.	2*s*. 6*d*.	1*s*. 6*d*.
curate	3*s*. 4*d*.	2*s*. 6*d*.	1*s*. 6*d*.	2*s*. 6*d*.	2*s*.	1*s*.
wardens	13*s*. 4*d*.	5*s*.	2*s*.	10*s*.	3*s*.	1*s*.
clerk	2*s*. 6*d*.	1*s*. 6*d*.	1*s*.	2*s*.	1*s*. 6*d*.	1*s*.
bell and knell	6*s*.	2*s*. 6*d*.	1*s*.	4*s*.	2*s*.	1*s*.
gravedigger	2*s*. 6*d*.	2*s*.	1*s*.	2*s*.	1*s*.	8*d*.
	£1. 14*s*. 4*d*.	18*s*. 6*d*.	9*s*. 0*d*.	£1. 5*s*. 0*d*.	12*s*. 0*d*.	6*s*. 2*d*.

To bearers: for upper ground, in gowns, each 1*s*. 6*d*.; for other grounds, 1*s*.; without gowns, 6*d*. less. Sexton to have paid him by churchwardens out of bell and knell fees, for upper and middle grounds, 1*s*.; for lower, 6*d*. All strangers to pay double fees unless cause to contrary appear to rector and churchwardens in respect of poverty. Poor of the parish receiving alms to be buried without any duty or fees.
Clerk to receive churchwardens' fees, and account to them every month. For late hours, if corpse be not at grave before 10 p.m. between Lady Day and Michaelmas, or before 8 between Michaelmas and Lady Day, an additional one-third of the duties shall be paid, provided it be not occasioned by any official's default.
2. Workmen's bills for 1723 compared with books of works and examined by Philipps and Peck; the books allowed and signed.
3. Michell represented that he laid out £36. 10*s*. 6*d*. on chapel of St John, Clerkenwell between its sale and consecration. Warrant to be prepared

for paying him, and another for £118, one year's interest to Michell for purchase money of the chapel.

416. [p. 342] 14 June 1725
1. Meller and Melmoth desired to examine and settle Stonehouse's bill of fees and disbursements for soliciting bill for maintenance in parliament.
2. Warrants signed for paying Michell £36. 10*s*. 6*d*. for money laid out on Aylesbury chapel while he was agent, and £118 for interest.
3. Read Treasurer's memorial for a further allowance in consideration of his extraordinary trouble of several kinds, and that he may be considered in same manner as the other officers. Commissioners allowed it to be reasonable, but deferred consideration to another meeting.
Mrs Skeat to be allowed her late husband's salary after rate of £60 p.a., in proportion, to day of his death.

417. [p. 343] 21 June 1725
1. Read petition from Mrs Moor for an allowance for her extraordinary trouble last year; to be paid £2. 10*s*. from Secretary's incidentals.
2. Warrant to be prepared for paying a £50 gratuity to Treasurer.
3. Surveyors to state accounts of every workman separately so Board may judge what sums may be safely impressed to them till works are measured.
4. £3. 9*s*. 10*d*. charged in Stonehouse's bill of disbursements to be allowed him, and 12 guineas for his trouble in soliciting the bill for providing a maintenance.

418. [p. 344] 28 June 1725
1. Signed warrants for paying £50 to Treasurer, a half-year's salary to the officers, and a half-year's rent for this house, due to Secretary.
2. Treasurer to report state of accounts this day fortnight, specifying moneys received and laid out and what is in his hands. Such an account to be brought in for the future at first meeting after every Christmas and Midsummer Day.
3. Warrant to be prepared for imprests to workmen for 1724.
4. Hawksmoor to report what is necessary at Spitalfields church by next meeting.
5. James to call on Tufnell to give a more particular account of what he demands in respect of stones carried to site purchased for a church in St Olave's Southwark, and report to next meeting.
6. Signed imprest warrant for paying workmen for 1724.

419. [p. 345] 12 July 1725
1. Hawksmoor reported on state of Spitalfields church, and what was necessary for finishing it.
2. Allowed Secretary's bill of incidents; blank warrant to be prepared to imprest him a further sum.
3. Ground for Limehouse churchyard to be walled in with a plain brick wall, as at Wapping.

4. Signed warrant for paying workmen whose accounts were not settled at last meeting.
5. Table of fees for St George Hanover Square referred to next meeting.
6. Tower and spire of Spitalfields church being nearly finished and scaffolding up, tower to be carried on and finished as less expensive now than hereafter.
7. Churchyard to be enclosed by a plain wall not more than seven ft. high.
8. West portico to be finished in plainest manner and at least expense that can be.
9. Surveyors to submit plan and estimate of house for minister, to be built on part of ground already purchased.
10. Surveyors brought an account of damages sustained by Tufnell in laying stone for building in parish of St Olave, which on fair calculation amounted to £350; but it being doubted whether any contract was executed by Tufnell, they were ordered to ascertain whether any contract was executed.
11. Surveyors brought in account of Heath's house, which he proposes to sell as a parsonage house for Limehouse. Peck to ascertain Heath's lowest price, and price for house distinct from four tenements mentioned in his proposal; and cost of putting it in repair.

420. [p. 347] 26 July 1725
1. Read memorial from Mr Molyneux complaining of damages to his stables, cellars, etc., by building church in Hanover Square. Surveyors to report.
2. Read petition from churchwardens of Wapping praying that their church may be finished speedily; they were called in and told it should be.
3. Treasurer delivered account of moneys issued out of Exchequer from Lady Day 1719. Mellor and Ellis to peruse account and report.
4. Inquiry having been made whether any contract for mason's work for new church in St Olave's parish was signed by late Edward Tufnell, it appears that by his death soon after his proposal no contract was signed. [Marginal note: 'This contract since found'.] But as it was resolved by minute of 8 May 1718 that Tufnell be employed, Board agrees that £350, as mentioned in minute [10] of last meeting, be paid to his executors, and entered in the accounts in such terms that reasons appear as plain as possible.
5. Signed warrant for impresting £50 to Secretary.

421. [p. 348] 9 Aug. 1725
1. Meller reported that he had perused Treasurer's account of issues from Lady Day 1719, amounting to £103,000, which agrees with account he had drawn up, with some remarks. To be considered at next meeting.
2. James reported on damage to Mr Secretary Molyneux's house by the building of church near Hanover Square. Garden wall and gutter to be made good speedily, and damage to cellar arches and street pavement to be repaired as soon as masons have set their steps at south end of porch. Molyneux to be informed.

3. Read petition from governors of St Olave's grammar school, praying that a party wall may be built to separate their ground from the Commissioners', they bearing their part of expense. To be put in hand.
4. Peck to dispose of pales of old fence about Spitalfields church.

422. [p. 349] 3 Sep. 1725
1. Meller's remarks on Treasurer's account of issues to be considered at next meeting, and Meller desired to be present.
2. Consideration of site for minister's house, Limehouse, referred to next meeting.
3. Agent to inquire for a proper house to be purchased for minister of Bloomsbury.
4. Warrant to be prepared for paying Chas White £300 for Bethnal Green site.
5. Secretary to pay £5 to Newsham, watchman for Hanover Square church.

423. [p. 350] 8 Oct. 1725
1. Read petition from inhabitants of Bermondsey that a church may be built on site bought there. Referred to further consideration.
2. James presented the books of works; referred to a committee to meet this day week at 10.
3. Treasurer to inquire amount of revenue on coals from Michaelmas 1724 to Michaelmas 1725 and report to next meeting.
4. Secretary to advance £5 to Hall, watchman at Spitalfields church.
5. Plasterer at Bloomsbury church to attend next meeting.
6. Fence about Bloomsbury church to be removed inward as far as it can be done conveniently.

424. [p. 351] 22 Oct. 1725
1. Ellis reported that he and Dean of the Arches had examined the books of works and workmen's bills so far as bills had been passed by Surveyors, and found them right, except that for decoration of Bloomsbury church, which they submitted to the Board's consideration.
2. Treasurer reported produce of revenue on coals from Michaelmas 1724 to Michaelmas 1725 to be £65,514. 13*s*. 0½*d*.
3. Secretary reported he had inspected the books in Bishop of London's office, and that one and three-quarters acres of ground purchased by Commissioners of Dr Proctor in St Pancras parish were not consecrated.
4. Signed warrant for paying White £200 for site in Bethnal Green, title having been approved by Solicitor.
5. Mansfield attended and promised that plasterer's work at Bloomsbury church should be finished expeditiously.

425. [p. 352] 12 Nov. 1725
1. Affair of decorations of Bloomsbury church put up by Hawksmoor to be referred to another meeting.
2. Board to consider at next meeting what quantity of ground purchased of Dr Proctor should be allotted for a churchyard for new parish of Bloomsbury.

3. Petition from inhabitants of Bethnal Green urging that a church be built there referred to further consideration when churches now building are completed.

Warrant to be prepared for paying Mansfield £100.

Adjourned to this day fortnight.

[One folio, numbered 353–4, cut out of book].

426. [p. 355] 26 Nov. 1725

1. Approved table of burial fees for St George Hanover Square:

	Every corpse interred above ten years old			under ten years		
Ground:	Upper	Middle	Lower	Upper	Middle	Lower
To wardens	£2	10*s*.	1*s*. 6*d*.	£1	5*s*.	1*s*.
rectore	£1	7*s*.	4*s*.	£1	3*s*. 6*d*.	2*s*. 6*d*.
clerk	10*s*.	4*s*.	2*s*.	6*s*.	2*s*.	1*s*.
sexton	7*s*.	2*s*.	1*s*. 6*d*.	6*s*.	2*s*.	1*s*.
gravemaker	2*s*.	2*s*.	1*s*.	1*s*.	1*s*.	6*d*.
bearers	2*s*.	1*s*.	1*s*.	1*s*.	1*s*.	6*d*.

Still-born child or abortive, to wardens 1*s*., sexton 1*s*., gravemaker 6*d*. All strangers to pay double fees unless cause appear to rector and wardens in respect of poverty. Poor of parish receiving alms to be buried as such, without any fee. If corpse be not at the grave by 10 o'clock between Lady Day and Michaelmas or 8 between Michaelmas and Lady Day to the officiating minister an additional 7*s*. if the rector, 5*s*. if the curate, provided it be not occasioned by their default.

2. Surveyors to wall in one acre of the ground bought of Proctor for a churchyard for Bloomsbury.

3. Signed warrant for paying Mansfield £100.

4. Secretary to wait on Bishop of London's register for evidences and instrument of consecration of Ormond chapel for satisfaction of Board in some particular points.

5. Treasurer to prepare draft memorial to Treasury for opening a loan for taking in £40,000 for discharging Commission's present debt, the largeness of which has been occasioned by great despatch made in past year towards finishing the churches already begun.

6. Agent to inquire for proper ground for a churchyard for Millbank.

7. The Board, taking into consideration decorations of Bloomsbury church, viz. statue, lions, unicorns, festoons and crowns which were put up by Hawksmoor's order without their direction or privity (though some sort of decorations were necessary in those places), will allow no more than £368 on that account; and admonish Hawksmoor not to engage Board in similar expense without their consent on pain of bearing the cost.

427. [p. 358] 10 Dec. 1725
1. Books of works for 1724 examined by a committee and approved; to be delivered to Treasurer for his perusal in order to be signed by Board.
2. Churchwardens of Limehouse delivered petition that parishioners were desirous to agree to a reasonable pound rate towards endowment, but praying Board's assistance to procure competent share of parliamentary grant because of poverty of the inhabitants.
3. Treasurer read draft memorial to Treasury for a loan of £40,000, which with amendments was engrossed and signed.
4. Agent reported viewing a site for a churchyard for Millbank in Dean and Chapter of Westminster's Artillery Ground; to attend trustees and vestry of St Margaret Westminster and ascertain their demand for one acre.
5. Churchyard for St Mary le Strand: site in Bridges Street offered for £750, including old houses worth above £100. Surveyors report that no other site so convenient, and £700 not unreasonable for building site. Board resolved to pay £600 if parishioners would pay rest and clear site; parishioners agreed. Board instructed Solicitor to lay title before counsel, and, title being approved, was ordered to prepare conveyance. Now reported conveyance ready. Warrant to be prepared for paying £600 to James Lesley, Judith his wife, Patrick Maigham, Elizabeth his wife, and John Essington.

428. [p. 360] 7 Jan. 1725/26
1. Agent reported attending vestry of St Margaret Westminster: Sir Thos Crosse in the chair desired Board would direct Agent by a minute to apply to the trustees for their consent to dispose of the ground; so ordered.
2. Peck reported that he had seen Heath about purchasing house and garden at Limehouse for minister; he demands £550, which James thinks not too dear.
3. Heath to lay title deeds before Solicitor to consult counsel, Commissioners agreeing to pay £550.
4. Secretary to pay Agent £3. 1*s*. 6*d*., being overpayment to late Agent's widow.
5. Treasurer reported he had laid memorial for a loan before Lords of the Treasury, who had ordered a warrant for a loan to be made at Exchequer accordingly.
6. Signed warrants for paying half-year's salary due at Christmas to officers and half-year's rent for office.
7. Signed warrant for paying £600 to Jas Lesley and others.
8. Treasurer to examine books of works so that they may be signed at next meeting.

429. [p. 363] 28 Jan. 1725/26
1. Agent delivered resolution of trustees of the Military Ground in St Margaret Westminster, with plan annexed, to part with one acre. Surveyors to estimate cost of walling in.
3. Marshall delivered a report how the money for buying pews in

Ormond chapel has been laid out; referred to Deans of Chichester and the Arches, to report as soon as convenient.
3. Agent to inquire whether there is any other ground for a churchyard for Millbank, because of doubt whether Military Ground can be made to answer the purpose.
4. Meard having complained of a mistake in his proposal for church in Hanover Square, Surveyors to report.
5. Surveyors to report on petition of Sam Newsham, watchman.
6. Read petition of minister and churchwardens of Aldgate that site proposed by them may be bought for a church; Surveyors to view and report.
7. Petition of officers for an allowance for extra services last year referred to committee of Dean of the Arches, Philipps and Ellis, to report to next meeting.
8. The same officers elected 30 April 1724 to be continued to first meeting after New Year's Day next.
9. Petition of Devall and others, inhabitants of St Margaret Westminster, that there is no room to make a sewer to carry waste water from their houses because of drain made for Millbank church referred to Surveyors.

430. [p. 365] 4 Feb. 1725/26
1. Solicitor to deliver all papers about pew money for St George the Martyr to Deans of Chichester and the Arches.
2. Agent reported he could find no land proper for a churchyard for Millbank.
3. Surveyors reported estimate for walling Military Ground. Trustees to be asked whether they are willing to part with residue to south (about one and a half acres) on condition Commissioners wall in the whole and make posts and rails as required in their proposal.
4. Surveyors reported on Meard's complaint; his proposal included 25*s*. per square for ground flooring—at least 10*s*. per square less than ever has been offered. They think this was mistaken, because materials therein amount to upward of 25*s*., besides workmanship. Agreed that he be paid 35*s*. per square.
5. Petition of Devall and others to be complied with provided they bring waste water into the Commissioners' drain under Surveyors' direction.
6. Treasurer to pay £10 to Newsham, watchman at Hanover Square church.
7. Books of works done at the churches having been signed at last meeting, and that for Hanover Square church not then ready, it was now signed for 1724.
8. Solicitor to give Farrer the bill he prepared for enabling Commissioners to build in brick as well as stone, for purchasing chapels erected since the 9th of Anne, and for making clerks of new parishes, members of the Corporation of Parish Clerks, with copies to Speaker and some other MPs.
9. Lucas to be employed to finish brickwork of minister's house, Bow, *vice* Hester, deceased.

431. [p. 367] 11 Feb. 1725/26
Surveyors to report on house in Charles Street Comon [*sic*] Garden proposed for a minister's house for St Mary le Strand for £1,100.
2. Read petition for Hall, watchman, Spitalfields church. Treasurer to pay him by imprest £20, and £4 to Jonathan Durden, watchman at Wapping church.
3. Agree to accept proposal of trustees of Military Ground to convey one and a half acres for remainder of their lease if Commissioners can agree with Dean and Chapter of Westminster for freehold. Solicitor to attend Dean and Chapter and ask their terms.

432. [p. 369] 25 Feb. 1725/26
1. James submitted plan of another site for a churchyard for Millbank, proposed by Dean and Chapter of Westminster.
2. Read petition from Sir Fisher Tench; called in and told Board could come to no resolution until contract made with Johnson about site could be consulted, and Johnson discoursed with.
3. Hawksmoor submitted plan of house in Charles Street. Agreed that £1,100 be given for it on seller making good title; to lay title deeds before Solicitor.
4. On petition of White about executors of Edward Boswell, one of bricklayers for Bloomsbury church, ordered Treasurer not to pay Ford, the surviving contractor, without first acquainting Board.
5. Treasurer to pay £10 to Nich. Walker, watchman at Limehouse church.
6. Warrant to be prepared for paying Appleby, joiner for Spitalfields and Woolwich [Woolnoth] churches, as much as will make up £1,000 together with his imprest money, £75, already paid, and what is entered in the books of 1724 and not yet paid.
7. Surveyors to give directions for building vestry room for St Mary Woolnoth, near place old one stood.
8. Read minute of 27 Nov. 1724 concerning purchase of a site at Bethnal Green; resolved that six months notice be given White before foundation of a new church be begun.

433. [p. 371] 4 Mar. 1725/26
1. Treasurer to pay Solicitor £100 towards expenses of bill in parliament for providing maintenance for minister for Strand church.
2. Read petition from churchwardens, etc, of Spitalfields offering to pay £200 p.a. towards minister's maintenance; called in and told that their church should be finished speedily, and their parish probably included with other new Stepney parishes in an endowment bill.
3. Officers who applied for an extraordinary allowance to lay a specific account before committee; Secretary to attend with minute books.
4. Read petition from churchwardens of Limehouse offering £50 p.a. towards a maintenance for their minister; approved.
5. Dean of the Arches submitted report, signed also by Dean of Chichester, on transaction with trustees of St George the Martyr. Referred to next meeting.

6. Bishop of Rochester reported that Dean and Chaper of Westminster had decided a price for Millbank churchyard and were notifying Solicitor for Board's information.
7. Appleby to finish joiner's work at Spitalfields church with all possible speed.
8. Stonehouse to be employed to solicit bill for building churches with brick, and for other objects.
9. Zacharius Hamlyn to be employed to solicit bill for settling a maintenance on minister of Strand church.
10. Considering circumstances of new parish of St Mary le Strand, £2,500 a proper sum to be allowed out of moneys appropriated [for endowment] in act of the 5th of the King.

434. [p. 373] 11 Mar. 1725/26
1. Churchwardens, etc., of Wapping willing to settle £120 p.a. to maintain minister as an inducement to Commissioners to be at the charge of a bill for endowing church.
2. Petition of Geo. Crochly complaining of damage to his schoolroom by building Bloomsbury church referred to Surveyors.
3. Solicitor to prepare a bill for endowing the five new churches in Stepney with all possible speed.
4. Churchwardens, etc., of Stratford Bow willing to settle £45 p.a. to maintain minister.
5. Signed warrant for paying Appleby £392. 19*s*. 10*d*. by imprest.
6. Signed memorial to Treasury that fictitious tallies may be struck at four per cent for what remains of the loan of £40,000 for discharging debts to the workmen.

435. [p. 375] 17 Mar. 1725/26
1. Good reason to apprehend that upon an application to parliament by Dean and Chapter of Westminster there is a design to take some part of the fund appropriated to use of the Commissioners, to employ it on Westminster Abbey. There are several large parishes in Winchester diocese and within the bills of mortality which greatly need additional churches, and have petitioned, which cannot be so well accommodated if such diminution be made. Notice to be given to Bishop of Winchester of the application, and to Dean and Chapter of St Paul's, there being need of two churches in Cripplegate parish under the jurisdiction of the Dean and Chapter, building of which Commissioners may not be able to effect if diminution made.

A true state of this case to be drawn up, Bishop of Carlisle and Chichester and Dean of the Arches making a draft for next meeting.
2. Solicitor and Treasurer to attend this committee. Treasurer to apply to Jodrell, Clerk of House of Commons, for a copy of first application to parliament of Dean and Chapter of Westminster for money to repair Abbey.

Treasurer to apply at Exchequer for an account of annual produce of coal duty from 14 May 1716 to Lady Day 1719.

3. Treasurer to apply to Treasury for copy of last application of Dean and Chapter of Westminster for money for repair of the abbey.
4. Allowed Secretary's bill of incidents; warrant to be prepared.
5. Application to Treasury signed at last meeting cancelled for some mistake therein, and another signed desiring the striking of fictitious tallies for £20,000 at four per cent on the loan for £40,000.

436. [p. 377] 25 Mar. 1726/27
1. Read petition from rectors of St Dunstan's Stepney; told them that it should be considered when endowment bill shall be brought in.
2. Bishop of Carlisle and Dean of the Arches delivered report, signed also by Bishop of Chichester, on application of Dean and Chapter of Westminster that either their proportion of the £360,000 may be allotted them, or that the £4,000 p.a. may be continued to them out of the fund of £21,000 p.a. for 32 years from Lady Day 1719.

The committee think themselves concerned only with former part of petition, this Board having nothing to do with the surplus of fund. Dean and chapter have no claim to further share of the £360,000, having received all that was intended them by acts of 9th Anne and 5th Geo. I. Greenwich Hospital likewise having received full allotment, remainder is wholly appropriated to the Commission's uses. Expense of building with stone, and purchasing sites is so great, and so far exceeds calculations formerly made, that it will be utterly impracticable to build half the churches first purposed, even employing whole sum as it now stands. Necessity of having many additional churches about London still continues: several parishes containing 30,000 or 40,000 souls, many at too great a distance from the parish church and having no place to attend divine service, as appears by their repeated applications. Lastly, taking away any part of what remains of the £360,000 will defeat pious intentions of late Queen and present King, and parliament's principal design, tending to benefit of the Church of England and advancement of religion, and will deprive many thousands of convenience of worship and disappoint their just expectations of relief, to which they have so largely contributed in coal duty since 14 May 1716.

Committee submit that Board ought therefore to give utmost opposition to do so unreasonable an application.

Referred to same committee to frame a report with representation to be made as soon as there is occasion.
3. Petition from minister and churchwardens of St Olave's praying for a church to be built on site bought; shall be considered in proper time.

437. [p. 380] 28 Mar. 1726
1. Thanks of the Board to committee of Bishops of Carlisle and Chichester and Dean of the Arches for drawing up representation, which is forthwith to be printed.
2. Read petition of Lloyd, watchman at Bloomsbury church, complaining of disturbance to himself and workmen. Surveyors to report.

438. [p. 381] 1 Apr. 1726
1. Hawksmoor reported on petition of Griffith Lloyd. Solicitor to

support Lloyd in name of Board, he having acted in discharge of his office.
2. Minister's house to be built at Bloomsbury according to plan delivered by Hawksmoor at cost not exceeding £1,000.

439. [p. 382] 13 Apr. 1726
1. Considered report of Deans of Chichester and the Arches on pew money for St George the Martyr: trustees acknowledge on the balance of their last account £722. 9*s*. 9*d*. of moneys appropriated for purchasing pews remaining in their hands; and that £45 craved to be allowed to Moody and £6. 0*s*. 6*d*. charges at Doctors Commons ought not to be allowed by Commissioners but be added to account, making £773. 10*s*. 3*d*.

Treasurer to demand this sum from the trustees in order to purchase pews, and to acquaint them that the 13 pews purchased by them since 13 May last be forthwith placed in Commissioners' hands for use of parishioners.
2. Secretary to acquaint Marshall and trustees that they make take a copy of report if they wish.

440. [p. 383] 22 Apr. 1726
1. Hawksmoor submitted plan of site for a church in parish of St Botolph Aldgate, in Butcher Row, East Smithfield, for £2,300.
2. Cotes, agent for proprietor, to submit rent-roll of houses on the ground.
3. Read letter from Mrs Fewtrell to know if Board adhere to resolution of purchasing her ground in St Giles Cripplegate. Board do so adhere; warrant to be prepared for paying her £350.
4. Counsel signifying that conveyance of the ground from vicar etc. of St Giles Cripplegate may be accepted, agreed that conveyance be forthwith executed.
5. Warrant to be prepared for £1,100 for house in Charles Street, Convent Garden.
6. Instrument for investing patronage of St George Hanover Square in Bishop of London to be engrossed, executed and enrolled.

441. [p. 385] 29 Apr. 1726
1. Surveyors to view houses on Aldgate site, acquainting Rev. Dr Bray of the time.
2. Signed warrant for paying Mrs Catherine Fewtrell £350.
3. Read petition from Ety, complaining of damage to his house by building of Bloomsbury church; Surveyors to report.
4. Surveyors to deliver plan of Mrs Fewtrell's ground to Solicitor to annex to conveyance.
5. Solicitor reported Dean and Chapter of Westminster would sell site in St Margaret Westminster for £120. Agreed. Solicitors to apply to Chancery for confirming the contract, according to the act.

442. [p. 386] 6 May 1726
1. Signed warrant for paying £1,100 to Edward Hamstead, poulterer, for

house in Charles Street, Covent Garden, for minister of St Mary le Strand.
2. Hawksmoor delivered plan of Mrs Fewtrell's ground to be annexed to conveyance.
3. On Hawksmoor's report, ordered that £5 be paid Ety for damage to his house in building Bloomsbury church.
4. Surveyors to prepare plans for enclosing churchyards, together with the height and breadth of walls and depth of foundations, and also plans of ministers' houses to be built in Spitalfields, Wapping, Bloomsbury and Westminster, and bring estimates and proposals from workmen.

443. [p. 387] 23 May 1726
1. Minister's house to be built for Spitalfields according to plan submitted by Hawksmoor for not more than £1,000.
2. Surveyors to direct workmen to proceed to build parsonage houses on foot of contract made for that at Bow; and for walling in of churchyards on same foot.
3. Particulars of damage to Crochly's house and school to be referred to Surveyors.
4. Committee appointed to consider officers' application for a gratuity reported: Truth of petitions' allegations fully made out; work officers have had to do for two or three years past has far exceeded that of former years, and has required much more attendance than at first foundation of the churches when work was chiefly confined to masons, bricklayers and carpenters, but is now spread among all the artificers, carrying much more trouble in measuring works, drawing plans for new parishes, making up and examining the books and paying numerous artificers.

The original salaries, compared with what is allowed for like services in other places, are much lower, especially if it is considered that they are debarred of perquisites that persons in similar offices conceive themselves entitled to.

The Board some time since reduced certain salaries because of an intermission of business, but it has now increased more than ever. Committee consider that officers should be restored to original salaries.
5. Board agree with committee: officers entitled to their full salaries, to continue until Board direct to the contrary.

444. [p. 390] 18 July 1726
1. Signed warrants for paying officers a half-year's salary, £560, and gratuity from 14 Jan. 1725 to 14 Jan. 1726, £330; half-year's house rent £37. 10*s*.; to executors of Edw. Tufnell, mason, £350; to workmen from Lady Day 1724 to Lady Day 1725, £19,972. 6*s*. 8*d*.
2. Treasurer to pay workmen in tallies and orders with interest incurred between the date of order and time of issuing them, as in like case upon application to Treasury by order of 8 April 1723, as appears by minute of 24 May 1723.
3. Treasurer to pay Mrs Moor 50*s*. for last year's extraordinary services in cleaning Commissioners' rooms.
4. Signed warrant for laying out £2,500 in South Sea Annuities for rector of St Mary le Strand.

445. [p. 391] 11 Nov. 1726
1. Solicitor submitted his bill from 9 April 1725 to 1 Oct. 1726 of £289. 7*s*. 6*d*. Referred to Dean of the Arches, Melmoth and Ellis or any two of them.
2. Solicitor to prepare draft of bill for settling a maintenance for the five new churches in St Dunstan Stepney.
3. Turner's bill and petition referred to Surveyors.
4. Surveyors to prepare design for minister's house at Westminster suitable to ground purchased, with estimate.
5. Agent to inquire into state of houses on ground purchased of Fewtrell and report to next meeting.
6. Solicitor to procure enfranchisement of house and ground purchased of Heath on the best terms he can.
7. Treasurer delivered two receipts dated 18 Aug. 1726 for £2,500 laid out in South Sea annuities for endowment of St Mary le Strand.

446. [p. 393] 2 Dec. 1726
1. Hawksmoor to report on Cleave's petition.
2. The books of works from Lady Day 1725 to Michaelmas 1726 being prepared by Surveyors, resolved that Sir J. Philipps, Dean of the Arches, Ellis and Peck examine them.
3. Considered petitions of Durden, Walker, Newsham and Hall, watchmen; Secretary to pay each £3.
4. Treasurer to imprest £10 to Turner on account of his bill for £21. 7*s*. 6*d*.
5. Workmen's petition for interest on their tallies to be considered when a warrant is signed for works done between Lady Day 1725 and Michaelmas 1726.

447. [p. 394] 19 Dec. 1726
1. Secretary to allow Cleave to inspect the books concerning smith's work done by him at several churches, to enable him to show Board what works were done by other smiths that should have been done by virtue of his contract.
2. Read Agent's report on houses on Fewtrell's ground. Agent and James to sell materials of the houses to highest bidder for pulling them down.
3. Secretary to pay £4 to Durden, watchman at Wapping church.

448. [p. 395] 9 Jan. 1726/27
1. Money given to Ormond Street chapel trustees to be considered at next meeting; Deans of Chichester and the Arches and Peck desired to be present.
2. Petition of Sir Isaac Tillard to be considered when Bishop of Chichester and Peck present.
3. Signed two warrants for paying officers' salaries for half-year to Christmas and half-year's rent.

449. [p. 396] 19 Jan. 1726/27
1. Deans of the Arches and Chichester appointed to meet any two of the

proprietors of pews in Ormond Street church to adjust differences between Board and proprietors. Notice to be given to Marshall.
2. James reported that books of works made up to Michaelmas last amount to about £24,000.
3. Warrant to be prepared for paying 6*s*. 8*d*. in the pound to the artificers on present debt in tallies and orders together with interest due thereon from date of orders to paying of the workmen; but the watchmen being very indigent to be paid all that is due to them.
4. Philipps and Ellis to examine Secretary's bill of incidents and report to next meeting; warrant to be prepared to imprest him a sum for occasional charges.
5. Board being informed of great damage at Limehouse and Wapping churches done by pilferers, churchwardens to attend next meeting to consider best means of prevention.
6. Several papers referred to Surveyors.

450. [p. 398] 27 Jan. 1726/27
1. Churchwardens of Limehouse and Wapping promised to prevent, as far as in their power, damages by pilferers.
2. Ormond Street affair to be considered at next meeting in order to give Deans of Chichester and the Arches instruction to confer with trustees. Secretary to submit relevant papers.
3. Petition of churchwardens of St John Clerkenwell about an endowment to be considered at next meeting.
4. Signed two warrants for paying £8,699. 10*s*. 3*d*. to workmen, and £50 imprest to Secretary for incidentals.

451. [p. 399] 3 Feb. 1726/27
1. Read petition of minister and wardens of St John Clerkenwell. Michell attending was told Board will adhere to usual method of endowing by a pound rate.
2. Read petition of Edward Baldwin for saving clause in Stepney churches endowment bill preserving his present rights as clerk of St Dunstan Stepney.
3. Solicitor read draft of Stepney churches endowment bill.

452. [p. 400] 10 Feb. 1726/27
1. Dean of the Arches reported that he and Dean of Chichester had met gentleman from Ormond Street chapel, and that they were disposed to give the Board satisfaction without further trouble.
The two deans to meet persons appointed by Ormond Street church trustees to settle matters in dispute in best manner they can.
2. James to prepare plan showing boundaries of Poplar hamlet for making it a parish.
3. Read Dr Warren's representation complaining of damage to his cellars in new house at Bow by water from roads; £15 allowed for making a drain under Surveyors' directions.

453. [p. 401] 20 Feb. 1726/27
1. Read petition from churchwardens, etc, of Spitalfields, setting forth

things unfinished in church, particularly spire and portico. Hawksmoor to direct proper workmen to finish these speedily.
2. Read memorial from principal inhabitants of intended new parish in St Margaret Westminster, proposing to raise £125 for maintenance of minister if £2,500 be allowed out of parliamentary fund; and praying that towers of church and some other uncompleted works may be speedily finished.
Board approved proposal and directed Solicitor to prepare a bill for endowing church without loss of time. Surveyors to consider best method of finishing towers and other works.
3. James presented plan of hamlet of Poplar with its boundaries for enrolment and being converted to a separate parish.

454. [p. 403] 27 Feb. 1726/27
1. At general reduction of salaries, Agent's (at first £100) was by minute of 2 March 1720 reduced to £60, and on Skeat's death the Board, observing labour of the office was considerably lessened, made a further reduction on 14 Sept. 1724, but on 23 May 1726 restored officers to their former salaries. Doubt whether the intention was to allow Agent £60 or £100.

Resolved to allow no more than £60 p.a. to person who shall be chosen *vice* Prichard, deceased.

Ordered John Sherman to be appointed Agent.
2. Melmoth having examined Solicitor's bills, settled at £282. 14*s*. 2*d*. Warrant to be prepared.

455. [p. 404] 10 Mar. 1726/27
1. Warrant signed for paying Solicitor's bill.
2. Dr Shippen, principal of Brasenose College Oxford, and Dodd, rector of Stepney, to be desired to attend at next meeting, to state how much Easter offerings and other perquisites are likely to amount to in hamlets after they become distinct parishes.

456. [p. 405] 16 Mar. 1726/27
1. Secretary to attend Crosse for original instrument describing boundaries of new parish in St Margaret Westminster and deliver it to Batley for the perusal of Dean and Chapter.
2. Principal of Brasenose College and rector of Stepney delivered amount of perquisites in hamlets.
3. Whereas Spitalfields offered to settle £200 p.a. for minister's maintenance, it now appears that £150 p.a. is as much as can be expected because of decay of trade and fall of rents.
4. Dean of Chichester reported that he and Dean of the Arches had agreed with representatives of trustees of Ormond Street chapel that moneys undisposed of and remaining in trustees' hands shall be paid to order of the Board for purchasing pews. Rector and churchwardens shall be empowered to treat for pews and lay terms before trustees. Trustees shall certify approbation to such person as Board directs, who shall have power finally to agree for purchases and order the money upon proper conveyances being made.

Resolved that Deans of the Arches and Chichester or either be empowered to settle the account with trustees and direct money remaining in their hands to be lodged with Hoare and Co. subject to the Board's further orders, and empowered to receive accounts of purchases and direct money to be issued for such as they approve. [Footnote: 'Alterations in the minutes made by the Board on second reading, Friday 24th March 1726/7'.]

457. [p. 407] 24 Mar. 1726/27
1. Warrant to be dated 4 March 1725/6 for £100 which Treasurer paid Solicitor by minute for paying expenses of bill in parliament for Strand church; and for £400 to Solicitor for defraying fees and charges in pursuing bills now depending for endowing church in St Margaret Westminster and Stepney churches.
2. Ordered that spire at Spitalfields be finished according to design sent in by Hawksmoor, and that his estimate of charge for portico be considered at next meeting.

458. [p. 408] 27 Mar. 1727
1. Read two precepts from House of Commons, ordering Treasurer to submit an account of all sums issued towards bulding church of St Margaret Westminster and for site of church [Millbank]; and ordering Secretary and Surveyors to submit plan of district of Millbank and orders of this Board relating to that district.
2. Signed warrants for paying Solicitor £100 and £400.
3. Secretary submitted minutes about district taken out of St Margaret's parish, Westminster.

459. [p. 409] 6 Apr. 1727
1. Commissioners, having been informed that opposition is intended against a pound rate in new parishes in Stepney, desire churchwardens and others who made the proposals to attend committee of House of Commons on Monday next, to be ready if necessary to declare on what authority they made such proposals in the name of the inhabitants.
2. Treasurer to advance two guineas to Durden, watchman.

460. [p. 410] 10 Apr. 1727
Solicitor to fee counsel to attend bill of endowment now depending in parliament.

461. [p. 411] 12 Apr. 1727
Resumed consideration of bill of endowment now depending in parliament.

462. [p. 412] 17 Apr. 1727
Read order from House of Commons dated 15 April about new districts in Stepney, and Secretary presented several orders of the Board about them.

463. [p. 413] 28 Apr. 1727
Secretary to advance £5 to Hall, watchman, on his bill for carrying rubbish out of church.

464. [p. 314 (*sic*)] 5 May 1727
1. Hawksmoor submitted plan of site of church and parsonage house at Bloomsbury. The kitchen and cellars being dark and small, ordered that a small shed be built for a wash-house in Little Russell Street at further end of churchyard, next the ale house, for not more than £30.
2. Portico and entablement at Spitalfields church to be made of wood and brick.
3. Surveyors to prepare a model and estimate of a church and parsonage house not to exceed £10,000 together with enclosing the ground.

465. [p. 415] 9 June 1727
1. Surveyors submitted their respective models for a new church. Ordered that they jointly prepare by next meeting a model of a church tower that may be built as cheap as possible.
2. Read letter of Cleave, the smith. Surveyors to report by next meeting, and Cleave to have a copy.
3. Treasurer to prepare memorial to Treasury for opening a loan of £25,000 for Board's use.
4. Treasurer's account of money issued from Exchequer since Lady Day 1719 to be inserted in book of muniments.

466. [p. 416] 19 June 1727
1. Deans of the Arches and Chichester presented account of £1,500 formerly paid to trustees of St George's chapel, there remaining due upon the balance £693. 14*s*. 10*d*. Approved.
2. Agreed by Commissioners and trustees that the balance be deposited with Hoare and Partners for purchasing pews for such parishioners as want them.
3. Resolved that the balance be put into hands of Hoare to be applied conformable to resolutions of 16 March, and that the deans be enabled to draw sums desired by trustees for purchasing pews.
4. Copy of last two minutes to be delivered to Hoare and Partners.
5. Signed memorial to Treasury for loan of £25,000.
6. Hawksmoor and James presented memorial in answer to Cleave's complaints; delivered to Cleave to consider and return to next meeting.

467. [p. 418] 23 June 1727
1. Read petition from minister and wardens of Stratford Bow. Dr Warren and others were called in. Petition to be considered at a fuller meeting.
2. Stonehouse's bill for soliciting the endowment bill referred to Solicitor to examine and settle.
Crochly's petition to be considered at a fuller meeting; Hawksmoor to report.

4. Surveyors to take new survey of Mrs Fewtrell's ground in St Giles Cripplegate.
5. A plan for a new church to be erected in parish of St Olave Southwark was laid before Board, and another plan of a church to be built in Old Street in parish of St Giles Cripplegate; both approved.
Surveyors ordered to direct workmen to begin digging foundations without loss of time.

468. [p. 419] 30 June 1727
1. The doors opening into churchyard of new church at Ratcliff Highway to be shut up unless reason to the contrary shown at next meeting. Wm Noble, Widow Cowley, John Stringer, Dr Harries and Russel to be informed.
2. Secretary to present at next meeting petition of Tufnell's executors about removing the stones from ground in St Olave's, Surveyors' report, and entry in book of works for £350 allowed to executors on the account.
3. Newsham to be paid till Lady Day last as watchman at Hanover Square church at 1*s*. 6*d*. per day, totalling £5. 6*s*. 6*d*., to be paid him by Secretary.
4. Same officers to be continued till first meeting after Christmas 1727.
5. Signed warrants for paying officers' salaries to Midsummer, and half-year's rent.
6. Agent to inspect books and inform himself what houses and lands have been purchased by Commissioners, and by whom possessed.
7. Agent to demand of executors and administrators of Skeat and Prichard the moneys received by them for Commission's use and unaccounted for.
8. Agent to demand arrears of rent due from the several tenants.

469. [p. 421] 7 July 1727
1. Paper concerning £350 paid executors of Tufnell to be entered in minute book: for loss by stone laid down by building church in St Olave Southwark and not proceeded with, 570 tons at £1. 3*s*. 6*d*. delivered. Loss by present value of stone together with carriage and wharfage, 8*s*. 6*d*. per ton, making £242. 5*s*.; plus interest for 4 years, £134, making whole loss £376. 5*s*. If any stone remain on ground when the church shall be built, 8*s*. 6*d*. per ton to be deducted from mason's bills.
2. Solicitor, having examined Stonehouse's bill, to pay him £16. 7*s*.
3. All private doors to be shut up in churchyard wall of Wapping, except entrance at west and that on south towards the east.
4. Solicitor to examine Johnson's lease and report whether anything is to be altered when it is renewed, his term expiring next Christmas.
5. Vestry act of St George the Martyr today delivered to be referred to Deans of the Arches and Chichester.
6. Solicitor to consult counsel whether contract with late Capt Tufnell, his executors and administrators, without mention of his assigns, for stonework of church in St Olave, be obligatory on Board, as contract now assigned to son of deceased.

470. [p. 424] 24 July 1727
1. Read opinion of counsel about Tufnell's contract; consideration deferred.
2. Read petition of Durden, watchman; Treasurer to pay him £4 if so much due.
3. Agent delivered account of yearly rents of Board's tenants. To demand arrears now due, and rent due by Marshall. In future, to collect rents yearly at proper times and pay them to Treasurer. If any refuses to pay, Agent to inform Solicitor, that he may act.
4. Goff's proposals for smith's work at Old Street church approved; Solicitor to prepare contract.
5. Advertisement ordered for masons' proposals for Old Street church.

471. [p. 426] 4 Aug. 1727
1. Masons' proposals for Old Street church referred to Surveyors.
2. Read case of Tufnell, with Ward's opinion. Case again to be referred to Ward.
3. Treasurer submitted bills for passing accounts in Treasury and Exchequer, from 7 June 1722 to Christmas 1725, £83. 8*s*. 10*d*. Warrant to be prepared for next meeting.
4. Signed warrant for paying workmen from Lady Day 1725 to the end of December 1726, £18,166. 1*s*. 6*d*.

472. [p. 427] 25 Aug. 1727
1. Surveyors having examined masons' proposals for Old Street church, Thos Shepherd to be employed.
2. After full inquiry, allow Crochly £100 in consideration of damages from building of Bloomsbury church; warrant to be prepared.
3. Wexholm and Barr to be employed to make and furnish bricks for Old Street church.
4. Signed warrant for paying Treasurer £83. 8*s*. 10*d*.

473. [p. 429] 11 Sep. 1727
1. Solicitor to pay £31. 10*s*. for charges in enfranchising house purchased of Thos Heath for minister of Limehouse.
2. It appearing by Agent's report that Skeat died indebted to the Board £54. 14*s*. 6*d*., Agent to demand payment of Mrs Skeat.
2. Signed two warrants for paying Crochly £100 and Heath £500.
4. Read petition from churchwardens, etc., of Bethnal Green, praying that a church may be built on site purchased of White. Agent to give White notice to clear the ground by Lady Day next.
6. Solicitor to prepare contract with Jas Wilson and Benj. Prosser, bricklayers, for Old Street church.
7. Vestry room to be built at north-west angle of church ground in Bloomsbury over offices already directed for minister, it appearing the least expensive way.
8. Surveyors to report on damages at alms- and engine-houses at Spitalfields.

474. [p. 431] 22 Sep. 1727

1. Read petition from Thos Ross, victualler, of St Giles in the Fields, complaining his house likely to suffer damage by brewhouse intended to be built for minister. Surveyors to report.
2. Read memorial from Carteret, Postmaster-general, about passage from the Post Office to gallery in St Mary Woolnoth. Surveyors to report.
3. Copy of memorial and minute to be communicated to parish vestry.
4. John Bever to be employed as watchman, Old Street church.

475. [p. 432] 9 Oct. 1727

1. Read report from the churchwarden, etc., of Spitalfields, setting forth damage done by building of new church; told that Surveyors should be ordered to view and consider.
2. Surveyors to inspect accordingly and report to next meeting.

476. [p. 433] 27 Oct. 1727

1. Surveyors submitted report on damage to parish house and shed for engine in Spitalfields. Expense of rebuilding, about £90. Consideration referred to next meeting.
2. Several inhabitants of Bermondsey attended with petition for having a church built on site purchased. Told that Board was inclined to comply with their petition; Secretary to keep it with office papers.
3. Read petition from Wilson, now in prison, praying he may be permitted to go on with brickwork of Old Street church. Surveyors to learn what proposals he will offer about finding security for his performance.

477. [p. 434] 10 Nov. 1727

1. Act of vestry of St Mary Woolnoth concerning passage from Post Office to gallery to be delivered to Postmaster-general by Secretary.
2. De la Motte, an assignee of estate of Jas Wilson, bricklayer, a bankrupt, declared on behalf of creditors that he had no objection to Commissioners discharging Wilson from his contract and agreeing with another.
3. Hawksmoor and James having some time ago complained to Wilson of his not setting about bricklayer's work at Old Street church, and he promising to set about it and to bring good security to Board this day for performing the contract, or he would be content to waive it; and Wilson not having begun it, or brought any security, and being a bankrupt and prisoner in Ludgate for upwards of a year, Commissioners judge that he ought not to be employed at Old Street church.
4. Benj. Prosser and Wm Cooper, bricklayers, proposing to do the work on the terms in Wilson's contract, proposal is accepted; Solicitor to prepare contract.

MINUTES OF THE BUILDING COMMITTEE, 1711

Lambeth MS 2690

These minutes are written at the back of the volume containing the minutes of the Commission (above, **1–202**). The page references given below are to the modern numbering from the front of the volume. The contemporary numbering of the pages from the back of the volume is confused.

478. [p. 446] 10 Oct. 1711, Banqueting House, Whitehall
William Dickinson (Surveyor) and Minister and churchwardens of Stepney called in.

Surveyors to report on sites for four churches proposed by parishioners of Stepney by 16 Oct.

Skeat (Agent and Solicitor) to attend surveyors.

479. [p. 445] 16 Oct. 1711, St Dunstan in the West
Trustees of St George's chapel, Ormond St, delivered answer to Commissioners' letter; desired more time for designating boundaries, if made a parish church.

Resolved that chapel be made parochial; and that trustees' proposals are reasonable.

Surveyors presented surveys of Stepney hamlets; minister and churchwardens of Stepney examined thereon.

Resolved that five of the 50 new churches should be erected within Stepney; that the chapels of Bow and Poplar, in Stepney parish, be made parochial.

That one of the five new churches be at Bethnal Green, with a parish of the hamlets of Bethnal Green and Mile End New Town; and that a convenient site for church, churchyard and minister's house is a freehold estate of two acres called Hare fields, priced at £200.

That another new church be at Limehouse, with a parish of that hamlet; and that West's field, a freehold of near three acres for £400, is a convenient site.

That other new churches be erected in Upper Wapping, Lower Wapping and Spitalfields.

Surveyors and Agent to discourse proprietors of sites proposed for new churches and deliver account of the lowest prices; and to inquire whether any other sites in the hamlets obtainable at lower rates.

Churchwardens of Deptford delivered reply to Commissioners' letter; resolved that one of the new churches be erected in Deptford.

480. [p. 443] 19 Oct. 1711
Read, act for confirming to Brasenose College Oxford purchase of advowson of Stepney.

A motion to be made at next meeting of Commissioners that a letter be written to Brasenose College, desiring concurrence in division of parish of Stepney under New Churches Act; as this Committee does not consider itself empowered to do so.

Read, Dr Lamb's representation about Bow chapel. Dr Lamb requested to make it fuller and attend Committee on 23rd inst.

Surveyors to survey parishes for sites for churches, cemeteries and ministers' houses, acquainting parish authorities that they are authorized to expedite the matter: Dickinson to survey St James Westminster and St Martin in the Fields for two and three sites respectively; Hawksmoor to survey St Andrew Holborn and St Giles in the Fields for two sites each. Surveyors to consider a proper number of houses for each parish, and where the divisions should be made.

Read, representation from parish of St Saviour Southwark; Surveyors to view site proposed before next meeting.

Surveyors to provide a large map of London, Westminster and suburbs, showing parishes where new churches are intended to be built, and adding buildings erected since making of map.

Agent to go to parishes written to by Commissioners to quicken their returns, which should have parish plans annexed.

481. [p. 441] 23 Oct. 1711
Dr Lamb and Mr Hardesty attended.

Read, answer of churchwardens of St Botolph Aldersgate to Commissioners' letter.

Agent reported visiting churchwardens of St Clement Danes, St James and St Margaret Westminster, St Andrew Holborn, and St Giles and St Martin in the Fields, to quicken their returns, which should be ready within three weeks.

Dr Marshall, minister of St George's chapel, Ormond Street, and several inhabitants, delivered account of proposed new parish, with plan. Resolved that the plan contained a convenient district for the new parish.

Commissioners be moved to write to Sir Nathaniel Curzon to inquire terms on which he will sell freehold of the chapel.

482. [p. 440] 26 Oct. 1711
Resolved, to move Commissioners for general power to correspond with persons for expediting work.

Read, representations of minister and parishioners of St Botolph Bishopsgate and inhabitants of Hatton Garden, Norton Folgate, and Old Artillery Ground.

Resolved, that one of the new churches be built in parish of St Botolph Bishopsgate and the precincts of Norton Folgate, Old Artillery Ground, St Mary le Spittle.

Minister and churchwardens of St Botolph Bishopsgate and

inhabitants of Norton Folgate and Old Artillery Ground desired to attend again on 6 Nov.

Consideration of Hatton Garden representation postponed until return received from St Andrew Holborn.

Hawksmoor reported on St Andrew Holborn and St Giles in the Fields, with plans of sites. Further consideration postponed till parish returns received.

Dickinson to survey parish of St Botolph Bishopsgate and precincts of Norton Folgate and Old Artillery Ground, and report on proposed sites on 6 Nov.

Dickinson reported on St Martin in the Fields and St James Westminster; consideration postponed till parish returns received.

483. [p. 438] 27 Oct. 1711
Read, petition of several inhabitants of Limehouse that proposed new church be erected on Rigby's Garden.

Hawksmoor, accompanied by Sherlock and Isham, to survey and report on this and previously-proposed Limehouse site, inquiring values.

Read, Mr Walkden's petition proposing site in Grays Inn Lane, parish of St Andrew Holborn; resolved, not a proper site.

Read, representation from inhabitants of St Sepulchre Without for dividing parish, with plan. Hawksmoor to view site proposed.

Hawksmoor to survey following parishes for sites, ascertain parish boundaries and number of houses in proposed new parishes, and prepare plans.

Secretary to write to overseers of poor for White Friars for account of constitution and condition of that precinct.

Names of the several parishes with the number of churches at present proposed to be erected in them:

St Andrew Holborn	3	St Mary Whitechapel	2
St Botolph Aldgate	1	St Paul Shadwell	1
St Botolph Bishopsgate	1	St Ann Westminster	1
St Bride	1	St Clement Danes	1
St George Southwark	1	St James Westminster	3
St Giles Cripplegate	4	St Margaret Westminster	2
St Saviour Southwark	2	St Martin in the Fields	4
St Olave Southwark	2	Lambeth	1
St Sepulchre	2	White Friars	1
St Dunstan Stepney	5	St Mary le Strand	1
St Giles in the Fields	4	Deptford	1
St James Clerkenwell	1		
St Leonard Shoreditch	2		
Bermondsey	1		

484. [p. 436] 6 Nov. 1711
Read, offer from Dean and Chapter of Westminster of site in Tothill Fields or any other waste ground belonging to them for new church etc in St Margaret's parish. Commissioners to be moved to return their thanks.

Request from Rev. Sir George Wheeler that nothing be done respecting Norton Folgate till he could be heard. Consideration of Norton Folgate deferred to 16th inst.

Curate of St Giles Cripplegate reported that churchwardens and parishioners could not agree on return to Commissioners' letter.

Read, representations from St Mary le Strand, St Giles in the Fields, St Ann Westminster and Bermondsey.

Hawksmoor to report on site proposed for new church in Bermondsey.

Resolved that it is not proper for the Commissioners to present petition annexed to representation from St Mary le Strand to the Queen.

Dean of Carlisle to acquaint Commissioners with request of Dean of Rochester and several inhabitants of St Mary le Strand to state in petition to Queen that it is the Commissioners' opinion that one of the new churches should be erected for the parishioners of St Mary le Strand.

Read, letters from Brasenose College and Nathaniel Curzon Esq. Henry Box to discourse John Kent Esq about purchase of freehold of St George's chapel [Ormond Street].

Read, Dickinson's report on St James Westminster, St Martin in the Fields, Norton Folgate and Old Artillery Ground. Sir C. Wren, Archer, Vanbrugh and Mr Wren to view the three sites in St James parish proposed by Dickinson, who is to inquire after further sites.

Agent to inquire into value, etc., of sites in Windmill and Warwick Streets proposed by Dickinson.

Consideration of report on St Martin's parish deferred to 9th inst.

Skeat to inquire whether Lord Conway willing to sell his house in Queen Street as site for church, etc.

485. [p. 433] 9 Nov. 1711

Read, representations of St James Clerkenwell, St Martin in the Fields, St Clement Danes, St Leonard Shoreditch and St James Westminster.

Thomas Elford, churchwarden, reported that there are about 7,200 souls in St James Clerkenwell, and two proper sites for new churches, etc, viz. Vinegar house, Woods Close (Lady Northampton's), and St John Close.

Representation from St Martin's computed population at about 29,600; site proposed vested in Mercers' Company and leased to Mr Vandeput.

Inhabitants of St Clement Danes left a map, computed population at about 10,140, and proposed as site Grange Inn (freehold vested in Mr Hewer of Bushey Hall, Herts).

Population of St James Westminster computed at about 20,000. Read, certificate relating to chapel in Hatton Garden.

Mr Russell, Rector of St John Wapping, delivered petition and plan; resolved, that one of the fifty new churches should be erected in parish of St John Wapping.

Inhabitants of Spitalfields delivered plan of one and a half acre site and stated population of hamlet at 18,000 or 20,000; there is one French church there, fit to be made parochial.

Representation from St Botolph Aldgate computes population of manor of East Smithfield at about 9,000, and of whole parish at about 21,000; and proposes two sites: one at or near the May Pole, East Smithfield, 150 ft × 70 ft, on which are 15 old houses, rent under £100 p.a., freehold vested in parishioners of St Mary at Hill; the other, in same street, larger but cheaper, the property of Mr Paradice of Wiltshire. Archer proposed third site, waste belonging to the Crown, on Little Tower Hill at end of Minories.

Read, report from trustees of King Street chapel, in St James Westminster.

Box reported on interview with John Kent, who would write.

Hoskins reported that Lady Russell promised to reply soon to the Commissioners' proposals made to her by Bishop of London.

Archer reported on sites referred to him: at upper end of Haymarket; where the Bowling Green is, at the upper end of Marlborough Street; and at end of St James Street, Covent Garden. The first two (both in St James Westminster) he judges suitable, but the third not convenient.

Sherlock and Isham reported on the two sites proposed in Limehouse, judging West's fields preferable.

Consideration of representations deferred to this day adjourned to Tues. next.

Hawksmoor reported in favour of site proposed in Bermondsey, and that Lord Salisbury's steward promised to discuss it with his lordship.

Skeat to inquire of Mr Manly or his deputy about any further grant of the ground at the end of Windmill Street, at upper end of Haymarket, after Madam Panton's interest expires.

486. [p. 429] 13 Nov. 1711
Commissioners to be recommended to build a second new church in Spitalfields, the population being about 20,000.

Read, representations from Lambeth, White Friars Precinct, St Giles Cripplegate, St Sepulchre, and St Olave Southwark.

Read, answer from Lady Russell about proposed site for cemetery for St George's chapel; and for site for a church, etc. in Bloomsbury; to be laid before the Commissioners.

Refered to Commissioners, whether representation from King Street chapel trustees be laid before Archbishop of Canterbury, its benefactor.

Hawksmoor to survey Rotherhithe for a proper site for church, etc.

Dickinson to report on site for church etc. in St James Clerkenwell, proposed by Rev. Francis Browne.

Resolved, that there should be a cemetery wherever it can be had at a convenient distance from a new church.

Resolved, that a second new church should be built in Upper Liberty of manor of East Smithfield within St Botolph Aldgate; and that site on Little Tower Hill at end of Minories is proper for church and minister's house.

Hawksmoor to inquire for more proper site for lower part of manor of East Smithfield than either of those proposed.

Jennings to inquire about interest of Duchess of Portsmouth in Monmouth House, Soho Square, St James Westminster.

Resolved, that church for St Mary le Strand should be built at or near the Maypole in the Strand.

Hawksmoor to report on the ground.

Resolved, that one of the new churches for St Giles in the Fields should be built in Lincoln's Inn Fields, provided there be no churchyard, intramural burials or ring of bells.

Secretary to deliver to Surveyors a list of parishes wherein the Commissioners have agreed new churches should be built, and number allotted.

Vanbrugh to view chapel in Hatton Garden, and site proposed at north end of Hatton Garden.

Resolved, that one of the new churches should be built in that part of St Sepulchre's called St Sepulchre Without.

487. [p. 426] 16 Nov. 1711

Secretary reported offer by Sir John Thornicroft, lord of the manor of Stockwell, of two acres of waste at Stockwell town end.

Surveyors to report on site proposed in plan delivered by rector of Whitechapel.

Read, representations from St Andrew Holborn, St Giles Cripplegate, and trustees of new chapel in Tothill Fields.

Mr Hayes delivered offer of ground belonging to Red Lion and Green Dragon Inns, Holborn, for site for church, etc., in St Giles in the Fields.

Read, petition of some inhabitants of St Leonard Shoreditch; Mr Francis Coleman offered site in Holywell Lane.

Rev. Sir George Wheeler delivered representation and plan concerning his chapel in Spitalfields.

Rev Mr Brookes, minister of St Alphage, delivered petition and plan.

Skeat reported that Lord Conway was not in town; and that Mr Manly promised an answer in about a week concerning ground at upper end of Haymarket. Read, petition of some inhabitants of Bethnal Green; resolved, that their reasons are insufficient to alter opinion about place to build church. Resolved, that parish of St James Westminster ought to be divided into four distinct parishes; and that the chapel in Berwick Street is not fit to be made parochial.

Resolved, that parish of St Martin in the Fields ought to be divided into four distinct parishes.

Resolved, that a second church ought to be erected in St Saviour Southwark; Hawksmoor to attend vestry of St Olave Southwark next Thurs.

Surveyors to attend Committee next Tues., with such maps and plans as they have.

488. [p. 423] 20 Nov. 1711

Surveyors to examine what approaches there are for coaches from Bethnal Green to Hare Fields.

Dickinson reported in favour of Farthing [Pardon] Churchyard site in St James Clerkenwell proposed by Rev. Mr Browne, who stated he would sell the remaining nine years of his lease for £200.

Dickinson laid plan of site in Norton Folgate proposed for one of the churches to be erected in Spitalfields.

Resolved, to determine first the sites for churches before considering division of parishes.

Hawksmoor to report on site proposed in Nightingale Lane for upper part of St John Wapping.

Vanbrugh reported that chapel in Hatton Garden was not fit to be made parochial. Ordered, that debate about the chapel be deferred until Lord Thanet comes to town.

Vanbrugh reported in favour of site at north end of Hatton Garden.

Resolved, that West's Fields is the most proper site in Limehouse for a church etc. Skeat to inquire owners and value, and for a house or ground for the minister.

Resolved, that site next Ratcliff Highway and Cannon Street is convenient for a church, etc, for Upper Wapping. Skeat to ask Mr Watts his price for it, and inquire for a house or ground for the minister.

Surveyors and Skeat to look for a house or ground for minister of Bow and Old Ford, Stepney.

Skeat to inquire whether there is any house belonging to chapel at Poplar.

Sir C. Wren, and Archer, Vanbrugh and Wren, Esqs., to survey and report on sites already or hereafter agreed upon by Surveyors. Secretary to give them list of sites already proposed, and whether approved or disapproved by this Committee.

Commissioners to be consulted, whether any site should be approved on which church cannot be built east and west.

Hawksmoor to inquire for a second site for a church etc in Bermondsey.

Resolved, that site on Little Tower Hill at end of Minories is a proper site for one of the two new churches for St Botolph Aldgate, and Archer to ask John Jefferys Esq. of Sheen his terms.

489. [p. 419] 23 Nov. 1711

1. Trustees of St George's chapel to be asked how much money necessary to make the church parochial, and to inquire for ground for a churchyard.
2. Resolution relating to proposed parish for St George's chapel to be laid before next meeting of the Commission.
3. The Committee resolved:
4. That Three Cups Inn, Holborn, is a proper site for one of the new churches for St Andrew Holborn.
5. Skeat to inquire about the site.
6. That a solicitor should be appointed to inquire into value of sites selected.
7. Hawksmoor to inquire for two more sites in St Andrew Holborn.
8. Surveyors to attend Committee at three o'clock every day they meet.
9. Surveyors to look for site for churchyard in out parts of St Ann Westminster.

10. Surveyors each to have a copy of Commissioners' resolution relating to placing churches east and west.
11. Approved, sites for two churches and ministers' houses in St Olave Southwark, one in Stony Lane and Vincorne [Unicorn] Yard, the other in Horsleydown Lane.
12. Approved, districts proposed by Dickinson for the two new parishes.
13. Surveyors to inquire for ground for one or more churchyards for the two new parishes.
14. That two acres should be allowed for each church yard when possible.
15. That site at the Maypole in the Strand is a proper site for a church for parish of St Mary le Strand.
16. Hawksmoor to inquire for sites for minister's house and churchyard for St Mary le Strand.
17. That Grange Inn is a proper site for church and minister's house in St Clement Danes.
18. Hawksmoor to inquire for ground for a church yard.
19. Gastrell and Cross to apply to Mr Ewers, proprietor of Grange Inn, for his terms.
20. Hawksmoor to settle a district for new parish with parishioners of St Clement Danes.
21. Hawksmoor reported that the approaches for coaches from Bethnal Green to Harefields may be made good.
22. Read proposal for house for minister of Bow and Old Ford.
23. Read Mr Kemp's proposal for site for house for that minister.
24. Hawksmoor to view Kemp's site, and if it is a proper one obtain Kemp's terms.
25. Skeat to inquire for site for house for minister of Poplar.
26. Mr Watts delivered his demand for site for church and minister's house in Upper Wapping.
27. Resolved that the demand is reasonable.
28. Hawksmoor to inquire for ground for a churchyard.
29. Skeat to inquire for sites for churchyards for the two new parishes to be taken out of St Botolph Aldgate.
30. Skeat to send to Mr Paradice for his terms for site in Lordship part of St Botolph Aldgate.

490. [p. 415] 27 Nov. 1711
1. Read proposal of Sir Nathaniel Curzon and John Kent Esq for freehold of St George's chapel, Ormond Street.
2. Resolved that the proposal is unreasonable.
3. Read, the case of the inhabitants of Lambeth Deane and Stockwell.
4. Resolved, that the new church in Lambeth parish should be erected in or about Stockwell.
5. Sir John Thornicroft offered two acres in Stockwell for building a new church.
6. Commissioners to be moved to thank him for his offer.
7. Mr Peterson delivered a proposal for an acre on which to erect a church in Upper Wapping.

8. Mr Watts offered two acres in Upper Wapping for £400.
9. Resolved that Watts's proposal should be preferred to Peterson's.
10. Read John Jefferys' demand for £400 for a site for a church and minister's house on Little Tower Hill at end of Minories.
11. Jennings to try to persuade Jefferys to abate his demand.
12. Henry Hoare delivered proposal from Rev. Dr Bray for districts of the two intended new parishes in St Botolph Aldgate.
13. Resolved that proposed district for the lower parish is a proper one.
14. Resolved that to district proposed for the middle parish there should be added all houses on both sides of the way from north side of Trinity Minories to Whitechapel Street, and all south side of Whitechapel Street from Aldgate to the Bars.
15. Read, Mr West's demand for £400 for three acres in West's Field, Limehouse for a church, etc.
16. Resolved that the demand is reasonable.
17. Hawksmoor proposed a district for a new parish to be taken out of Bermondsey, and a site for a new church, etc.
18. Resolved that district and site are proper.
19. Commissioners to be moved to desire one or more members to apply to Lord Salisbury to set moderate price for proposed site.
20. Hawksmoor proposed a district for parish to be taken out of St Sepulchre.
21. Resolved that St Sepulchre should be divided into two parishes by a line drawn through centre of Long Lane, across Smithfield on north side of the sheep pens and down middle of Cheek Lane to Fleet Ditch.
21. Crosse to apply to Sir John Robinson for his terms for site in St Sepulchre.

491. [p. 412] 30 Nov. 1711
Skeat to obtain Widow Moore's terms in writing for site agreed on in Limehouse.

Dickinson to inquire for another site within proposed district for St George Ormond Street.

Upon Skeat's report from Manley about proposed site at upper end of Haymarket, agreed he should enquire further of Madam Panton and Mr Taylor about any reversionary grant.

Hawksmoor reported in favour of site proposed by Kemp for house for minister of Bow, at £150. Hawksmoor or Skeat to obtain his written demand.

Secretary to give Mr Beckley a list of sites approved by the Commissioners.

Resolved that the Borough Liberty and part of the Clink Liberty from Dead Man's Place and Stony Street to the Thames ought to be continued to St Saviour Southwark.

That the Tenterfields on north side of Castle Street is a proper site for a church, etc, for a parish to be taken out of St Saviour's.

Resolved that the district for the middle parish to be taken out of St Saviour's be bounded by Bandy Leg Walk, Maiden Lane, the Bear Garden, down Rope Alley to the Thames. Site proposed in Pye Garden, on south of Maiden Lane, is a proper one for another church, etc., in St Saviour's, and its district should consist of the remaining part of parish, lying south-west of Maiden Lane.

Hawksmoor to inquire about two last-mentioned sites.

Mr Sclater delivered demand of £300 for three acres in Hare alias Cross Fields, Bethnal Green, as set out by Hawksmoor. Resolved that demand is reasonable.

Read, representation from Common Councilmen of St Bride's.

Barker delivered his demand for £2,200 for Three Cups Inn, Holborn. Resolved that demand is unreasonable.

Nelson to acquaint Lord Thanet with objections to making the chapel in Hatton Garden parochial.

Skeat to inquire for another site for church, etc. in Lower Wapping, Ballard's demand of £900 being unreasonable.

Skeat delivered demands of Mr Jackson and Mr Henshaw for site proposed in Stony Lane and Vincorn [Unicorn] Yard, St Olave's Southwark. Crosse to view site and inquire after a cheaper site near that place.

Resolved, that it should be reported to Parliament that part of St Giles Cripplegate should be added to St Alphage.

Skeat to obtain Mr White's demand for two sites proposed in St Giles Cripplegate, and details of the precincts of parish, and number of houses in each.

Resolved that Mr Smith's ground in St Margaret's Westminster is a proper site for a church and minister's house.

492. [p. 408] 4 Dec. 1711
Read, a second proposal from Sir N. Curzon and John Kent Esq. for the freehold of St George's chapel. Resolved, that the £1,000 demanded is reasonable.

Isham to try to persuade Barker to abate his demand for Three Cups Inn, Holborn.

Surveyors to report on chapel in Noble Street, St Giles Cripplegate.

Resolved that Plow Yard near Bloomsbury Market is a proper site for one of the churches to be built in St Giles in the Fields, containing 110 ft in front and 164 ft in depth. Hoskins to apply to Lady Russell for her terms.

Resolved that Hawksmoor's design for church to be erected within the great square in Lincoln's Inn Fields be laid before Commissioners. Sir Trenchman Masters and other inhabitants of Red Lion Square declared they were unwilling that a church should be built in that square.

Wm Cullpeper, Esq., delivered a written offer of a site for church etc. in St Leonard Shoreditch. Consideration adjourned until other sites are proposed in that parish.

Skeat to desire Ironmongers' Company's terms for a site for church house for Bow. Resolved that it ought to be accepted, as commodiously situated, and no other thereabouts.

Dickinson to inquire for site for church etc. in that part of St Bride's parish to the north of Fleet Street.

Skeat to desire Ironmongers' Company's terms for a site for church etc. in Old Street, within St Giles Cripplegate.

Duchess of Monmouth's demand for £3,000 for site in Soho Square is too high; Soho Square is the properest site for a church, so long as there is no peal of bells or church yard. Skeat to inquire who the proprietors are, and also for a site for a minister's house.

Skeat to inquire for sites for churches etc. in the following parishes: one in St Botolph Bishopsgate; two in St Leonard Shoreditch; two in St Mary Whitechapel; two in Spitalfields hamlet; one in St John Wapping; one in St Paul Shadwell.

Resolved that the site near the Swan with Two Necks in Tothill Street is proper for one of the new churches etc. in St Margaret Westminster. Dickinson to make a plan, showing approaches. Skeat to ask Mr Smith for his written demand for the sites of both the new churches, etc.; that near Millbank to be for a square of one acre and a quarter. Churchwardens to propose appropriate districts.

493. [p. 405] 7 Dec. 1711
1,2. Received representations from churchwarden of St Saviour Southwark, and minister, churchwardens and parishioners of Rotherhithe.
3,4. Resolved that St Saviour's representation ought to be laid before Commissioners; and that Rotherhithe's case be particularly represented in Commissioners' report.
5. Hawksmoor's proposed division of St Clement Danes is convenient.
6. White delivered written demand for site in St Giles Cripplegate.
7. Skeat to inquire for another site for church etc. in Lower Wapping besides that proposed by Johnson.
8,9. Skeat delivered Rous's demand of £350 for site in St Paul Shadwell; Sir R. Hoare desired to discourse Rous about price, exclusive of nine houses mentioned in his proposal.
10,11. Hawksmoor's division of St Paul Shadwell is convenient; as well as the five parishes he proposes for St Giles in the Fields.
12,13. Chapel in Hatton Garden not fit to be a parish church, but districts proposed by Hawksmoor for the other four parishes into which St Andrew Holborn to be divided are convenient.
14. Dr Gastrell delivered rental of site of Grange Inn, St Clement Danes, for Mr Ewers, the proprietor, who required 15 years' purchase for freehold, besides lessees' interest.
15. Hawksmoor to inquire for another site in St Clement Danes.
16,17. Read a second proposal from Mr Thos Jackson for one of sites agreed on in St Olave Southwark. Skeat to apply to Henshaw for his demand for the freehold, exclusive of six houses fronting the street.
18–20. Hy Smith, Esq., delivered written demands for two sites he proposed in St Margaret Westminster. That in Vine Garden, near Millbank, at £500 is reasonable. Dickinson to survey the ground adjoining Swan with Two Necks and report.
21. If part of St Giles Cripplegate is added to St Alphage, three new churches will be sufficient for the parish.

494. [p. 402] 11 Dec. 1711
1. Resolved that one new church is sufficient in St Leonard Shoreditch.

2. Three new churches sufficient in St Giles Cripplegate.
3. A church ought to be built for the use of the inhabitants of Norton Folgate, Old Artillery Ground and St Mary le Spittle; site proposed by Dickinson in Spittle Square near Lord Bolingbroke's house a convenient one.
5. A second church ought to be erected in Lambeth.
6,7. Site proposed near Brown's Lane is proper for one of new churches in Spitalfields; and that opposite Pater Noster Row for the other.
8. Hawksmoor's proposed division at Deptford is convenient.
9. Mr Wise's demand for £400 for three acres of Deptford is reasonable.
10. Site at upper end of Holywell Lane, St Leonard Shoreditch, convenient.

495. [p. 400] 14 Dec. 1711
Approved Rous's demand for £350 for site for church and minister's house, St Paul Shadwell. Hawksmoor to inquire for church yard.

Read second representation from trustees of St George's Chapel [Ormond Street]; consideration postponed.

Coleman delivered written demand for £450 for two acres for church etc. for St Leonard Shoreditch.

Robinson proposed to sell his site viewed in St Sepulchre Without for £600 without the materials on it, or £650 with them.

Mr Sheriff Stewart to be desired to inquire if City will part with their interest in the square within the rails, West Smithfield, for a church for St Sepulchre Without.

Several inhabitants of St Giles Cripplegate delivered written reasons against adding part of that parish to St Alphage. Surveyors to view St Alphage church and report how many it will contain decently.

Governors of Free School, St Olave Southwark, made written demand of £300 for site in Horsley Down, exclusive of leases thereon. Consideration postponed until leasees make their demands.

Report to Queen and Parliament to be general, praying further time and powers.

496. [p. 398] 18 Dec. 1711
Hooper, on behalf of Wm St John, Esq., Lord Bolingbroke's executor, and Mr Jeremy Sambrook, mortgagee in possession of the earl's lands in Norton Folgate, delivered written demand for land and houses proper for site for church, etc. of £2,117 15*s*. for the whole, or £1,603 15*s*. for part. Skeat to inquire for another site.

Read petition of ministers and some inhabitants of St Clement Danes; to be laid before Commissioners.

Approved demand for £80 by Exton and Chandler for site for minister's house at Poplar.

Skeat, Beckley and the Surveyors to proceed with all possible expedition during interval between Commissions, so that business will be ready when new Commission meets. In their inquiries, they are to fix on sites that lie amongst or near the better sort of inhabitants.

Mr Merrick delivered written demand for £720 for cemetery for the middle parish intended to be taken out of St Botolph Aldgate; consideration postponed until site for third church settled.

Read demand for £500 for site for a minister's house in St Margaret Westminster, including old house, etc. of which materials valued at £150 or £200.

Commissioners to be moved to appoint members to distribute the £200 advanced by Her Majesty towards defraying incidental expenses.

497. [p. 396] 21 Dec. 1711
Secretary to deduct for his own and messenger's expenses £19. 18*s*. 4*d*.; pay Brown, keeper of Quest Room, St Dunstan in the West, £8; Agent and Surveyors £40 each on account; Crocker £10; to discharge bill of Brooks, doorkeeper at Whitehall, and allow him 3*s*. for attendance every Commission day; and retain remainder in his own hands on account.

MINUTES OF THE BUILDING COMMITTEE, 1712–16

Lambeth MS 2693

498. [p. 1] 11 June 1712, at Whitehall
The Committee came to the following resolutions:
1. The most speedy way to put into execution the powers granted by the second Act for Fifty New Churches will be for the Commissioners to confirm what they formerly did in pursuance of the first Act, and thereby make it their present act.
2. A plan to be drawn out in columns of such things as were agreed upon, in relation to each parish.
3. Hawksmoor to submit a plan of the ground of old church and churchyard of Greenwich, with an upright plan or draught of new church, and a particular estimate, and valuation of old materials fit to be used about the new church.
4. The Commissioners should appoint some person to settle purchase of ground upon which St George's Chapel [Ormond Street] stands, on the terms previously approved.
5. The like to be done for all other proposals formerly made, or to be made, and agreed on by Commissioners.
6. Commissioners should consider of some proper way to treat with patrons of parishes where new churches are to be built.
7. Commissioners should assign certain times and places for their meetings, and give notice in *Gazette* so that all concerned might know when and where to apply to them.

499. [p. 3] 4 July 1712
1. Considered two plans for East Greenwich church, submitted by Hawksmoor and by James.
2. Hawksmoor was called in and ordered to correct his plan, pursuant to verbal directions.
3. Hawksmoor to give an account at next meeting of dimensions of parish churches of St James and St Ann, Westminster, and compute the number each will conveniently contain for the decent performance of Divine Service.

500. [p. 4] 11 July 1712, at Mr Thomas Rous's in Doctors' Commons
1. Beckley submitted a proposal of 9 July under Mr N. Curzon's hand.
2. Resolved that Commissioners should express surprise that Curzon's demand differs so much from that of 30 Dec. 1711, since that was an abatement of £600 of his first demand, and proposing to take £1,000 for the ground rent and reversion of St George's Chapel [Ormond Street]

without any further demand. As Commissioners then agreed, and still do, they expect he will stand to his offer. If not, they will look for another site.

3. By Commissioners' order, considered site proposed by Wise for site for new church, churchyard and minister's house, Deptford.

4. Resolved £400 be given to Wise for his three acres with two houses that must be pulled down to make an approach, according to the offer made by him to the Dean of Canterbury and Hawksmoor; and that they reject the proposal delivered this day.

5. Hawksmoor to view Mr Vokins's three acres in Deptford, and any other proper for a site, and take dimensions and price thereof.

6. Hawksmoor and Skeat to view the chapel in Hatton Garden and see what houses are fit to be bought to make that a convenient site for a church; and enquire value of the houses and the leases and inheritances after expiration of the leases.

7. Dickinson to attend next Tuesday with account of what sites he has viewed in Whitechapel.

8. Rev. Dr Browne to be desired to make a demand for ground in St James Clerkenwell parish proposed by him as site for church, etc.

9. Skeat to bring on Tuesday next what proposals he has for sites.

The Committee came to the following resolutions:

'10. That one General Modell be made and Agreed upon for all the fifty new intended Churches.

11. That the Scituation of all the said Churches be Insular where the Scites will admit thereof.

12. That the Ministers House be as near the said Churches as conveniently may be.

13. That there be at the East end of Each Church two small Roomes. One for the Vestments, another for the Vessells & other Consecrated things.

14. That there be at the West end of each Church a convenient Large Room for parish business.

15. That the Fonts be so large as to be capable to have Baptism administered in them by dipping, when desir'd.

16. That the Churches be all built with Stone on the Outside, and Lined with Brick on the Inside thereof.

17. That the Pews be all of Equal height, so low that every person in them may be seen, either Kneeling or Sitting, and so contrived that all Persons may Stand and kneel towards the Communion Table.

18. That the Moveable forms be so contrived, as to run under the Seats of the Pewes, and draw out into the Isles upon occasion.

19. That, the Chancels be raised three Steps above the Nave or Body of the Churches.

20. That, there be handsome Porticoes at the West end of each church where the Scite will admit of the same.

21. That no Person shall be admitted a General Undertaker to Build any of the said New intended Churches, but that every Artificer be separately agreed with, to perform the Work belonging to his particular Trade or business.'

501. [p. 7] 15 July 1712
1. Skeat presented demand under Edward Buckley's hand of £600 for site for Whitechapel, which Dickinson reported proper and convenient.
2. Skeat to ask Buckley to attend on Friday next to discuss site.
3. Commissioners to be moved to appoint one of Surveyors to wait on Sir John Thornicroft about setting out ground he formerly offered for a site in Stockwell.
4. Hawksmoor to submit at next meeting plans of sites he has viewed.
5. An offer of a site in St John Wapping made by Mr Davie and Mr Meredith.
6. Hawksmoor to view it and report.
7. Skeat to inquire and report who are proprietors of the following proposed sites:
8. Upper end of Bond Street leading to the pest house within St James Westminster.
9. Upper end of Marlborough Street now or lately a bowling green, in the said parish.
10. Tweed Street, between Poland and Berwick Streets, in the said parish.
11. Skeat to inquire after executors of Mr Powell, supposed proprietors of site proposed at corner of Warwick and Glasshouse Streets; and obtain their demand in writing.

502. [p. 9] 18 July 1712
1. Pursuant to Commissioners' order, considered Wise's demand for Deptford site.
2. Recommend agreeing to demand, except for having a pew in the church, settled to himself and his family, and Samuel Priestman's being sexton, neither of which are in Commissioners' power to grant.
3. Bulstrode to procure written proposals from Lord Hatton and his tenants of their demands for their interests in two houses in front and six in rear of chapel in Hatton Garden.
4. Rev. Dr Browne delivered demand of £200 for his interest in Pardon churchyard, approved heretofore by this Committee for a church in St James Clerkenwell.
5. Dr Browne's demand deemed reasonable, provided tenants have customary right to renew lease for 21 years at any time before expiration for the sum of £3. 10*s*.
6. Jennings to inquire to Mr Paine, Treasurer of the Charterhouse, how Commissioners should apply to the governors about purchasing inheritance of a site proposed by Dr Browne for new church in St James Clerkenwell.
7. No site ought to be approved for new church, etc., until viewed by some of Commissioners.
8. Skeat to inquire what the owners of the houses to be pulled down near Goulston Square to make a proper site for one of the new churches in Whitechapel will take for their interests.
9. Secretary to write to Sir James Etheridge asking his demand for his interest in two houses in Goulston Square next the Snuff House, now in the possession of Mr Cowley.

10. Skeat to inquire what the several proprietors of the grounds in Lemon Street will take for their interests.

503. [p. 11] 25 July 1712
1. Brooke, minister of St Alphage, delivered a plan with dimensions of that church.
2. The said church will conveniently contain 800.
3. Minister and churchwardens of Cripplegate to be so informed.
4. Two sites proposed for new churches in Spitalfields: against Paternoster Row, and Brown's site—
5. To be viewed by Hawksmoor, and value of lands near them to be inquired into, and the quantity of ground necessary, exclusive of churchyard, and report with all convenient speed; the proprietors to have an answer in three weeks time at the farthest.
6. Mr Campbell delivered several designs for new churches for consideration.
7. Any persons delivering estimates are to set down the thickness of stone they design to use in each part of the church, and the sort of stone.

504. [p. 13] 29 July 1712
1. Hawksmoor to set out ground to be bought of Sclater in Bethnal Green, and bring plan to have it annexed to conveyance.
2. Hoskins and Hoare to view the said ground.
3. A time ought to be fixed by Commissioners for persons to lay designs or models for churches before them.
4. White delivered two written proposals of £1,200 and £1,800 for two pieces of ground in St Giles Cripplegate.
5. White to be desired to submit a rental of the houses and ground.
[6.] Crosse and Vanbrugh to view the sites, attended by Dickinson.
7. Mr Hambleton delivered written proposal of £1,200 for site in St Giles Cripplegate.
8. Freedom part of St Giles Cripplegate parish ought to be kept entire to the mother church, except such part of parish as may hereafter be allotted to St Alphage.
9. Brooke, minister of St Alphage, to be desired to propose at next meeting what part of St Giles Cripplegate he desires added to St Alphage.

505. [p. 15] 12 Aug. 1712
1. Curate on behalf of vicar and others of St Giles Cripplegate presented two petitions against annexing part of parish to St Alphage; which were read; and they and the minister of St Alphage were heard severally.
2. Petitions and reasons to be laid before Commissioners tomorrow.
3. Rev. Dr Marshall submitted plan of ground in St Pancras proposed as churchyard for new parish to be allotted to St George's chapel [Ormond Street], with a demand for same.
4. Resolved that the two acres proposed (for which £400 are demanded) are a convenient spot for churchyard for the said intended parish.
5. Tuffnell and Strong, masons, Hues, Billinghurst and Woolfe & Partner, bricklayers, delivered proposals for building East Greenwich church.

6. Proposals referred to Mr Wren and Vanbrugh to report to next meeting of Commissioners; the persons to attend, together with Hawksmoor and Dickinson, at Vanbrugh's house in Scotland Yard at 9 a.m. tomorrow.
7. Hawksmoor to lay before Commissioners an estimate of whole charge of building Greenwich church according to design fixed upon by them on 6 August, exclusive of paving.
8. Bulstrode delivered demand of £1,340. 15*s*. from Lord Hatton, Mr Bennet and others for their respective interests in houses and ground adjoining chapel in Hatton Garden.
9. Same to be laid before Commissioners at their next meeting; if houses be not purchased, church will not be insular. Materials of chapel worth about £200.

506. [p. 17] 15 Aug. 1712
1. Several waiting for an answer about the two sites in Spitalfields, they were informed that Committee was not yet ready with an answer.
2. Nelson reported that he and Jennings had viewed the chambers in Lincoln's Inn, pursuant to Commissioners' desire, and judged them very proper for their meetings. To make agreement for them for one year from Michaelmas next.
3. Read a letter from Kent, about ground on which St George's chapel stands.
4. Beckley to acquaint Kent that Mr Curzon has complied with Commissioners to accept £1,000 for inheritance, pursuant to Kent's and Curzon's former demand, and they expected he would not recede therefrom, and desired his final answer.
5. Hawksmoor, pursuant to Commissioners' order, submitted draft contract to be signed by masons and bricklayers employed on Greenwich church.
6. Draft referred to Beckley to perfect, and he to wait on Annesley and Jennings, or one of them, for their approbation.
7. Hawksmoor to direct masons and bricklayers to begin with all possible expedition.

507. [p. 19] 22 Aug. 1712
1. Ordered Hawksmoor to finish model for Greenwich church in all its parts, so as to have particular and exact plans drawn therefrom to be annexed to the agreement to be made with artificers.
2. Dickinson and Skeat to view Harris's ground in St Giles Cripplegate and take a rental, and his demand, and report.
3. Skeat delivered Bartlett's proposal for three acres for site in St George Southwark at £400.
4. Nelson and Crosse to be desired to view said ground and report; Skeat and Dickinson to attend them.

508. [p. 20] 26 Aug. 1712
1. All papers or models delivered to Commissioners or Committee and

approved by either to be kept by Secretary and not redelivered without order.
2. Secretary to read the minutes to Commissioners or Committee every day before they rise; chairman to sign before they depart.
3. Secretary to write to minister and churchwardens of Greenwich for lead from old church to be weighed and delivered to Osmond, the plumber, against his receipt; he to dispose of it as Commissioners shall direct.
4. Medlicott to acquaint Lady Mordaunt that Commissioners are informed that she has caused materials belonging to Greenwich church to be taken away, and that they expect she will return them. Since she would have been obliged to build chancel herself if Public had not built the church, they hope she will contribute something towards building chancel.
5. Medlicott to inform minister and churchwardens that when churchyard wall is pulled down for laying new foundation, Commissioners expect that suitable fence shall be made before the churchyard at parish expense as shall enable artificers to carry on their work conveniently.
6. Crosse reported that he and Nelson had viewed proposed site in St George Southwark and judged it proper.
7. Secretary to invite the proprietor, Bartlett, to attend with a proposal.
8. Dickinson to survey ground of the late Earl of Bolingbroke within Norton Folgate Liberty, and report on Friday next what part is necessary for a church and house, with the price demanded.
9. Crosse and Box to view site proposed in St Paul Shadwell and report on Friday.

509. [p. 22] 29 Aug. 1712
1. Crosse and Box reported they had viewed two sites proposed for a church in St Paul Shadwell.
2. Dickinson to view Rous's ground and report whether it will permit a good foundation.
3. Dickinson reported he had viewed Earl of Bolingbroke's ground.
4. Hooper has promised to give Sambrook's answer about price in a week or fortnight.
5. Medlicott reported that Lady Mordaunt had readily agreed to return old chancel materials [Greenwich]. She had removed them only to prevent their being stolen.
6. Medlicott also reported that minister and churchwardens of Greenwich had promised to set up such fence as Committee require.
7. Offered £300 to Mr Bartlett for his ground in St George Southwark, viewed by Nelson and Crosse, he clearing it from lease now on it. He took time to consider.
8. Skeat delivered rental of Harris's ground in St Giles Cripplegate.
9. Dickinson to view said ground and report.

510. [p. 24] 3 Sep. 1712
1. Dickinson and Skeat to view two sites in St Paul Shadwell—belonging

to Dean of St Paul's, and Mercers' Company's Matchwalk—report and, if suitable, receive proprietors' proposals.
2. Dickinson and Skeat to view Dethick's ground in Poplar, and inquire whether and for how much proprietors would sell enough for minister's house.
3. Proposal of Goldsmiths' Company (£800) for Primrose Alley site, St Botolph Bishopsgate, read and rejected.
4. Dickinson and Skeat to view Ironmongers' Company's ground in Cripplegate and receive their demand for as much as is required for a site.
5. No person to be employed by Commissioners till he has stood proposed a week at least.
6. Osmond acknowledged receipt of 11 tons, 2 cwts, 3 qtrs, and 17 lbs of old lead from Greenwich.

511. [p. 26] 10 Sep. 1712
1. Dickinson and Skeat to view ground of Humphreys, Heath, Wood and Michell in Red Lion Street, Spitalfields, see what part would be convenient, treat with proprietors and report.
2. Dickinson and Skeat having viewed Rous's ground reported that no good foundation could be obtained. Committee rejects his proposal.
3. Proposal from Hastings for St Paul Shadwell delivered.
4. Consideration thereof postponed.
5. Skeat to attend Essington and inquire whether Mercers' Company will part with so much of Matchwalk, Ratcliff Highway, as is sufficient for a church, etc., and on what terms, and report.
6. Dickinson and Skeat reported that Dean of St Paul's ground not proper for church foundations.
7. Dickinson and Skeat reported that Dethick desired a week to consider what proposal to make for a site for minister's house in Poplar.
8. White offered to sell his estate at upper end of White Cross Street, St Giles Cripplegate (yearly rent £82) for £1,000.
9. Dickinson and Skeat to view White's other ground and report on Wednesday.
10. Harris's proposal further considered.
Commissioners to be summoned to meet at Secretary's house next Wednesday, as Whitehall room is employed for other business.

512. [p. 28] 24 Sep. 1712
1. Wise delivered proposal of £400 for two-and-a-half acre site at Deptford, with house, smith's shop, etc. Agreed.
2. Beckley to make abstract of title and lay it before Jennings.
3. Bulstrode reported he had spoken with Serjeant Bennet about Greenwich church chancel; he would do all in his power with Lady Mordaunt.
4. Bulstrode reported that he and Nelson found the site in Red Lion Street proper; they had discoursed with the proprietors who refused to take less than £1,260 as formerly proposed.
5. Skeat delivered Ironmongers' Company's proposal for church near Old Street, Cripplegate.

6. Mr Wren and Manlove desired to view sites belonging to White (2), Harris and Ironmongers' Company in St Giles Cripplegate, and report.
7. Archer and Jennings to view site proposed by Lady Russell in Plow Yard in St Giles in the Fields, and report.

513. [p. 30] 31 Oct. 1712, at Lincoln's Inn
1. Mr Wren and Manlove delivered written report on Ironmongers' Company's site.
2. King, Mr Wren, and Manlove to treat with Ironmongers' Company.
3. Skeat to acquaint White that Commissioners had viewed his site at lower end of White Cross Street, and they desire his lowest demand.
[4.] Dickinson to view site proposed by King near Goswell Street, St Giles Cripplegate, and report.

514. [p. 31] 7 Nov. 1712
1. King reported he, Manlove and Mr Wren had offered Ironmongers' Company £500 for their site in St Giles Cripplegate, and they insisted on £600.
2. Dickinson to examine back part of ground and report whether proper for foundation, and compute extraordinary building charges occasioned by raising the ground; and whether ground proposed for churchyard is proper.
3. All reports in future to be in writing, and signed by persons making the reports.
4. White's proposal rejected as unreasonable: 14 years' purchase for old houses and sheds, in all £1,800; besides a further demand for one other old house at same rate.
5. Mr Wren and Manlove to view site proposed by Sambrook and Hooper in Norton Folgate, and report.
6. Dickinson to attend them.
7. Agreed to give proprietors of Red Lion Street, Spitalfields, site £1,260 if title good; proprietors to attend on Monday next with title deeds.

515. [p. 33] 10 Nov. 1712
1. Proprietors of Red Lion Street site signed minute of their agreement to sell for £1,260.
2. Hawksmoor to wait on Mr Baron Price and take an account of what ground he has in Wapping, and see whether any part be proper for a new church.

516. [p. 34] 17 Nov. 1712
1. Skeat and Dickinson to inquire whether minister and churchwardens of St Olave Southwark will part with their burying place over against Paris Street for a new church, if Commissioners buy them another.
2. Manlove and Mr Wren to view site proposed by Goldsmiths' Company in St Botolph Bishopsgate, and report.
3. Dickinson to attend them.
4. Westmoor to be employed to value crop on Wise's ground at Deptford, being recommended by Dean of Canterbury and Gastrell.

5. Considered and rejected site in Plow Yard, St Giles in the Fields, proposed by Lady Russell, as inconvenient and her demand extraordinarily high.
6. Rous's ground in St Paul Shadwell to be reviewed by Surveyors, with workmen to assist them. Also to inquire after and view any other sites to be had in the parish.
7. Nelson and Jennings to inquire whether Mr Brewster will part with the rest of this floor, and consider what other conveniences are wanting in and about the chambers for the use of the Commissioners, their officers and servants.
8. To meet next Friday to consider what officers must necessarily be employed, and what salaries and gratifications it will be proper to allow. Notice to be given to all Commissioners in their summons by the Messenger.

517. [p. 36] 21 Nov. 1712
1. Rous's salary as secretary to be £200 p.a. from 28 September, 1711.
2. Manlove and Mr Wren delivered written report on two sites in Spitalfields and Norton Folgate: consideration postponed.
3. No further occasion for Thomas Brooks's attendance as Door-keeper.
4. Thomas Crocker, Messenger, to serve as Messenger and Door-keeper.
5. Brooks to bring in his bill as soon as convenient.
6. Crocker's salary to be £30 p.a. from Michaelmas 1711.
7. Skeat's salary as Agent and Solicitor to be £100 p.a. from Michaelmas 1711.
8. Sums already paid to Officers to be taken as payments on account.
9. No Officers to be allowed perquisites.
10. Rest of the salaries deferred to Monday.

518. [p. 38] 24 Nov. 1712
1. Balloting box to be provided, and all questions arising at this Board to be determined by ballot.
2. Dickinson to set out the quantity of ground belonging to the several proprietors for site proposed in St Olave Southwark by Jackson and Henshaw, and their respective demands, and for the strip not included in Jackson's lease.
3. Also to view the 12 acres belonging to parish and report what part thereof proper for burying places.
4. Committee after some debate about salaries to be allowed to Hawksmoor and Dickinson ordered them to be called in and offered each £200 p.a., including all incident charges.
5. King and Vanbrugh to view site proposed by Mr Davy in lower part of St Botolph Aldgate parish and report.
6. Skeat to receive proprietors' demands for four front houses adjoining Goldsmiths' Company's site in Norton Folgate.
7. Jefferys to be informed that Committee ready on Monday next to make agreement with him for site he proposed for church on Little Tower Hill for St Botolph Aldgate.

519. [p. 40] 1 Dec 1712
1. Kent, proprietor of the freehold of St George's chapel [Ormond Street], delivered proposal to alienate freehold for £100.
2. Kent to be paid £100 for alienation of freehold.
3. Beckley to wait on Curzon, the mortgagee, for his title deeds, and make abstract to lay before Annesley.
4. Beckley to submit his bill for work done as Solicitor to the Commission.
5. Jennings acquainted Committee that he had a letter from the Bishop of London about making Aylesbury chapel in St James Clerkenwell a parochial church. Dickinson called in: he had viewed the chapel and it could no ways be made proper for the purpose.
6. Secretary to write to governors of Charterhouse to see if they will part with a piece of ground in St James Clerkenwell, and report on what terms.
7. Jennings delivered letter from Hawksmoor about his salary. Dickinson called in; said they would accept Committee's offer.
8. £200 p.a. to be allowed Hawksmoor and Dickinson as Deputy Surveyors and Clerks of the Works under this Commission, including all incident charges, except for making wooden models, opening ground, and travelling beyond parishes where new churches are to be built.
9. Their salary to start at Michaelmas 1711; payments already made to be deducted from salary.
10. Henry Smith Esq., Treasurer of the Commission, delivered a paper concerning his salary. After consideration resolved:
11. That further consideration be adjourned to Monday.
12. Tuffnell and Strong, masons for Greenwich church, petitioned Commissioners to provide sheds for sheltering workmen; they were called in and asked the cost—about £50.
13. £25 to be allowed the masons for providing sheds to shelter their workmen from weather.

520. [p. 43] 8 Dec. 1712
1. Read King's and Vanbrugh's written report on site proposed by Davy in East Smithfield in St Botolph Aldgate; requested to inquire more particularly and report further.
2. Harris's proposal for site in St Giles Cripplegate to be returned to him.
3. Davy's proposal for site in East Smithfield to be returned to him.
4. Secretary submitted letter to be sent to governors of Charterhouse about site in St James Clerkenwell.
5. Said letter to be laid before Commissioners at their next meeting.
6. Commissioners to be moved to desire Lord High Treasurer to issue and pay by way of loan on Coal Duties £5,000 to Commission's Treasurer.
7. Consideration of Treasurer's salary postponed to this day fortnight: notice to be given to the Commissioners.

521. [p. 45] 15 Dec. 1712
1. Beckley to lay before Box abstract of Sir John Thornicroft's title for site in Lambeth.

2. Box to peruse abstract and report.
3. Beckley delivered his bill.
4. Bill referred to Jennings, Annesley, and Box to report.
5. Gerrard delivered written proposal of Samuel Hawkins for £150 for three houses in Unicorn Yard in St Olave Southwark.
6. Skeat delivered second written proposal for Hayes: £1,000 for Green Dragon Inn within St Giles in the Fields.
7. Consideration deferred until other proposals of houses required to complete the site submit demands.

522. [p. 47] 22 Dec. 1712
Debated Treasurer's salary; determination adjourned till Michaelmas next. Treasurer called in and told that Committee expected he should take no perquisites because they design him such salary as shall be sufficient to give him full satisfaction for his trouble.

523. [p. 48] 29 Dec. 1712
1. Bertie, Annesley, Jennings and Nelson to treat with patrons of parishes where new churches are to be built, about the patronage, and report from time to time.
2. Dickinson to open Smith's ground in St Margaret Westminster, and report whether it will admit good foundation.

524. [p. 49] 5 Jan. 1712/13
1. Dickinson delivered two reports, on Smith's ground at Millbank and the Ironmongers' Company's in St Giles Cripplegate.
2. Will agree with Ironmongers' Company if they will make the street leading to front of new church forty feet wide.
3. King, Manlove, and Mr Wren to treat with Ironmongers' Company about breadth of street.
4. The several Commissioners named to be desired to inquire particularly after sites in the specified parishes:
St Margaret Westminster: Smalridge, Crosse.
St Clement Danes: Sherlock, Jennings.
St Andrew Holborn: Bulstrode, Hoskins.
St Giles in the Fields: Annesley, Child.
St James Westminster: Nelson, Mr Wren.
St Martin in the Fields: Medlicott, Archer.
5. Surveyors and Agent to inquire particularly for sites within said parishes, and acquaint Commissioners appointed to each what sites they find.
6. Secretary to send minute to each of the said Commissioners of what already done or proposed in each of the said parishes.
7. Secretary also to submit account of what had been done relating to St Mary le Strand at next meeting.
8. Jennings and Nelson reported in writing on agreement with Mr Brewster: read and agreed to:
9. Commissioners and Committee to have use of Great Room as now fitted up and all other rooms on the same floor except the little closet

backwards; and also use of some rooms below stairs for their servants and a vault for coals, for £40 p.a. payable quarterly by Treasurer without further application.

525. [p. 51] 12 Jan. 1712/13
1. Hawksmoor delivered report signed by himself, Dickinson, Tufnell and Hughes on Millbank site, certifying it will admit of good foundations for a church.
2. Dean of Carlisle, Crosse and Vanbrugh to confer with Smith about the place for the new church, and the avenues to be made thereto.
3. Moss and King to examine Secretary's bill, and report.
4. Secretary submitted a minute of what Commissioners had done about St Mary le Strand.
5. Moss desired leave to offer a proposal for the more speedy and effectual employing the churches to be built, in the worship and service of God, so soon as any of them shall be ready for use.
6. Leave so given.

526. [p. 53] 19 Jan. 1712/13
1. Skeat to wait on Earl of Scarborough about a site within St James Westminster.
2. Moss offered a proposal [as above, 12 January].
3. Consideration deferred to next meeting.

527. [p. 54] 27 Jan. 1712/13
1. Hawksmoor or Dickinson to attend Nelson and Bulstrode to view site of Hatton Garden chapel.
2. Hawksmoor to attend on Johnson, churchwarden, and other inhabitants of St Clement Danes, to take plan of churchyard for site for new church, and an account of what the parish desire may be done on parting with the churchyard for that purpose.
3. Crosse and Vanbrugh to be added to the Commissioners desired to treat with Ironmongers' Company on Cripplegate site; they or any two to meet Ironmongers on Thursday next to set out site; notice to be given to King, Manlove and Mr Wren. Dickinson to attend them.
4. Humble application to be made to Her Majesty for leave to build a new church for St Mary le Strand at the Maypole in the Strand.
5. Skeat [smith] recommended to the Committee to serve ironwork to be used in building Greenwich church, and Jeffs, Cordwell and Groves as carpenters.
6. Notice to be given in *Gazette* next Saturday that all who desire to be employed in the smith's, carpenter's and plumber's work of Greenwich church bring their proposals to Committee this day fortnight.
7. Consideration of Moss's proposal adjourned to this day week.

528. [p. 56] 1 Feb. 1712/13
1. Vanbrugh submitted new plan for removing Ironmongers' Company site, Cripplegate, 110 ft further from the street than formerly proposed.
2. Commissioners appointed to view the said site to treat upon the new plan, and report as soon as convenient.

3. Child and Hoare to be desired to apply to Lord Mayor, President, Vice-President and Treasurer of the Artillery Company whether a site can not be obtained for a church, etc. in Artillery Ground.
4. Osmond to deliver to Greenwich church masons so much of old lead as they shall require.
5. Consideration of Moss's proposal adjourned to next week.

529. [p. 57] 9 Feb. 1712/13
1. Sir James Bateman submitted the form of several warrants to be issued by Commissioners to the Treasury, for payment of Officers' salaries, etc. Read and agreed to; to be transcribed fair and submitted at next meeting.
2. John Skeat, Edward James, Robinson, Cowrey and Bullen severally delivered proposals for smith's work for Greenwich church.
3. William Ogburn, Jas Grove, Jeffs and John James likewise for carpenter's work.
4. Osmond, Roberts, Cocks, Knight and Matthews likewise for plumber's work.
5. Hawksmoor to prepare particular schemes of work to be done in the building by the several artificers, and submit the same on Monday next, in order to their making more exact proposals.

530. [p. 59] 16 Feb. 1712/13
1. Trustees of Ormond Street Chapel delivered a third proposal about making chapel parochial. Read, with former proposal of 14 December 1711.
2. Agree with proposal of 14 December 1711.
3. Read Hastings's proposal for ground in St Paul Shadwell.
4. Same to be considered at next meeting; Dr Higden to have notice. Hawksmoor to report on Rous's ground at the same time.
5. Hawksmoor to survey Wise's ground in Deptford on Friday next and report the exact quantity thereof; Beckley to go with him.
6. Beckley to engross all writings that are ordered to be engrossed by the Commission.
7. Hawksmoor delivered particulars of carpenter's, smith's and plumber's work for Greenwich church.
8. Secretary to make transcripts and deliver them on Wednesday morning to the workmen for them to deliver their prices on Monday next.
9. Crosse delivered proposal about Smith's ground in St Margaret Westminster: read and agreed to.
10. Smith to lay abstract of title and his deeds before Solicitor, to be laid before counsel.

531. [p. 61] 23 Feb. 1712/13
1. Considered Hastings's and Rous's sites in St Paul Shadwell. After debate, Jennings, Nelson and Crosse desired to treat with persons who attended about Hastings's ground to try whether they would abate anything of their last demand.

2. Model proposed for Greenwich church considered; after debate ordered:
3. That Hawksmoor should make an estimate of whole charge of new church as it is new modelled, for Monday next.
4. He should also estimate the difference between carrying or not carrying on the two arcades or breaks on north and south sides.
5. Workmen to proceed no further upon said arcades till ordered by Commissioners to do so.
6. Hawksmoor also at same time to give account of how many squares of building whole church as it now stands modelled contains, and number of people it will contain decently when built.
7. Smiths, carpenters and plumbers to deliver their proposals to Committee at five in the afternoon.
8. Committee will then consider artificer's proposals.

532. [p. 63] 24 Feb. 1712/13
1. Read proposals of sundry persons for plumber's work at Greenwich.
2. Said persons need not attend further until they have notice.
3. Carpenters who have proposals to attend on 5 March.

533. [p. 64] 2 Mar. 1712/13
1. Samuel Priestman, owner of the crop on Wise's ground, Deptford, attended with valuer; he was called in, and after some time ordered to withdraw.
2. Priestman to be given £70 for his crop, he delivering it on the ground to Commissioners' order when required.
3. Beckley to send to Wise for his deeds and an abstract to lay before counsel.
4. Beckley to lay deeds and abstract of Smith's ground, Westminster, before Jennings for his approbation.
5. Hawksmoor to view and report on site proposed near St Giles's pound, wherein Mr Bourne is concerned.
6. Hastings's and Rous's ground in Shadwell again considered, but no resolution taken.
7. Bartlett delivered a second proposal offering to take £350 for his site in St George Southwark.
8. Dickinson to survey and report what part thereof belongs to the Mint, and what part of parish may be most conveniently allotted for a district to proposed church.
9. Committee will consider sites in St Olave Southwark on Monday next.
10. Dickinson to attend with plans and drafts relating to parish and sites proposed.
11. The workmen to go on with arcades on the north and south sides of Greenwich church as formerly proposed by Hawksmoor.

534. [p. 66] 5 Mar. 1712/13
1. Smiths and carpenters for Greenwich church gave in their prices to the schedules delivered by the Committee's direction.

2. Considered plumbers' proposals. After debate, ballot determined by majority of three for Graysbrook (12) over Cox (9 votes).
3. Graysbrook shall give £1,000 security for performance of the plumber's work in a good and workmanlike manner; if he fail of due performance, whatever Commissioners have to pay over and above his contract prices shall be deducted from moneys due to him.
4. A convenient place to be assigned him to lay his lead.

535. [p. 68] 9 Mar. 1712/13
1. Nelson delivered a bill of Green, a joiner, for work done for the Commissioners. Referred to Nelson and Jennings.
2. Hastings's agent delivered proposal of £1,200 for site in Shadwell, provided Commissioners comply with condition therein.
3. Agent to be told that unless he hears from Commissioners in a fortnight he may dispose of his site as he pleases.
4. Dickinson to inquire whether any other site may be had nearby.
5. James to be employed as carpenter and Skeat as smith at Greenwich.

536. [p. 69] 23 Mar. 1712/13
1. Wise's title deeds to the site in Deptford he sold to Commissioners to be produced whenever he have occasion for them, at his expense.
2. Notice to be given to Hawksmoor that Commissioners and Committee expect his attendance every time they meet.
3. Skeat and Hawksmoor to attend committee of Mercers' Company on Friday next, to discuss Matchwalk, Shadwell.

537. [p. 70] 30 Mar. 1713
1. Agree to Ironmongers' Company proposal of 23 March for site in St Giles Cripplegate, provided Company contract to build street leading thereto from Old Street before 25 March next. Otherwise, agree to proposal of 24 September last.
2. Beckley to lay title to Red Lion Street, Spitalfields, before attorney-general for his approbation.
3. Beckley to attend Webb and take his opinion of the title to site of Ormond Street chapel.
4. Bulstrode and Nelson delivered their report on Hatton Garden chapel site.
5. Nelson reported that he and Jennings had amended bill of John Green, joiner, for work in and about Commission's rooms. [The sum of] £6. 7*s*. 4*d*. ought to be paid him in full of his bill of £7. 8*s*. 0*d*. Agreed.
6. Archer reported that he had viewed Davall's ground proposed for church etc. in lower part of Aldgate parish, which was convenient.

538. [p. 72] 13 Apr. 1713
1. Mr Carpenter for Richard Wise delivered a proposal for selling the Commissioners four houses to make an avenue to site purchased in Deptford at £240. Agreed.
2. Thos Crocker, Messenger, to be discharged from his attendance to look after and show the models.

539. [p. 73] 23 Apr. 1713
1. Dickinson to attend on Thursday next with maps of St Martin in the Fields and St James Westminster.
2. Notice to be given in Commissioners' summons for Thursday next that Committee intend to pitch upon models for the churches to be built on the site proposed by Henry Smith, Esq, in St Margaret Westminster, and that purchased of Wise in Deptford.
3. Beckley to draw conveyance for Smith's ground with all convenient speed.
4. Brewster to be allowed £10 to fitting up rooms let by him to Commissioners; a warrant to be made out.
5. Agreed with Thos Lucas to build wall on one side of site at Deptford according to Hawksmoor's draft, at rate of £5 per rod and 4*d*. per yard digging.
6. Secretary to submit estimate of what moneys will probably be wanted to defray charge of purchases, etc., this year.

540. [p. 75] 6 July 1714, at house of Henry Smith, Esq., in Old Palace Yard
The pillar to be erected near the Maypole to be a Corinthian pillar 15 ft in diameter.

541. [p. 76] 2 Nov. 1714: Committee appointed 15 July, at Smith's house. Vanbrugh and Gibbs submitted two designs for the church to be erected near the Maypole.

Both designs are proper to be put into execution. Referred to Commissioners to make choice.

[Two leaves removed; pp. 79 and 80 are blank]

542. [p. 81] 7 Feb. 1715/16, at Lincoln's Inn
The minutes of Committee of 4 February referred to this Committee were read.
1. Committee took into consideration Gibbs's account. Several articles therein were excluded by order of the former Commissioners when Surveyors' salaries were settled. Account to be re-delivered to him with copy of order of the former Commissioners, and Gibbs to make a new account.
2. [Following entry crossed out] Board should be moved to direct Treasurer to submit at every meeting an account of moneys received from Exchequer and sums issued by him, and produce his vouchers, whereby balance in hand will always appear.
3. Committee report they found annual salaries given to Officers as follows: Treasurer £300; Secretary £200; Agent £100; Solicitor £80; Messenger £30. Also an order by former Commissioners that their officers should be elected yearly.
Secretary to examine Minute Books of last Commission and draw up report on what conditions salaries were given.

543. [p. 83] 14 Feb. 1715/16
Minutes of last meeting were read.

Gibbs delivered a new account of his expenses in trying several pieces of ground, making wooden models, etc. £221. 19*s*. Bill to be allowed.

544. [p. 84] 20 Feb. 1715/16
Hawksmoor pursuant to Commissioners' order of 4 February submitted account of churches building and sums due, totalling £23,133. 15*s*. 7*d*. and a further £1,712. 15*s*.

INDEX OF PERSONS

An asterisk (*) indicates a member of one of the Commissions for building fifty new churches. Dates of first and last attendance and number of attendances are given for:

A: First Commission, 1711
B: Second Commission, 1712–15
C: Committee of the 1711 Commission
D: Committee of the 1712 Commission
E: Third Commission, 1715–27

Vestrymen nominated for the new vestries (228, 347, 355, 365, 403, 414) have not been individually indexed.

INDEX OF PLACES

INDEX OF SUBJECTS

LONDON RECORD SOCIETY

The London Record Society was founded in December 1964 to publish transcripts, abstracts and lists of the primary sources for the history of London, and generally to stimulate interest in archives relating to London. Membership is open to any individual or institution; the annual subscription is £7 ($15) for individuals and £10 ($23) for institutions, which entitles a member to receive one copy of each volume published during the year and to attend and vote at meetings of the Society. Prospective members should apply to the Hon. Secretary, Miss Heather Creaton, c/o Institute of Historical Research, Senate House, London, WC1E 7HU.

The following volumes have already been published:

1. *London Possessory Assizes: a calendar,* edited by Helena M. Chew (1965)
2. *London Inhabitants within the Walls, 1695*, with an introduction by D. V. Glass (1966)
3. *London Consistory Court Wills, 1492–1547*, edited by Ida Darlington (1967)
4. *Scriveners' Company Common Paper, 1357–1628, with a continuation to 1678,* edited by Francis W. Steer (1968)
5. *London Radicalism, 1830–1843: a selection from the papers of Francis Place,* edited by D. J. Rowe (1970)
6. *The London Eyre of 1244,* edited by Helena M. Chew and Martin Weinbaum (1970)
7. *The Cartulary of Holy Trinity Aldgate*, edited by Gerald A. J. Hodgett (1971)
8. *The Port and Trade of Early Elizabethan London: documents,* edited by Brian Dietz (1972)
9. *The Spanish Company,* by Pauline Croft (1973)
10. *London Assize of Nuisance, 1301–1431: a calendar,* edited by Helena M. Chew and William Kellaway (1973)
11. *Two Calvinistic Methodist Chapels, 1743–1811: the London Tabernacle and Spa Fields Chapel,* edited by Edwin Welch (1975)
12. *The London Eyre of 1276*, edited by Martin Weinbaum (1976)
13. *The Church in London, 1375–1392*, edited by A. K. McHardy (1977)
14. *Committees for Repeal of the Test and Corporation Acts: Minutes, 1786–90 and 1827–8*, edited by Thomas W. Davis (1978)
15. *Joshua Johnson's Letterbook, 1771–4: letters from a merchant in London to his partners in Maryland,* edited by Jacob M. Price (1979)
16. *London and Middlesex Chantry Certificate, 1548*, edited by C. J. Kitching (1980)

17. *London Politics, 1713–1717: Minutes of a Whig Club, 1714–17,* edited by H. Horwitz; *London Pollbooks, 1713,* edited by W. A. Speck and W. A. Gray (1981)
18. *Parish Fraternity Register: fraternity of the Holy Trinity and SS. Fabian and Sebastian in the parish of St. Botolph without Aldersgate,* edited by Patricia Basing (1982)
19. *Trinity House of Deptford: Transactions, 1609–35,* edited by G. G. Harris (1983)
20. *Chamber Accounts of the sixteenth century,* edited by Betty R. Masters (1984)
21. *The Letters of John Paige, London merchant, 1648–58,* edited by George F. Steckley (1984)
22. *A Survey of Documentary Sources for Property Holding in London before the Great Fire,* by Derek Keene and Vanessa Harding (1985)
23. *The Commissions for Building Fifty New Churches,* edited by M. H. Port (1986)

All volumes are still in print; apply to Hon. Secretary. Price to individual members £7 ($15) each; to institutional members £10 ($23) each; and to non-members £12 ($28) each.